Balanced Leadership

Balanced Leadership

Making the Best Use of Personal and Team Leadership in Projects

Ralf Müller, Nathalie Drouin, and
Shankar Sankaran

OXFORD
UNIVERSITY PRESS

OXFORD
UNIVERSITY PRESS

Oxford University Press is a department of the University of Oxford. It furthers
the University's objective of excellence in research, scholarship, and education
by publishing worldwide. Oxford is a registered trade mark of Oxford University
Press in the UK and certain other countries.

Published in the United States of America by Oxford University Press
198 Madison Avenue, New York, NY 10016, United States of America.

Library of Congress Cataloging-in-Publication Data
Names: Müller, Ralf, 1957– author. | Drouin, Nathalie, author. | Sankaran, Shankar, author.
Title: Balanced leadership : making the best use of personal and team
leadership in projects / Ralf Müller, Nathalie Drouin, Shankar Sankaran.
Description: New York, NY : Oxford University Press, [2022] |
Includes bibliographical references and index.
Identifiers: LCCN 2021030357 (print) | LCCN 2021030358 (ebook) |
ISBN 9780190076139 (paperback) | ISBN 9780190076122 (hardback) |
ISBN 9780190076153 (epub) | ISBN 9780190076146 | ISBN 9780190076160
Subjects: LCSH: Leadership. | Teams in the workplace. | Project management.
Classification: LCC HD57.7 .M853 2021 (print) | LCC HD57.7 (ebook) |
DDC 658.4/092—dc23
LC record available at https://lccn.loc.gov/2021030357
LC ebook record available at https://lccn.loc.gov/2021030358

DOI: 10.1093/oso/9780190076122.001.0001

1 3 5 7 9 8 6 4 2

Paperback printed by Marquis, Canada
Hardback printed by Bridgeport National Bindery, Inc., United States of America

Contents

List of Illustrations

Figures

Tables

Boxes

Preface

This book is about contemporary leadership in projects. It adds two new perspectives to the leadership literature. The first is that of horizontal leadership. This occurs when the project manager empowers a team member to lead the project through a crisis or to solve a particular issue that the project manager might not be able to do. Once the horizontal leader is empowered, the project manager follows this temporary leader, but also governs the activities of the empowered leader.

The second new perspective is balanced leadership, the dynamic and timely shift of leadership authority between project managers and team members to ensure the best possible leader at any point in time in the project.

Together, these two new perspectives pave the way to a deeper understanding of the particularities of leadership in temporary organizations, such as projects. The reader will be presented with an overarching theory for balanced leadership, which is then broken down into its five events and their coordination mechanisms, which is called the socio-cognitive space. Three case studies are provided to illustrate the theory.

The content of the book is based on a program of many research studies, all contributing to the same objective: understanding balanced leadership. Dozens of researchers from all over the world contributed with their local studies to the global results described by the authors in this book.

This program of studies, and the resulting new theories, would not have been possible without the generous research grant from the Project Management Institute (PMI®). Their vision and belief in our study has opened the door to the new project-specific theories described herein. We are grateful to PMI for their support and encouragement.

We also thank all the researchers who worked with us. The particular contributions of most of them are listed in the acknowledgments at the end of each chapter.

Last, but certainly not least, we thank all the practitioners for spending time with us in interviews or in filling out surveys. What is presented in this book is their story about the reality of leadership in projects.

1

Introduction

Few concepts exist that have so many different definitions and are so widely used as *leadership*. Therefore, we should always relate the use of the term to a particular context. In this book, the context is projects and their management. Projects are temporary organizations whose assigned resources undertake a unique and collaborated effort to deliver a beneficial outcome. Accomplishing this outcome requires leadership, which we define herein as an interpersonal, person-oriented, social influence (Endres & Weibler, 2017) to guide the resources in direction, course, action, and opinion (Bennis & Nanus, 1985). So, leadership is for, with, between, and about people. That makes it different from management, which is about tasks, such as goal setting, planning, and controlling.

Leadership in projects has been looked at for decades, almost exclusively from leadership theories derived from research in permanent (as opposed to temporary) organizations. That has given us much insight into what goes on between project managers and project steering groups, project managers and teams, within teams, and so on. However, it raises the question of whether possible particularities in leadership theory in temporary organizations have not been found because the research was mainly done in more permanent organizations. The research done on leadership in projects followed to a large extent the existing streams of either looking at the project manager's leadership or at the leadership that emerges from the project team. The former we often call *vertical leadership*, which is the project manager's top-down leadership over the project team. The latter stream of research looks at the different ways in which leadership emerges from the project team.

In 2016, the Project Management Institute (PMI®) commissioned the authors of this book to study the relationship between these two research streams in the context of projects. When we presented this project at conferences, our colleagues reacted enthusiastically and asked to join us. Within a short time, we were able to assemble teams in nine countries, scattered all over the world, and at least 25 researchers who strongly supported us. A large number of publications resulted from this concerted effort and are summarized and brought together in a cohesive "story" in this book. The authors and the country teams are still working on further studies and associated publications. By the time of writing this book, we had looked at many qualitative and quantitative studies, including approximately 80 in-depth case studies, around 300 interviews, global surveys with hundreds of responses, and so forth. It is fair to say that this is one of the largest studies ever conducted in project management research in general and leadership in projects in particular.

During these studies, we found a great deal of support for the findings from earlier studies. However, we also found new leadership approaches, which had not been found in the leadership literature before. Before we start with these yet unknown leadership approaches, we first define what we mean by leadership approach and leadership style and clarify which of these we will use in this book.

Leadership approaches

In this book, leadership approach refers to the level at which leadership is located, or the direction where leadership comes from, at any point in time in the project. By extending the research streams mentioned earlier, we distinguish between vertical, horizontal, team-based, and balanced leadership approaches. Within each approach, different leadership styles are possible.

Vertical leadership is done by the project manager. It refers to the top-down approach from a formally appointed leader to the project team. It is the most traditional way of looking at leadership in projects. Earlier studies have given insights into project managers' preferred leadership styles, such as the transactional style over transformational style (Keegan & Den Hartog, 2004). Other studies revealed the psychological profiles of project managers regarding their intellectual, emotional, and managerial intelligence (IQ, EQ, and MQ, respectively) and the associated leadership styles. These studies revealed the significance of project managers' EQ for formal project success (Müller & Turner, 2010), as well as for collaboration satisfaction within the team (Zhang, Cao, & Wang, 2018).

Horizontal leadership is a new approach found in projects. In horizontal leadership, the project manager empowers a project team member to lead the project temporarily. This becomes necessary because the team member possesses a particular skill set crucial for overcoming technical or other issues in the project that is not possessed by the project manager himself or herself. When the empowered team member takes on the horizontal leader role, the project manager starts to follow the temporary leader to solve the project's current issue. Simultaneously, the project manager observes whether the horizontal leader performs the task in the project's best interests and terminates the horizontal leader's assignment if that is not the case. The horizontal leader can apply a range of leadership styles, depending on the project needs. Chapter 2 provides an overview of the popularity of autocratic, democratic, and laissez-faire styles in different project types and geographies.

Team-based leadership refers to an approach where leadership emanates from within the team. Earlier studies addressed, for example, the emergence and visibility of team-based leadership styles, such as distributed leadership (Lindgren & Packendorff, 2009), or shared leadership in projects (Crevani, Lindgren, & Packendorff, 2007). Team-based leadership and horizontal leadership are the main themes of the book. They are enabled by the project manager, and together with vertical leadership, they constitute the main building blocks of balanced leadership.

Balanced leadership is another approach observed so far only in projects. Balanced leadership is the dynamic and temporary shifting of leadership authority between the vertical leader (i.e., project manager), horizontal leader, or leading subteams to accomplish desired states in the project. Earlier, we gave the example of a technical specialist appointed as a horizontal leader to lead the project through a particular issue or crisis. This shift of leadership is one of many different shifts in balanced leadership. Another example could be the need for a creative solution to a design issue found in a project. Here, a team of highly creative people might be needed. Appointing the team members as a leading subteam would be a typical solution. This appointment leads to a temporary *team-based leadership* in the project. The rest of the project team, including the project manager, is led by the empowered team. The particular leadership style, such as shared or distributed leadership, is up to the empowered team to decide. In other words, through balanced leadership, the best suitable leader is appointed for the project at any point in time.

Figure 1.1 depicts some exemplary situations for balanced leadership to arise. The dark circles refer to the most likely leadership approach. Within each approach, various leadership styles are possible. Examples include projects for innovative new products. In the concept phase of such projects, the team members' combined creativity is required to come up with real new ideas and solutions. Hence, as shown in Figure 1.1, team-based leadership approaches, such as shared or distributed leadership, are most likely. However, if a particular specialist skill is required, leadership may shift temporarily to a horizontal leader. Similarly, in the planning phase, the project manager leads the planning team but cannot be the number-one specialist in all aspects of the project's scope. Here, a horizontal leader might be needed to clarify the

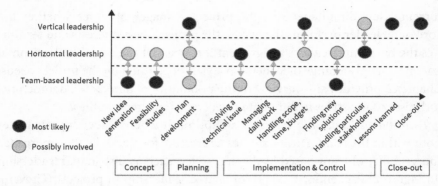

Figure 1.1. Examples of balanced leadership.

types of technologies available for a particular part of the project and to steer the team to an agreed-upon decision in the project's best interest.

Leadership styles

Many different leadership styles exist, and this book is not meant to address all of them. Instead, we focus in the upcoming chapters on those leadership styles that we identified through our studies. These include transactional and transformational leadership, autocratic, democratic, and laissez-faire styles, as well as shared and distributed leadership. We briefly introduce them in the following.

Transactional leadership builds on the notion of contingent reward. Here, leaders exchange things of value to the followers against a certain behavior or performance expected of them. It is often coupled with *management-by-exception*, whereby a leader mainly focuses on corrective criticism, negative feedback, or negative reinforcement. This can be done actively by observing followers for their mistakes in order to correct them, or passively by waiting until their performance goals are compromised. A study by Keegan and den Hartog (2004) showed that transactional leadership is the most popular style among project managers. Later studies indicated that in complex projects, such as organizational change projects, more transformational styles are preferred, while project managers of simpler projects, such as engineering-type maintenance projects, prefer transactional styles (Turner & Müller, 2006).

Transformational leadership attempts to develop followers to their full potential. Transformational leaders exhibit engagement with their followers. They use charisma, develop a vision, engender pride, respect, and trust, provide inspiration, motivate by creating high expectations, and model appropriate behaviors (Bass, 1990). Transformational leadership is often referred to as being based on four factors (Northouse, 2007):

- *Idealized influence*: The leader acts as a role model for followers, who identify with and emulate them. These leaders typically show high standards of moral and ethical conduct and are deeply respected by their followers.
- *Inspirational motivation*: The leader communicates high expectations and motivates followers to become committed to a shared vision. Through emotional and symbolic means, they aim to have their followers achieve more than what they would if they were driven solely by self-interest.
- *Intellectual stimulation*: The leader stimulates the use of creativity and innovation, thereby challenging existing beliefs and values so that followers think out of the box and come up with new solutions and ideas.
- *Individualized consideration*: The leader provides a supportive climate and listens carefully to the needs of the followers. He or she tries to assist the followers through coaching in becoming fully engaged.

Autocratic leadership is characterized by central decision-making by the leader, coercion, and a general lack of democratic processes. These leaders decide on their own without asking for opinions or suggestions from others (Yukl, 2002). Their style is strongly related to the leader's traditional image as the "boss" (Frame, 1987). This style is often chosen for efficiency reasons, such as in high-risk situations (Kocher, Pogrebna, & Sutter, 2013). Angus-Leppan, Metcalf, and Benn (2010) maintain that these leaders show reward-and-punishment behavior or rely on process and position to influence others. In line with English philosopher Thomas Hobbes (1588–1679), these authors argue that autocratic leadership is most beneficial in controlling selfishness in the commercial world, and that through their high level of control, autocratic leaders can effectively resolve and prevent social dilemmas. They argue further that autocratic leaders' voluntary teams show low levels of loyalty and high levels of fluctuation because this style "wears down" the staff.

Democratic leadership is a participatory style where leaders value their team members' inputs and receive their commitment in return. It is appropriate for building consensus within the team, but might be too time-consuming to apply in cases of risks or emergencies (Goleman, Boyatzis, & McKee, 2002). The approach might improve decision quality because it captures a broader range of opinions. However, even though these leaders seek input from their teams, they may not follow this input in their decision-making (Frame, 1987).

Democratic leadership is one of the literature's preferred styles because it is seen as relatively more successful by behavioral scientists. It is one of the preferred styles of project team members (Oke, 2013).

Laissez-faire leadership is characterized by the absence of leadership. The French word *laissez-faire* translates as "let it go" and implies a hands-off style, which gives almost all decision-making authority to the team (Frame, 1987). Laissez-faire leaders abdicate responsibility, give little feedback, and do not attempt to help their followers grow. It is also known as a non-leadership style (Northouse, 2007). Work planning, task assignment, and control in the project are mostly exercised by the teams themselves, making it a preferred style in cultures that oppose control, such as in micro and small companies and nations with low power distance (Turner, Ledwith, & Kelly, 2010).

Shared leadership is different from the preceding leadership styles because it emanates from within the team, rather than from the project manager. It emerges through a process of collaborative team interaction for the identification of an individual team member as a temporary leader, for example, to provide temporary leadership in solving a particular issue in the project (Cox, Pearce & Perry, 2003; Pearce & Sims, 2000). Team members engage in peer leadership by agreeing on one team member to be the leader (Crevani et al., 2007). One of the requirements for shared leadership is the team's authority to plan and manage, which requires the project manager's efficacy and empowerment by the team's appointed leader (Müller, Packendorff, & Sankaran, 2017).

Distributed leadership is related to shared leadership, as it is also leadership at the team level. It is different, however, in that distributed leadership emerges from the discourse within the team. Instead of appointing one individual as a leader, distributed leadership builds on the team's "collective brain" by encouraging team members to contribute ideas to build a broad base of different perspectives and possible solutions to a given issue. The discourse on these perspectives brings out the agreed-upon solution or decision, which the team then implements (Müller et al., 2017). However, it is not uncommon in such situations that the team's boundaries become blurred and individuals otherwise perceived as external stakeholders become involved in increasing the range of possible solutions and the resulting quality of the team's decisions (Lindgren & Packendorff, 2011).

This brief discussion of leadership approaches and styles is not meant to be an exhaustive list. It is provided as an introduction or refresher for the chapters and discussions to come. This starts with Chapter 2, which provides a more in-depth discussion of horizontal leadership's nature and its application in construction and information technology projects on three different continents (North America, Europe, and Oceania). This chapter will also provide an overview of the preferred leadership styles in these projects and the nature of the decisions made by both project managers and horizontal leaders in delivering their projects.

Chapter 3 outlines the theory of balanced leadership. It does this by informing the readers of its underlying philosophical and theoretical lenses and then describes the theory in terms of its five events (as detailed in the following) for balanced leadership, processes, the reasons for their functioning, as well as the limitations of its use. This provides a middle-range theory, which is refined in each subsequent chapter through models that fit seamlessly into the overall theory described in Chapter 3.

Chapter 4 describes the first of the five events in balanced leadership: the nomination of team members to a project. The variety of approaches for nomination and their popularity are discussed, as well as the tactics used by project managers to influence the nomination decisions made by other managers.

Chapter 5 describes the identification of possible horizontal leaders, which is the second event in balanced leadership. Here, the nature of team leadership and required competencies of appointed leaders are discussed, as well as the ways to identify them in organizations.

Chapter 6 addresses the third event, the selection and empowerment of a horizontal leader or a subteam. The different selection and empowerment concepts are discussed. A subsequent look at practices in projects identifies four different empowerment types which, together, provide for a career development framework for future managers.

Chapter 7 discusses the fourth event, the empowered leadership performed by the horizontal leader or leadership team and its influence on performance, together with the parallel process for the governance of the empowered leader(s). The differences between leadership and governance and their application in practices are also discussed.

Chapter 8 presents the fifth event, the transition of leadership authority at the end of a horizontal leadership assignment. Using transition theory and realist social theory, the chapter outlines the processes and criteria for decisions regarding horizontal leadership assignments in the future.

Chapter 9 addresses the coordination of the five events of balanced leadership in a socio-cognitive space. It outlines the need for and characteristics of the particular information that must be shared between the project manager and team for balanced leadership to occur.

Chapter 10 is a case study of a project using balanced leadership in a public organization in Australia. It describes how decisions are made at different levels of an organization that have a bearing on projects, how the five events of balanced leadership interact, and how they are coordinated through the socio-cognitive space.

Chapter 11 describes two large projects as case studies in Canada and provides an in-depth account of the ways the socio-cognitive space coordinates the leadership in these projects.

Chapter 12 concludes the story and discusses the future outlook of balanced leadership.

Summary

This chapter has introduced the concepts of balanced leadership and horizontal leadership and has set them in relation to existing leadership concepts, such as vertical leadership and team-based leadership. It also has provided a short introduction to the leadership styles addressed later in this book.

2

Horizontal Leadership and Its Scenarios

The role of leaders is not to get other people to follow them but to empower others to lead.

—Bill George (George & Sims, 2007, p. 36)

Introduction

The complexity of projects rises continuously (Maylor, Vidgen, & Carver, 2008) as the pace of change affecting organizations increases (Yukl & Mahsud, 2010). This situation intensifies the need to adjust leadership styles and it becomes imperative for managers and project managers in these complex and changing environments to adopt more malleable and adaptive leadership approaches (Yukl & Mahsud, 2010; Burke & Cooper, 2004). As mentioned in Chapter 1, leadership style has been recognized as the driver in a project manager's rate of success or failure (Cunningham, Salomone, & Wielgus, 2015). According to Ojokuku, Odetayo, and Sajuyigbe (2012), the leadership style of a manager influences the performance of team members as well as the motivation of the team to reach organization or project goals. Leadership is a social influence process in which leaders seek the participation of team members to reach specific goals (Bhatti, Maitlo, Shaikh, Hashmi, & Shaikh, 2012). In addition, Nanjundeswaraswamy and Swamy (2014) determined that a relationship exists between leadership style, work satisfaction, and organizational commitment, which are essential for project management success. Therefore, it is important for project managers to develop leadership skills. In this regard, Müller and Turner (2010) determined in their research the need for project managers to be trained not only in technical and management skills, but also in the development of leadership competencies. However, the project manager cannot be a specialist and the sole decision-maker in all areas from technology to business and strategy. Project managers must rely on team members and their specific expertise for appropriate and timely decisions for

Table 2.1 Leadership Approaches

Leadership Approach	Definition	Source
Vertical	By an appointed or formal leader of a team	Pearce & Sims (2002, p. 172)
Shared / distributed	A group process in which leadership is distributed among, and stems from, team members	
Horizontal	Executed by a team member upon nomination by the project manager (vertical leader), and governed by the vertical leader for the time of the nomination	Pretorius et al. (2017)
Balanced	Emerges from the dynamic, temporary, and alternating transitions between vertical, shared, distributed, and horizontal leadership for the accomplishment of desired states in, for example, a task outcome, or the entire project	Müller et al. (2018)

complex projects in a competitive market. Existing leadership theory takes a static perspective by theorizing either the leadership of a project manager as vertical leader or the leadership in a team (shared or distributed leadership), but not both in parallel. Table 2.1 defines various leadership approaches.

In actuality, both types of leadership prevail in projects, but little academic work has been found on this phenomenon from the literature reviewed (Müller, Packendorff, & Sankaran, 2017).

As mentioned in Chapter 1, there is a need to investigate the balance between the vertical leadership (of a senior or project manager) and horizontal leadership (of a team leader or team members) and the context in which the balanced leadership occurs to lead to project success. It brings us to the following question: How do horizontal leaders execute their leadership task in the context of balanced leadership? We were interested in looking at the nature of the leadership style when it is split between the project manager and the horizontal leader, and the nature of the decisions made by the two parties when executing their particular leadership approach. Figure 2.1 depicts horizontal leadership as positioned within the balanced leadership framework.

In this chapter, we further present scenarios to illustrate how leadership is balanced in projects. First, we identify the circumstances that call for the empowerment of team members to become horizontal leaders for the good of the project; we will learn about the nature and the split of leadership styles across the two leadership levels, which helps to find a balance across the two levels. Second, we will learn about the types of decisions that are delegated to teams, as well as those that typically remain at the project manager's level. Third, we hope to provide a more dynamic and realistic theory about leadership in projects, in particular horizontal leadership, for new opportunities

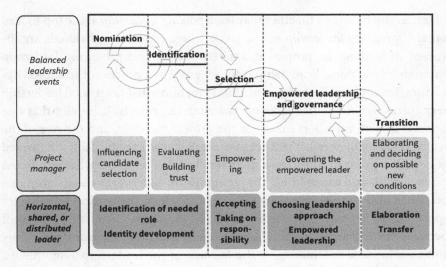

Figure 2.1. Locating horizontal leadership in the balanced leadership framework.

for theorizing. This includes the relative weight of leadership by vertical and horizontal leaders as manifested in their decision-making power, or their accountability as shown by the nature of the decisions they make.

Horizontal leadership

What is horizontal leadership? We realized that, to date, there has been limited use of the term "horizontal leadership" (Pretorius, Steyn, & Bond-Barnard, 2017). Since very few authors use this term, we decided to base our understanding on the most recent research on the topic conducted by Müller, Zhai, and Wang (2017). Müller et al. (2017) mentioned that some research has looked at leadership that emerges from teams or individuals in a team. This leadership complements the leadership of the vertical leader and it includes, for example, the studies on shared leadership (Pearce & Conger, 2003). Müller et al. (2017) explain that traditional vertical leadership approaches are supplemented by approaches that include horizontal, and thereby collective, leadership. The point here is to show that, in practice, leadership could also involve several individuals "acting simultaneously and that these actors do not necessarily have to be formal managers or leaders" (p. 190). Denis, Langley, and Sergi (2012) identify four streams of research based on such a perspective. These authors talk about *sharing leadership* (or its related concept of distributed leadership) for team effectiveness, an approach based on members of teams and how they together may lead; *pooling leadership* at the top to lead others; *spreading leadership* across levels where different individuals are involved in leading the project at different stages; and *producing leadership* through interactions. Leadership is thus viewed as a process of relational dynamics. In addition, Pretorius et al. (2017) mention that horizontal leadership recognizes the *distributed form of leadership* in projects. It implies that one or several team members influence the project manager, and the rest of the team complete the project in a set manner. Because specific skills are needed at a certain point in time, team members become temporary leaders, based on their skills and capabilities. They temporarily take over the leadership role on behalf of the project manager (as vertical leader). The vertical leader is responsible for keeping the general vision and direction, encouraging the shift between vertical and horizontal leadership by including the team in the pursuit of solutions, and managing the fairness of the leadership assignments. Horizontal leadership is facilitated through empowerment by the project manager, and is accomplished through self-management of the horizontal leader.

Thus, horizontal leadership is practiced by a team member after he/she has been nominated by the project leader (vertical leader). In addition, the project manager governs this leadership for the duration of the nomination and decides when it is time to pull it back to the project manager. The project manager may have several reasons for pulling it back. The decision is made when there is no longer a need to delegate the decision-making to a horizontal leader, when the horizontal leader should no longer lead the decision-making based on their expertise, or when the horizontal leader does not want to lead the process for various reasons (Müller et al., 2017). Figure 2.2 (from Müller et al., 2017) illustrates this sequential process model that starts in quadrant 1 (*qualification and selection*) with the qualification of possible candidates for horizontal leadership and the selection of a candidate when the need for horizontal leadership arises. In quadrant 2 (*enabling*), the vertical leader appoints or grants the authority to one or several horizontal leaders. The horizontal leader therefore has the opportunity to develop self-management capabilities. Quadrant 3 (*exercising horizontal leadership*) makes visible the leadership by the horizontal leader, namely, the vertical leader's handover of leadership authority and the acceptance of it by horizontal leaders. Finally, in quadrant 4 (*monitoring and control*), once the horizontal leader has taken over, the vertical leader's monitoring and control of the horizontal leaders sets in.

Chapter 1 has covered the variety of leadership styles cited in the literature. We will not repeat this here, but will summarize some key points that will be used in this chapter. For instance, Frame (1987) proposed three basic

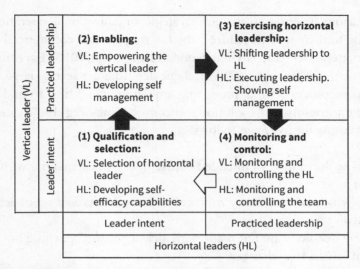

Figure 2.2.   Leading and leadership, vertically and horizontally.
Source: Müller et al. (2017).

leadership styles: autocratic, laissez-faire, and democratic. *Autocratic* leadership is associated with the traditional image of the manager as the "boss" (Frame, 1987, p. 73) and is associated with highly centralized decision-making. *Laissez-faire* lies at the other extreme. When this style is adopted, nobody is in charge, and project members decide by themselves. A laissez-faire approach might be used by project managers to encourage creativity in team members. *A democratic* style is a participative approach. Democratic leaders value team members' inputs to be included in decision-making processes. It is important to understand the leadership style of our vertical leaders since it could have an impact on the delegation and empowerment of the horizontal leader. It is also important to identify the nature of decisions that are delegated to the horizontal leader. These will be further discussed in the scenarios section.

Nature of decisions

Every project has decisions that are made at different hierarchical levels, with the responsible actor operating in a certain number of fields of action corresponding to certain decision types. Decisions could be characterized as unstructured or complex. Although the concept of a decision remains ambiguous and ill-defined (Nutt & Wilson, 2010), decisions could be classified under various types (strategic, non-strategic, organizational, operational) or according to their specific nature (whether they involve commercial or economic matters) (see Morris, Greenwood, & Fairglough, 2010). For Mintzberg, Raisinghani, and Theoret (1976), strategic decisions are seen as large, expensive, and precedent setting, producing ambiguity about how to find a solution and uncertainty in the solution's outcomes. Mintzberg (1987) categorizes decisions using the five *Ps*, as follows:

Plan: the decision is an intended course of action carried out with a clear purpose.

Ploy: (which has a military root) refers to decisions as a set of actions to outwit the competition.

Pattern: decisions are not made with a clear planned purpose but exhibit similarities to each other.

Position: a decision is meant to realize a match between the organization and the environment.

Perspective: decisions are a reflection of how strategists in an organization perceive the world and their organization.

At the project level, strategic decisions are important because they may affect the objectives and project goals. For the purpose of this chapter, these strategic decisions are defined as: *strategic and political decisions* that involve, for instance, the budget allowance, management of political issues within the organization; *business management decisions* that affect the overall logic of the firm's bundle of services and markets (Nutt et al., 2010); the *administration of contractual agreements*; key *human resource* policies and resource allocation; and, finally, the *governance structure* (e.g., the selection and development of project-management practices). These strategic decisions deal with overall project effectiveness and adequate resource utilization so that the organization can obtain expected benefits (Bourgault, Drouin, Daoudi, & Hamel, 2008). Tactical or operational decisions relate to the day-to-day functioning of the project. These tactical decisions require a lot of inputs to establish an efficient vision of the project, making certain that project goals are pursued as planned, e.g. solving technical problems, fine-tuning project planning (Bourgault et al., 2008, p. 57). These decisions are related to *technical decisions* that are usually made by an expert; *stakeholders management*; the *daily tasks* attached to the management of the project; and *changing* or *unforeseen* events that occur throughout the life cycle of the project. These decisions, which are more task-oriented, are usually under the responsibility of the horizontal leader (Müller et al., 2017). According to Zabojnik (2002), it may be optimal to let workers decide how to do their jobs, even though managers may have better information. Zabojnik (2002) further argues that decentralization of decisions is recommended when quick responses to changing technologies and environments are required, and new information flows upward through the hierarchy. Decisions could be made by an individual or by team members as a group.

Examples of scenarios using case study descriptions

To illustrate some scenarios, the following section describes case studies with Canadian, Scandinavian, and Australian firms. The firms and their specific projects are described in Boxes 2.1, 2.2, and 2.3, followed by a discussion of the scenarios for balanced leadership.

Box 2.1. Canadian Cases

Utilities. Project 1 (Canada) is worth around C$500 million and involved the rehabilitation of the intake and spillway at a generating station. This undertaking was intended to ensure long-term facility operability. The project took 10 years and involved at its peak a dozen people from the company plus external stakeholders such as contractor teams. The on-site team was led by a senior manager, in charge of a portfolio of five major projects in a specific geographical region. The senior manager reported directly to his immediate superior, who was based at the headquarters of the company. The project manager was responsible for all project-related activities and reported directly to the senior manager. The security adviser was a team member in charge of the construction safety and relations with the contractors. The on-site engineer was accountable for all mechanical and technical engineering issues, and reported directly to the project manager and frequently collaborated with the engineering division based at the headquarters. Finally, the clerk was mainly in charge of buying equipment that supported the management of the teams and on-site facilities. External stakeholders were mostly contractors (three or four depending on the phase of the project) and the team of the turbine manufacturer. The Canadian company leading this project is a world leader in the field of hydroelectricity. It focuses on the refurbishment of generating and transmission hydroelectricity facilities to meet the needs of its clients.

Construction/Public Sector. Project 2 (Canada) involved the construction of a sports stadium. With an allocated budget of slightly over C$50 million, the stadium had to

Box 2.1. Continued

house both an indoor and an outdoor field. The building of a state-of-the-art sports stadium was the result of an election promise several years prior to its formal authorization. The completion of Project 2 stretched over eight years and involved an architectural contest to select a design that would become a symbol of creativity and innovation. Initially under the sole charge of the city's Sports Department, the project was later carried out jointly with the Property Planning and Management Department, as the latter was more experienced in the fields of project management and infrastructure construction. Operating under a matrix structure, Project 2 was supervised by senior managers from both departments, who were also in charge of other projects and programs simultaneously. Under their authority, two project managers were assigned full-time to the project, one each from the two departments involved. The project manager attached to the Sports Department was mainly in charge of communications, public relations, and fostering relationships with sports associations, while the project manager from the Property Planning and Management Department was assigned to oversee the activities related to the planning and the building of the infrastructure. When the construction phase began, an on-site engineer and on-site assistant junior engineer were added as full-time members of the project team to monitor the construction site and ensure compliance with contracts. As for external stakeholders, the primary parties were the architectural firm, chosen through the contest, and the building contractor, selected following a call for tender. A steering committee was formed in order to facilitate collaboration between the core project team and other stakeholders, such as representatives from other internal departments, sports associations, municipal regulatory bodies, and energy service providers. The organization commissioning the infrastructure project is a municipal government administering an urban city that has over one million inhabitants.

Box 2.2. Scandinavian Cases

Professional Services. Project 3 (Scandinavia). The organization plans, builds, operates, and maintains roads in Scandinavia. It is more than 150 years old, and a highly multidisciplinary organization of about 7,500 employees, including a wide range of analysts, engineers, and other skilled workers. This organization runs a large number of projects of varying size at any point in time. The unique geography and climate in Scandinavia present a number of challenges to road construction projects, such as subsea tunnels, long tunnels, and advanced bridge constructions. The case study was done on four large road construction projects in northern Scandinavia. In addition to the typical project execution processes that are widespread in

Box 2.2. Continued

infrastructure development projects, the focal projects contain a large number of stakeholders and are highly infused with local and regional political issues. The interviews were conducted with two senior managers, as well as project managers, and project team members of a wide spectrum of projects.

Engineering. Project 4 (Sweden). The organization is a global engineering corporation with more than 130,000 employees. Its focus is on development of technologies in the automation and power industry, for which it develops and supports a broad range of products and services. The organization maintains a global network of corporate research centers for the development of technologies for future products and services. The case study was done on one of these centers. Here, the focus of activities is very broad and covers technology development for automation, environment, machines, and new materials, as well as underlying services and processes, such as those for software architecture and processes. The research center does this by monitoring the market to identify opportunities for technologies needed for development, developing these, and then transferring them to the business areas of the wider corporation, where they are used in and for products. The employees in this center are typically engaged in collaborations with universities and other research centers internal and external to the corporation, and to a lesser extent with customers and their specific projects. The interviews were conducted with a senior manager, as well as project managers and project team members from a wide spectrum of projects. These include engineering and engineering studies, technical Research and Development (R&D), and IT projects.

Box 2.3. Australian Cases

Construction/Private Sector. Project 5 (Australia) is the IT department for a major international property and infrastructure group employing more than 12,000 people. Its business covers managing projects over their life cycle, including coming up with new ideas. It also invests in development projects and participates in construction. The IT department was mainly focused on solutions for internal departments like human resources, finance, and property development in helping to deliver technologies for business operations. There were two project teams managed by two delivery managers delivering close to 15 projects at any one time. The teams used both waterfall and agile methodologies, depending on the context in which the project was carried out.

Box 2.3. Continued

Financial Services. Project 6 (Australia) is a major financial services company in Australia with close to A$100 billion in assets and employing more than 15,000 people. Its business service is in banking and several types of insurance and wealth management. The people interviewed at this organization were part of a major business transformation IT-based project that was carried out over two years and estimated to cost more than A$300 million. The project was carried out in collaboration with a major technology partner and employed close to 600 people at its peak. Work was also outsourced to offshore service providers but was managed centrally from Australia. The project was aimed to increase efficiency, speed up transactions, and make better use of business intelligence. The major methodology used by the organization was agile due to its heavy IT emphasis. While the organization did not use a large-scale project management office, the project was supported by sponsors from technology and business areas at the top.

Leadership styles

Figure 2.3 presents the leadership style for each project by calculating the number of times a particular style was observed for vertical leaders (project manager or senior manager). A percentage was then calculated to identify the style by country and for the Scandinavian region. Sub-figures 1 through 3 show the results by country, and sub-figure 4 summarizes these results for all cases.

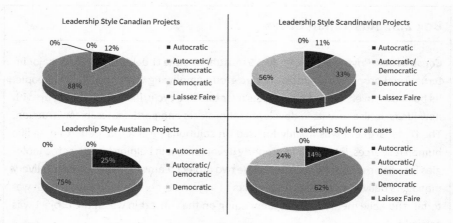

Figure 2.3. Leadership style by project and country/region.
Source: Drouin et al. (2018).

In their paper, Drouin, Müller, Sankaran, and Vaagaasar (2018) show that 62% of the vertical leaders (project managers or senior managers) use a mixture of democratic and autocratic approaches to manage their projects; 24% prefer a democratic approach; while 14% prefer an autocratic one. By country, they noticed that for the Canadian projects, the vertical leaders clearly preferred an autocratic/democratic approach in both projects (88%) where decisions seem more centralized by vertical leaders and, when delegated, they are either at the level of the project team or to individuals. Only one project manager in the utility sector (Project 1) was identified as having an autocratic style. This project manager particularly centralized the decision-making within his team, and his delegation to horizontal leaders was either at the individual level or to team members. The vertical leaders in the Australian projects were also characterized as using an autocratic/democratic approach (75%) and one project manager in Project 6 (construction sector) preferred an autocratic style. Delegation to horizontal leaders is mainly through the team, and a combination of individual and team delegation was observed for the autocratic leader. In Scandinavian projects the results are different. Drouin et al. (2018) noticed a 56% presence of democratic leadership style and a 33% combination of autocratic and democratic, which is a significantly lower percentage than what was observed in the Canadian and Australian projects. Only one project manager in Project 3 (Professional Services - Scandinavia) appears to use an autocratic leadership style (11%). As far as the delegation to horizontal leaders is concerned in the Scandinavian projects, the latter is done by all vertical leaders, mainly through individuals (Drouin et al., 2018).

Nature and frequency of decisions

Every project investigated had decisions that needed to be made. Decisions are also made at different hierarchical levels, with the responsible actor operating in a certain number of fields of action corresponding to certain decision types. Traditionally, strategic decisions (strategic planning) are made by upper management, tactical decisions (management control) by middle management, and operational decisions (operational control) by non-management employees (Bourgault et al., 2008). Again, based on Drouin et al. (2018), Table 2.2 lists the decisions that are made by vertical leaders in their study (*Strategic and political*; *Business management decisions*; *Administration of contractual agreements*; *Human resource policies*; *Governance structure*; and *Other*), and those that are delegated to horizontal leaders (*Technical decisions*; *Stakeholders management*; *Daily tasks*; *Unforeseen events*; *Improvement and*

Table 2.2 Nature and Frequency of Decisions Based on Total Number of Interviews

Canada	Scandinavia	Australia	Total (Decisions)			
Frequency	Frequency	Frequency			Nature of Decisions	
				% of All Interviews		
2	3	1	6	21%	Strategic / political	
9	8	6	23	79%	Business / management	**VLS**
10	4	2	16	55%	Administration / contract	
7	3	3	13	45%	Human resources	
8	3	1	12	41%	Structure	
1	1	0	2	7%	Other	
11	10	4	24	83%	Technical	
4	4	1	9	31%	Stakeholders	
10	5	6	21	72%	Daily tasks	HLS
3	0	2	5	17%	Unforeseen events	
0	1	2	3	10%	Improvement / change	
0	2	0	2	7%	Other	
			136	29		

Source: Drouin et al. (2018).
Note: VLS = Vertical leadership, HLS = Horizontal leadership

change; and *Other*). These authors analyzed the frequency of each decision made by vertical leaders and horizontal leaders. In total, 136 decisions were identified in 29 interviews. The percentage of each decision frequency was calculated by dividing the frequency of each type of decision by the number of interviews.

The results (Table 2.3) show that 83% of the decisions that are delegated to horizontal leaders are technical decisions. Senior and project managers

Table 2.3 Nature and Frequency of Decisions Based on Number of Decisions per Country/Region

Leadership Style / Nature of Decisions	Canada Autocratic / Democratic		Scandinavia Autocratic / Democratic		Australia Autocratic / Democratic		Total	
	Frequency	%	Frequency	%	Frequency	%	Frequency	%
VLS								
Strategic / political	2	5%	3	14%	1	8%	6	8%
Business / management	9	24%	8	36%	6	46%	24	32%
Administration / contract	10	27%	4	18%	2	15%	16	22%
Human resources	7	19%	3	14%	3	23%	13	18%
Structure	8	22%	3	14%	1	8%	12	16%
Other	1	3%	1	5%	0	0%	2	3%
Total number of decisions	37		22		13		74	
HLS								
Technical	11	39%	10	45%	4	27%	24	37%
Stakeholders	4	14%	4	18%	1	7%	9	14%
Daily tasks	10	36%	5	23%	6	40%	22	33%
Unforeseen events	3	11%	0	0%	2	13%	5	8%
Improvement / change	0	0%	1	5%	2	13%	3	5%
Other	0	0%	2	9%	0	0%	2	3%
Total number of decisions	28		22		15		65	

Source: Drouin et al. (2018).
Note: VLS = Vertical leadership, HLS = Horizontal leadership

count on the specific expertise of horizontal leaders to make such decisions. Similarly, decisions affecting the day-to-day activities of projects are the responsibility of horizontal leaders (72%), as well as stakeholder management, with a lower percentage of 31%. Vertical leaders control business-management decisions (79%), but seem to have less control over decisions related to the administration of contracts (55%), human resource management and resource allocation (45%), and governance structure of projects (41%). The lowest level of control for vertical leaders is for strategic and political decisions (21%), suggesting that these decisions are handled at higher hierarchical levels within the organization.

Leadership style was either found as a mixture of autocratic and democratic or as democratic per se. Linked to these leadership styles, the scenarios that emerge from Drouin et al.'s (2018) results are as follows:

- *Business management decisions* remain under the authority of vertical leaders, especially for the Scandinavian and Australian projects (per country/region: Canada, 24%; Scandinavia, 36%; Australia, 46%).
- *Contractual administration*: Particular to Canadian projects, the relatively low importance of vertical leader's authority on contractual administration (27%) and governance-structure decisions (22%) was observed, and these specific decisions seem to be made elsewhere within the hierarchy of the Australian and Scandinavian organizations.
- *Human resources*: In Australian projects it was observed that the management of human resources is under the authority of vertical leaders, with a score of 23%.
- *Technical decisions*: Despite slight differences in leadership styles, similar scenarios were identified by Drouin et al. (2018) for the delegation of authority to horizontal leaders. Delegations to horizontal leaders mainly occurred through technical decisions (technical decisions per country/region: Canada, 39%; Scandinavia, 45%; Australia, 27%) and decisions associated to the execution of tasks to deliver projects (daily tasks per country/region: Canada, 36%; Scandinavia, 23%; Australia, 40%).

Summary

This chapter has examined how horizontal leaders (within project teams) execute their leadership task in the context of balanced leadership and has described scenarios that occur when horizontal leaders are identified and empowered by the vertical leader (senior or project managers) and a project task is handed over to the horizontal leader to lead. Based on Drouin et al. (2018), it highlights the use of two preferred leadership styles in six projects: *a mixture of autocratic and democratic approach* (Canadian and Australian vertical leaders), and *a democratic approach* (Scandinavian vertical leaders). The vertical leader (project manager or senior manager) can be sometimes autocratic and sometimes democratic in the same context. Balanced leadership and the delegation of decisions occur in conjunction with different leadership styles that vary on a continuum between autocratic and democratic styles in some cases but that seem to be stabilized throughout a democratic leadership style for the Scandinavian vertical leaders.

In addition, this chapter has highlighted scenarios that connect vertical leadership styles and the nature of decisions delegated to horizontal leaders. Few research studies relate the vertical leadership style to its horizontal delegation through the lens of the nature of decisions (Müller et al., 2017). Drouin et al. (2018) clearly show a traditional task-oriented delegation with leeway and maneuvering for the horizontal leader.

This implies that delegation occurs when vertical leaders see horizontal leaders as competent relative to the demands of the specific task and sufficiently trustworthy, thus allowing the vertical leader to be confident in undertaking the risks associated with delegation to horizontal leaders (Schriesheim, Neider, & Scandura, 1998, p. 300). Although it was not discussed specifically in this chapter, Drouin et al. (2018) mention that vertical leaders distinguish between delegation to individuals or teams and highlight specific patterns. This was seen in one of the Scandinavian cases where the democratic leadership style favors delegation to individuals, and in one of the Australian cases where a mixture of autocratic and democratic leadership styles encourages delegation to teams. Difference in leadership styles may stem to a certain extent from the cultural differences between the countries (Müller, Zhu, Sun, Wang, & Yu, 2018). This seems to point toward a more people-oriented leadership approach in projects in Scandinavia.

In summary, this chapter has provided support on how horizontal leaders execute their leadership task in the context of balanced leadership in projects. It has revealed that balanced leadership is executed mainly through task-oriented leadership, and the switching of leadership authority is based on the trust that the vertical leaders place on the horizontal leader, as well as the evaluation of the horizontal leader's competencies. It also indicates that vertical leadership style is strongly influenced by cultural differences, and Scandinavian vertical leaders may use a more people-oriented leadership style compared with Anglo-Saxon countries such as Canada and Australia. Future research is needed to address the relationship between vertical leaders and horizontal leaders in more depth and with additional case studies in order to generalize the results. The scenarios illustrated in this chapter provide some insights to project managers and senior managers on what tasks are best delegated to horizontal leaders and what tasks should be handled by the project manager. This could help in empowering the horizontal leader to take up tasks that they are capable of managing so that the project manager can focus on tasks that s/he is better placed to manage. This can also help in better governance of the tasks and less interference into the "nuts and bolts" issues in projects when such tasks can be clearly delegated and managed by the team.

Acknowledgments

We would like to thank Drouin, N., Müller, R., Sankaran, S., and Vaagaasar, A. L. (2018) for allowing the use of the results of their article titled: Balancing vertical and horizontal leadership in projects: Empirical studies from Australia, Canada, Norway and Sweden, published in the *International Journal of Managing Projects in Business*, 11(4), 986–1006.

Reflection questions

1. How do horizontal leaders execute their leadership task in the context of balanced leadership?
2. What is the nature of the leadership style when it is split between the project manager and the horizontal leader?
3. What is the nature of the decisions made by the two parties when executing their particular leadership approach?
4. What could make horizontal leadership more efficient?

3

A Theory of Balanced Leadership

Nothing is so practical as a good theory.

—Kurt Lewin (1945, p. 129)

Introduction

This famous quote by Kurt Lewin captures the purpose of this book. Throughout all the chapters, we present theories based on research results obtained through various methods, with the goal of helping practicing managers, leaders, and team members better understand day-to-day leadership situations in projects. We are thus trying to enable our readers to make better-informed decisions.

But what makes theories practical? Andrew van de Ven (1989, p. 486) argues that "good theory is practical precisely because it advances knowledge in a scientific discipline, guides research toward crucial questions, and enlightens the profession of management." In this book, we address all of these arguments. We advance leadership knowledge in projects by adding a new dimension: the shift of leadership approaches over time, which we call balanced leadership. Simultaneously, we provide new avenues for researchers to investigate: What goes on in balanced leadership? What are the enablers, triggers, implications, and consequences of this approach to leadership? For this, we provide models and theories for further investigation, for example, at the detailed level of their constituting elements or relationships and their situational contingencies. Finally, we also provide insights for the profession of management, that is, for practicing managers, leaders, or temporarily empowered leaders. We do this by giving them the knowledge to recognize the dynamics of leadership in their projects and to subsequently apply the book's theories for predictable and comprehensible decisions and beneficial outcomes.

Examples of practical use of the theories described in this book include guidelines on the types of projects that benefit from balanced leadership, or the types of leadership styles to expect from empowered leaders in different industries or national cultures. Other examples include tools to assess team members for potential empowerment, or the method of empowerment that fits the project's circumstances, or the particular information that must be shared between a project manager and the team to make balanced leadership work, and many more. Given the wide variety of leadership situations in projects, we have not intended to write a "how to" book that describes a particular way of leading. On the contrary, we provide empirically based theories drawn from real data collected from hundreds of projects so that readers can develop a situational understanding of what happens in their own projects. Applying these theories and models gives guidance on handling leadership situations without being overly prescriptive. Through this, we make the leader understand the situation and give him or her room to maneuver most beneficially.

What is an empirically based theory? The term *theory* is defined in many different ways, which range from "observed regularities in data with procedural explanations, to an applied theoretical model, to a formal middle-range theory" (May et al., 2009, p. 1), or even grand theory. The first three of these definitions are important for this book. First, the theory we describe in the chapters of this book are all derived from observed regularities, that is, patterns of behavior in real-life projects that the interviewees and questionnaire respondents described when interacting with the researchers. Second, the models we present and the explanations of these are derived from these regularities. Finally, we aim to develop a middle-range theory of leadership in projects. Middle-range theory lies "between the minor but necessary working hypotheses that evolve in abundance during day-to-day research and the all-inclusive systematic efforts to develop a unified theory that will explain all the observed uniformities of social behavior, social organization, and social change" (Merton & Merton, 1968, p. 39). To this end, middle-range theories integrate theory development and their empirical testing for an explanation of a set of phenomena (such as balanced leadership).

Middle-range theories are located between substantive theories and grand theories. The former theories explain phenomena in their particular context, such as the balanced leadership events described in Chapters 4–8. Grand theories are highly abstract general theories that offer a comprehensive view of phenomena, which overcome empirical conflicts arising from empirical generalizations. Examples include Transaction Costs Economics (Williamson, 1985) or Agency Theory (Jensen & Meckling, 1976). Hence, middle-range theories possess a medium level of generalizability, sufficiently specific for the evaluation of observed phenomena, while simultaneously general enough for the development of broader theoretical statements (Morrow & Muchinsky, 1980).

Prerequisites for correct interpretation of theories

To interpret a theory correctly, we should have two sets of information in addition to the theory itself. The first set of information is related to the underlying assumptions in the studies on which the theory is based; we call this *research philosophy*. The second is related to the particular theoretical perspective taken during the studies, for example, a psychological perspective versus an economic perspective. This is called the *theoretical lens* and describes the nature of the explanation that the theory provides. Both research philosophy and theoretical lens are discussed in the following.

Research philosophy is a broad field, and we try to describe only the most rudimentary aspects that are needed to "make sense" of the theory described in this book. When using a theory, we should first know which type of a reality the theory describes. We call this ontology, that is, the study of the concepts of existence, being, becoming, and reality. In terms of reality, ontology distinguishes between objective and subjective reality—in our case, whether a theory describes an objective or a subjective reality. Objective reality is typically described in natural sciences, where a phenomenon's variables can be directly measured and observed. Examples include the outside temperature, measured objectively by a thermometer. Subjective reality cannot be measured directly. It is typical in the social sciences, where we observe, interview, or survey human beings, like when we aim to understand and predict hooliganism in a football stadium. In this case, we try to recreate the individuals' subjectivity in order to "make sense" of their behavior. Objective and subjective reality can be modeled as representing the two ends of a continuum. The balance between objective and subjective reality changes gradually from one extreme to the other, as shown in the left column in Table 3.1.

Associated with the gradual shifts from objectivity to subjectivity, different ways to find out what we can know about a phenomenon are applied. This is called *epistemology*—the study of knowledge and how we can know about something. Table 3.1 shows some typical associations between ontology and epistemology, such as a purely objective reality (e.g., the functioning of an automobile engine can be measured independent of the automobile). Researchers call this combination of ontology and epistemology a *positivism research paradigm*. When studies aim for high levels of objectivity but

Table 3.1 Research Philosophies and Their Meaning for Theories

Ontology	Epistemology	Paradigm	What It Means for the Theory
Objectivism	Measure independent of object	Positivism	All cars are always driven at 50 km/h, no matter the circumstances. It is a natural law.
Objectivism as ideal	Aim for objective statements from subjective individuals	Post-positivism	The respondents say they drive at 50km/h, knowing full well that cars are sometimes driven faster (or slower) than this. The theory describes a trend and may not hold when I am there.
Objectivism meets subjectivism	Look for evidence of the three layers of mechanisms, situation, and event	Realism	The respondents are of the opinion that they were driving at 50 km/h, in the particular situation that they were in when they were asked the question or the last time they observed it. Generalizations of the theory might be possible when set in relation to the underlying mechanics (i.e., the speed limit there, the frequency of speed tests, etc.).
Subjectivism	Reconstruction of the life-world of the informant	Social constructivism	The respondents think the cars are being driven at 50km/h, but this could be because: (a) "they accelerate even up to 50 km/h," as stated by a person who thinks the cars are being driven too fast as there is a kindergarten in the street (i.e., overemphasizing the perceived speed) (b) "we have to be as slow as 50 km/h, even though the road is wide and there is little traffic," as stated by a sports car fan living in that street (i.e., overemphasizing the speed reduction)
			Hence, both are extreme cases, which might be true on some occasions, but not reliably so in most or all cases. They are the subjective opinions of individuals and may be completely wrong. Hence, the theory holds only for the persons interviewed.
Subjectivism	Everything happens by chance	Post-modernism	Everything happens by chance. The cars may drive at 50 km/h at the time we looked at it, but they may have never driven at that speed before, nor will they ever drive at that speed in the future. The theory holds only for the very moment it was created.

can only obtain their data from (subjective) human beings, the objectivity is compromised and remains an ideal. These studies fall under the paradigm of post-positivism, and their results show trends, as opposed to natural laws, in positivism studies. Subjective ontology is typically associated with the "sense-making" of people's behavior by recreating what goes on in their sub-jective reality in the brain. These studies fall under the paradigm of social constructivism and give insights into an individual's subjective sense-making of phenomena. The extreme form of subjectivity is post-modernist studies. These are based on the assumption that everything in life and reality happens by chance, and predictability is impossible. These studies aim to explain a particular phenomenon without seeking for replicability or predictability for similar phenomena in the future.

This discussion leads to the question of why we should know about re-search philosophy when we use a theory. The answer is in the right column in Table 3.1. Let's take the example that a theory (based on empirical studies) says that cars are driven at 50 kilometers per hour (km/h) in the street where you live.

Looking at Table 3.1 shows that different research paradigms give different levels of "stability" for their resulting theories. This ranges from natural law (positivism paradigm), which means that a phenomenon always functions in the described way, independent of its circumstances, to the case where a phenomenon is occurring by chance (post-modernism paradigm) and will never happen like this again. Hence, knowing the underlying research phi-losophy allows us to set realistic expectations about the reliability and sta-bility of a theory. The column on the right side of Table 3.1 shows some typical assumptions for theories developed in the different paradigms. This includes theories describing trends when developed in a post-positivism paradigm; or describing one possible, but not the only possible, explanation when devel-oped in a realist paradigm. Those theories derived from studies using social constructivism identify the subjective meaning of individuals, and those in post-modernism explain how a perceived one-time phenomenon functioned. The column on the right uses the example of the preceding study on cars driving at 50 km/h as an example to show the implications of using different research paradigms for the interpretation of the theory.

Underlying philosophical stance: Critical realism

The studies on balanced leadership described in this book were done from a critical realism paradigm in the sense of Bhaskar (2009). This paradigm assumes that an objective reality exists, but that individuals subjectively in-terpret this reality. Critical realists distinguish between transitive and intran-sitive objects of knowledge. Transitive objects of knowledge are previously established facts, established methods, or theories that the researchers bring to the table to do the study; hence, the experience, techniques, and theoretical frameworks that the researchers are familiar with. Intransitive objects refer to the "events, situations, and mechanisms" that make up the phenomenon under study. Examples are molecular structures, suicide patterns, etc. They all exist independent of people's knowledge of them.

These intransitive objects are the phenomena under investigation. They are investigated for their underlying objective *mechanisms* (example in the following). The functioning of the mechanisms gives rise to a *situation* within which a phenomenon happens. The existence of the phenomenon in the situation then gives rise to the subjective interpretation by the individual, that is, an *event*. For example, we ask our colleague what it was like to drive to work in the morning, and he reports that he almost had an accident because someone took his right of way. From a research perspective, we can infer:

a. His car did start, and the engine was working; otherwise, he could not have been in the traffic at all. So the *mechanisms* were working (e.g., the car's engine).
b. He entered with his car into the traffic flow, which provided for the situation for the near-accident—another car almost bumped into his car. So the working mechanisms gave rise to the *situation*.
c. The colleague interpreted what happened as a mistake by the other driver, which is the *event*. So the situation gave rise to the event.

Critical realism is a systematic breakdown of phenomena from their subjective components to their objective components along the lines of event, situation, and mechanisms. While the data we collect from human beings are mainly about the subjective elements (e.g., the event, and to some extent, the situation), the objective elements are often recreated in hindsight, based on the situation's requirements or existing theories (e.g., that an engine must run before a car can be driven). Hence, this research paradigm uses both the subjective and objective reality of a phenomenon, which makes it "well-rounded" and balanced when compared with other paradigms.

What does it mean for a theory on balanced leadership? It means that the theory is one possible theory, but may not be the only possible explanation for the phenomenon. Hence, the future might bring other theories or further developed versions of the existing theory described herein.

It also means that the theory is based on empirical data that were analyzed using scientifically accepted methods, which counts for its validity. The fact that the theory derives from many different studies whose results converge adds to its reliability. The research methods, most often multiple case studies, are especially suitable for critical realism studies because the combination of this ontology and methodology provides for credible and robust results (Easton, 2010; Vincent & Wapshott, 2014). This provides a strong basis for a good theory.

The theoretical lens: Realist social theory

Previously in this chapter, we said that the correct interpretation of theories requires knowledge about the particular lens under which the theory is created. So is balanced leadership theory based on a psychology, management, or marketing lens toward the phenomenon? The answer is, it is based on realist social theory, which is a sociological theory. Sociology is the study of human social relationships and institutions, and this is what balanced leadership describes. Realist social theory is based on the critical realism paradigm and thus links seamlessly from underlying philosophy to applied theory. Realist social theory sees societies as open systems that constantly shape and become shaped by people's innovations and behavior (Archer, 1995). These open systems consist of three major elements: culture, structure, and agency. Of special interest for this book is structure and agency as the two key elements that explain what goes on in balanced leadership. Structure consists of the human and non-human parts of the societal system. It includes institutions, materials, expectations of higher-level managers, etc.—in short, everything that conditions our behavior. Examples are job descriptions, governance policies, managers' expectations, etc.

Agency describes peoples' actions within a structure, that is, their behavior and its "fit" with the given structure. The relationship between structure and agency has long been debated in sociology. While most philosophers agree that they are inextricably linked, Giddens, in his structuration theory, assumes that structure ultimately dominates agency (Archer, 2010). That means all people can be disciplined for a particular behavior if the structures are strong enough. But why do we have prisons, then? Even in the most stringent regimes? Archer addresses this by stating that structures "are mediated to people by shaping the situations in which they find themselves" (Archer, 1995, p. 196). Thus, structure and agency do not dominate each other. However, both can only be understood in relation to each other, that is, by looking at them simultaneously—the perspective adopted in this book.

The morphogenetic cycle

Central to realist social theory is the morphogenetic cycle, which analyzes the interplay between structure and human agency. Archer (1995, p. 5) explains morphogenetic as the following: "the 'morpho' element is an acknowledgment that society has no pre-set form or preferred state: the 'genetic' part is a recognition that it takes its shape from, and is formed by, agents, originating from intended and unintended consequences of their activities."

The morphogenetic cycle uses three elements: *structural conditioning*, *social interaction*, and *structural elaboration*. These elements describe a sequence of social structuring, human action within these structures, the consequences thereof, and the conditions that lead to maintaining or developing these structures further (Archer, 2020). In other words, the morphogenetic cycle explains what happens when a task is delegated to an individual and the consequences thereof for a similar situation in the future; for example, when a project manager empowers a team member to become a horizontal leader, and how the behavior of this empowered leader within the limitations of the conditions for empowerment will influence future decisions for empowerment (see the upper half of Figure 3.1).

It starts with *structural conditioning*, which conceptualizes the many different ways the "conditions" for executing a delegated task are conveyed to the candidate. As stated earlier, this can be, for example, in reference to a job description or a talk between the candidate and the delegating manager. It is this step in which the candidate is evaluated for being eligible to perform a task or not. The requirements and expectations for fulfilling the task are then communicated to him or her.

Once the candidate starts working on the delegated task, he or she becomes a human agent in *social interaction* with the task's conditions. This behavior can, but need not be, in line with the conditions imposed on the candidate, which leads to one of four possible situations:

1. The candidate's behavior is in line with the conditions. The delegating manager is happy with the candidate's behavior. Realist social theory refers to this as *necessary compatibility*.
2. The candidate's behavior differs from the conditions because of systemic differences between the candidate and the institution; for example, when the particular project control technique expected by the managers and stated in the conditions is not supported by the IT system of the company, and the candidate has to use a different one. This difference typically leads to a compromise between the conditions imposed

and the agency executed. Realist social theory refers to this as *necessary incompatibility*.

3. The candidate's behavior strongly contradicts the conditions given to him or her. This indicates extreme differences between the candidate and the delegating manager, which leads to attempts to eliminate one of the parties. This is referred to as *contingent incompatibility*.

4. The candidate does not behave in line with the conditions, but his or her behavior allows for constructing mutual benefits, which leads to opportunism. This situation is referred to as *contingent compatibility*.

These four outcomes are evaluated at the *structural elaboration* step, and lead to either morphostasis or morphogenesis.

Morphostasis—a process that works to maintain the status quo—describes the situation in which neither the criteria for selecting candidates, nor the conditions imposed on the candidates, nor the candidates themselves, will change the next time a similar situation for task delegation arises. Hence, the status quo is kept, and no change will be made to the three steps. This is likely in the cases described in points 1 and 4.

Morphogenesis—a process to further develop or change the status quo—describes the situation in which the criteria for selection of candidates, conditions, and/or choice of candidate will change the next time a similar situation for task delegation arises. This outcome is likely in situations described in points 2 and 3. The status quo will change. Depending on the experiences in the present iteration of the morphogenetic cycle, either one, two, or all three elements (i.e., criteria, conditions, and candidate) will be changed in the next iteration of the cycle.

Throughout this book, the three steps of the morphogenetic cycle provide the theoretical lens to look at and understand balanced leadership. Chapters 4–6 describe those balanced leadership events associated with *structural conditioning*, Chapter 7 the event associated with *social interaction*, and Chapter 8 the related event for *structural elaboration*. Chapter 8 emphasizes the morphogenetic cycle in detail and provides related examples.

Balanced leadership theory

Balanced leadership theory describes the dynamics in terms of processes and events that occur when leadership authority shifts between the project manager and his or her team members, or among team members. We describe this theory structured by its four essential elements, that is, the what, how, why, and when/where/who (Whetten, 2002). Hence we structure this section as follows:

1. The events in balanced leadership: This describes the *what*—the main components of the theory, its variables, and their relation to the morphogenetic cycle. These are the five main events of nomination, identification, selection, empowered leadership and governance, and transition (Figure 3.1).
2. The processes in balanced leadership: This describes the *how*—the logic and activity flow underlying the theory (see Figure 3.2 later in the chapter).
3. The functioning of balanced leadership: This describes the *why*—the underlying situational dynamics that support the theory's reasonableness.
4. The limitations of balanced leadership: This describes the *when, where,* and *who.* Hence, the conditions for the theory to hold, its enablers and disablers, and other boundary conditions.

This description concludes in the balanced leadership framework (see Figure 3.2 later in the chapter), which serves as a reference to the other chapters in this book.

Balanced leadership events

At the heart of the theory are the balanced leadership events. They were identified through several studies, observing what happens in projects and interviewing senior managers, project managers, and team members. Early on, an obvious finding was the "fit" of the data with the three steps of the morphogenetic cycle. The data allowed us to refine the three steps of the morphogenetic cycle into five events. The relationship between the morphogenetic cycle steps and the balanced leadership theory events is shown in Figure 3.1. The five events of nomination, identification, selection and empowerment, empowered leadership and governance, and transition are discussed in the following.

The *nomination* event refers to the appointment of resources as members of the project team. This happens initially at the outset of the project and recurs whenever new team members are required. Nominations happen quite frequently because projects typically have a steady inflow and outflow of resources, who are only called in for the time of their work on a particular project. Many different approaches exist in nominating resources. The

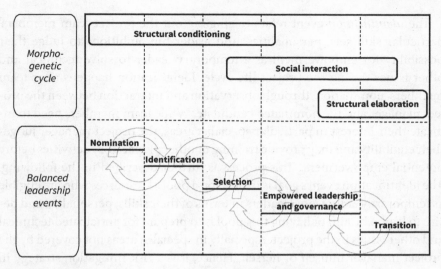

Figure 3.1. The balanced leadership events in the morphogenetic cycle.

organization's governance structure typically suggests a particular approach, but the circumstances of the project might lead to the adoption of a different approach. Most popular are nominations through functional managers in matrix organizations. They decide which person will work on what project and for how long. Despite this tradition, project managers are often not happy with this approach and the functional managers' associated decisions. A project manager often has already decided on a particular specialist who can serve as a temporary leader to guide the project through a crisis when the need arises. The desire for this "ideal candidate" is often based on past experiences with particular resources, similar projects, or technical issues similar to those anticipated in the new project. To pursue the nomination of their "ideal candidates," project managers use different tactics to increase their influence in the decision-making process. These include the use of their social relations with functional managers, or closely tracking when the desired resource is likely to be released by another project and then requesting them for their own project.

In terms of the morphogenetic cycle, the nomination event relates to structural conditioning. At this event, the conditions in terms of available resources, personalities, and specific skill sets are determined. Through this, the conditions for the potential use of empowered leaders in the project, the conditions that can be imposed on them, and the conditions for working toward successful accomplishment of the project plan and objectives are influenced.

The *identification* event refers to singling out the project team members' particular skill sets, personalities, and leadership ambitions to judge their possibility for empowerment as a temporary leader to solve technical and other issues during the project life cycle. Identification happens after team members' nomination, through observation and interaction between the project manager and the nominated candidate. While team members need to indicate their interest in particular specialist areas, the project manager judges their eligibility and may provide training or other preparatory activities before potential empowerment. This process is further described in the following. The identification event's goal is to develop a pool of resources who are eligible as temporarily empowered leaders in terms of their skills, personality, and desire to lead. The aim of having this pool is to prepare for anticipated technical and other issues in the project, especially in specialist areas not covered by the project manager himself or herself. Hence, it is a risk-mitigation strategy in terms of technical and leadership skills.

From a morphogenetic cycle perspective, the identification event is part of structural conditioning. Through the identification event, the scope of the possible conditions that can be imposed on empowered leaders is set. In the case of training and development of team members, their eligibility for specific tasks is increased. Hence, the scope of possible conditions is extended.

The *selection and empowerment* event refers to the point in time when a temporary leader, in the form of either an individual or a subteam from the project team, is empowered to lead. The event is enabled by the need for a leader other than the project manager. This is typically the case when the project has a severe issue or a crisis to solve and requires a different skill set than that of the project manager. Reasons for this can be manifold. One reason could be the need for the project team to follow a particular specialist in addressing a technical issue, which would lead to the appointment of a horizontal leader. Another might be that a creative or innovative solution is required for a problem. This typically leads to the appointment of a (sub-)team consisting of project team members, which would exercise either shared or distributed leadership to find a suitable solution. The selection of candidates for empowerment is typically made by situationally mapping the project's current requirements against the individual profiles of candidates established during the identification event. Occasionally, the selection decision is based on different reasons, such as providing a training ground for a soon-to-be manager to speed up his or her career development. So there is a range of different reasons for selection. These are addressed in more detail in Chapter 6. The subsequent empowerment of the selected leader(s) can also take place in many different ways. This typically ranges from a public announcement to all the major stakeholders, to informal updates of the project team, to a silent takeover by the empowered leader. The third form often happens when the empowered leader already has a position very close to the empowered role, such as deputy project manager.

From a morphogenetic cycle perspective, the selection and empowerment event is associated with the structural conditioning element. At this event, the conditions for the upcoming task are conveyed to the candidate(s), in order for them to adjust their agency to the expectations that come with the task that they are empowered to lead.

The *empowered leadership and governance* event refers to the appointed leader(s) taking over leadership authority by executing leadership and applying their leadership style. This is a critical point in the project because it requires the acceptance of the temporary leader(s) by the project team. This may not always happen. Some team members might disagree or may even be frustrated about the choice of the empowered leader(s). This must be anticipated by the project manager and carefully addressed during the empowerment event, for example, in one-on-one meetings with team members who may be frustrated about not being selected as a temporary leader. By the time the empowered leader(s) have taken over, the project manager subordinates to the appointed leader(s) and follows him or her through the task they are empowered to lead. However, the project manager is still formally accountable for the project results to the Steering Committee and other stakeholders. Hence, the project manager wears a second hat, which is the governance of the empowered leader(s), to make sure that the leadership exercised by the empowered leader(s) is in the best interest of the project. To this end, the project manager retains the right to correct the actions of the empowered leader(s), adjust their leadership style to the project's situation, and change or terminate the empowerment.

From a morphogenetic cycle perspective, the selection and empowerment event is associated with the social interaction element. During this event, the empowered leader(s) interact with the conditions imposed on them earlier. Depending on the personality of the empowered leader and the situation, his/her behavior(s) leads to the compatibilities or incompatibilities discussed earlier, which are then further elaborated in the next event.

The *transition* event marks the end of the empowerment. Here, an evaluation of the assignment is made, often in discussion between the empowered leader(s) and the project manager. Depending on the results of this evaluation, the criteria for selecting future leaders in a similar situation, the conditions imposed on them, or the selected person will be changed or held constant for future assignments in similar situations. Finally, the temporary leader(s) resume their former role in the project. Occasionally, they move on to other projects as formal project managers or functional managers somewhere in the organization.

From a morphogenetic cycle perspective, the transfer event relates to the elaboration element. It is here that the need for changes is elaborated, and the decision for a morphogenetic or morphostatic outcome of the appointment is made before the cycle enters its next iteration.

Balanced leadership processes

Balanced leadership consists of macro- and micro-processes. The macro-process relates to the level of events as described in the preceding section, whereas the micro-processes relate to the activity sequences within the individual events. This is summarized in Figure 3.2.

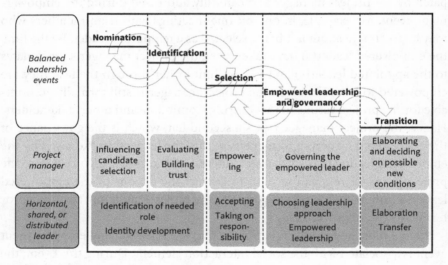

Figure 3.2. The balanced leadership theory framework.

Macro-processes

The outline of the five events suggests a sequential macro-level process from nomination to transition. However, this is almost never the case. The sequence can be broken at any time. For example, the nomination of new project team members can happen any time the need for a particular skill is identified, even shortly before the project's end. In this case, the new iteration of the events is nested in an existing flow of events. For example, a technical issue that threatens the project's progress during the implementation phase shows the need for bringing a new specialist on board. This triggers the nomination event, leading to the identification of further skill sets of the new team member, which changes the pool of candidates for empowerment. While the newly hired employee solves the problem, the need for another specialist may arise, which starts the nomination event again, leading to the identification event, and so on. But not all iterations of the five events start with a nomination. The decision for a morphogenetic outcome of a horizontal leader assignment may trigger a new selection and empowerment event, but not a nomination event, because no outside resource is needed. Or a morphostatic decision at the end of an empowered leader assignment may lead to the decision to continue with this leader for a further assignment. In these cases, the iterations of the events become nested within each other.

So the macro-process is made up of five events that need not follow the given sequence from nomination to transition in every occurrence. The flow of events can also be completely or partially reversed, as described in the preceding paragraph. This is why we called them events, not process steps, and indicated their relationships through circles in the background of Figures 3.1 and 3.2. Moreover, the events can be nested within each other, with the number of nested levels depending on various factors. These include the complexity of the tasks, the presence of required specialists in the project team, or the project's planning quality.

Thus, the macro-process for balanced leadership emerges in situational contingency and changes dynamically. It cannot be prescribed as explained in this book, as the sequence of events depends on the project and its circumstances. However, the five events will all appear in projects where balanced leadership takes place.

Micro-processes

At the micro-process level, we see basically two parallel processes: one executed by the project manager as a vertical leader, the other by the empowered horizontal leader(s). The content of each process differs by event (see Figure 3.2). These processes are explained in detail in Chapters 4–8. We provide a summary here.

During the *nomination event*, the project managers try to influence the appointment of resources to the project. They aim for the nomination of their "ideal" candidates. Given their authority level in this selection process, they may negotiate for and appoint their desired candidates if they have the authority to do so. More often, however, other managers make these appointments, so that project managers use politics, social relationships, or other means to influence these managers' decisions to appoint their desired candidates.

The candidates work in a parallel process, where they look out for a possible role for themselves in the project. They try to identify the skills needed and their ability to satisfy this need. Depending on the time the project has been going on, they may even develop and indicate an identity associated with the required skill sets for the project in order to become an "ideal" candidate for the project manager or other managers doing the nomination.

During the *identification event*, the project manager evaluates the fit between anticipated issues in the project and the skills, personality, professionality, and leadership attitude of the nominated resources. This is done through a preliminary evaluation, often based on reputation or former experience with the candidates. Following this evaluation, possible development needs are defined and offered to the candidates. After these developments, a further assessment is made to ensure the best possible fit between candidates and anticipated issues that require balanced leadership. This ends by associating with each individual in the team a certain level of trust in addressing the anticipated issues as a potential horizontal leader. This "trust level" becomes a major criterion for empowering the best possible leader during the selection event.

Project team members go through a separate process during the identification event. They start with a preliminary evaluation of their potential role in the project in order to develop an identity that allows them to contribute in a desired way to the project. This often leads to some rivalry among the team members until they find their particular comfort zone. Traditional leadership theory refers to this as the "Form, Storm, and Norm" phases in team building (Tuckman, 1965). This might be supported by some development activities encouraged by the project manager, as described earlier. Once the team members interested in becoming horizontal leaders are developed for their particular role, they wait for guidance and encouragement from the project manager to be ready for execution of the role when needed.

During the *selection and empowerment* event, the project manager maps the project's particular needs against the individuals in the team and the trust level established during the identification event. Criteria like skills, personality, professionality, and leadership attitude might be weighted and lead to a decision for an individual. Other situations might require more innovative approaches, leading to the selection of a team to solve the pressing issue. Yet other reasons for selecting and empowering individuals or teams might be to give them opportunities to develop their leadership skills, non-availability of better suitable resources, time, or budget constraints. Many different factors may influence the selection decision. Once this decision is made, the selected leader or leading team is empowered, and the decision is announced using the means described earlier.

The process followed by the team members during the selection and empowerment event starts with the acceptance of the role to which they are empowered. This includes clarification of the conditions for role execution. Depending on the project's situation, this can range from simply referring to a policy document to lengthy discussions about the assignment's scope, depth, and expectations of the project managers. Once the conditions are agreed upon and accepted, the candidate(s) take on the accountability for the role and the responsibility to fulfill the role in a professional manner, provide the agreed-upon level of transparency for their task, and perform their role within the ethical standards of the organization. In other words, they accept the four principles of good governance when executing their leadership role (Aras & Crowther, 2010). This event may end with some preparation work by the empowered leader(s) to ensure a successful start in their temporary role.

The micro-process followed by project managers in the *empowered leadership and governance event* pursues two objectives: following the empowered leader's leadership and governing the empowered leader to ensure the best outcome for the project. For the former, the project manager subordinates himself or herself to the empowered leader and follows his or her instructions to solve the issue at hand. For the latter, the project manager observes and governs the empowered leader's actions. Preferably, a governance approach based on the four principles named earlier is agreed upon between the project manager and empowered leader to ensure that the accountabilities, responsibilities, transparency, and fairness in the actions of the leader are in place. The process ends with the project manager's decision that the task the temporary leader was empowered to perform has been either completed or otherwise terminated.

The empowered leaders' process in this event starts with a decision on the most appropriate leadership approach. In cases where an individual is appointed as a horizontal leader, a decision will be made on the leadership style appropriate in the project's current situation. Is it an emergency that requires more central decision-making and authoritarian leadership styles by the project manager, or is it less of an emergency, which allows for more democratic styles? In case a subteam is appointed, they might have to decide whether they aim for a shared leadership approach, whereby a subteam member is to take the lead, or whether they aim for a joint discourse on possible ways to move forward, thus applying distributed leadership. Whatever the decision, the next step in the process is to implement the leadership approach and then adjust to changing circumstances during the remaining time of the event.

During the *transition event*, the project manager elaborates on fulfilling the task and the adherence to the conditions established at the outset. At this point, the processes of the project manager and empowered leader(s) converge for them to agree on the fulfillment of conditions and other expectations related to the appointment. This elaboration is decisive for the morphostatic or morphogenetic outcome of the balanced leadership assignment. Finally, the former empowered leader(s) transfer back into their team role or another assignment.

The functioning of balanced leadership theory

In the preceding sections, we addressed components (the *what*) and the processes (the *how*) of balanced leadership. This section addresses the question of the way it works; that is, *why* does balanced leadership work?

Traditional leadership theory claims that teams must work together over an extended period of time in order to become performant. Examples include the famous Tuckman model for team building, which claims that teams go through the phases of Form, Storm, and Norm, until they can start to Perform (Tuckman, 1965). Another popular theory is the Hersey and Blanchard model, which suggests that leaders should adjust their style to the team members' maturity (Hersey & Blanchard, 1988). These theories were derived from studies in functional organizations, for which they provided tremendous insights into the ways to maximize performance. However, projects are different. They are temporary, which means that team members see their appointment as one of many different appointments, not long-term employment as in functional organizations. Many team members and project managers work simultaneously in several projects, which has implications for their availability and the need to be temporarily substituted by someone if another project takes priority. Another large difference between employees in functional organizations and project team members is that the latter work for the project only as long as their service is needed. This can be as short as a couple of days (if not hours) in a multi-year project. That leads to constant inflow and outflow of project team members. Hence, from a Tuckman model perspective, the team can never reach its performance phase because it is always forming and norming.

Balanced leadership addresses this problem not by trying to optimize the working relationships and collaborations in the team, but by assigning the most appropriate, and thereby probably the most respected, leader at any point in time in the project. So rather than trying to achieve the impossible by having team members go through the team-building phases in ever shorter iterations, balanced leadership builds on the flexibility of individuals, stemming from their desire to deliver the project successfully, and having the team led by a respected leader who is the most appropriate person at the given time in a project. In other words, the collaboration of team members in the context of the given project situation is optimized for performance by using balanced leadership.

That leads to the question, how does this work? One possible explanation is given by contingency theory. This theory claims that an organization's performance can be optimized by adjusting the relationship between the internal characteristics of an organization to its context. It has its origins in the work of Donaldson (e.g., 1985) on organizational structures and life cycles of products, as well the studies on the contingencies between organizational structures and the characteristics of the markets these organizations are in. Examples include Burns and Stalker's (1994) findings that performance is optimized if organizations adjust their structures to their market's particularities. In stable markets, functional and merely mechanistic structures help optimize performance because they allow for fine-tuning their well-known processes and thereby maximize efficiency in production. Conversely, dynamic (i.e., frequently changing) markets are best addressed with more organic structures that allow building ad hoc temporary teams to quickly provide new solutions for emerging customer needs. Hence, contingency theory suggests that fitting the relationship between two variables (such as an internal and a context variable) can maximize a third variable (such as performance). More recent versions of contingency theory emphasize the broad range of possible relationships between these two variables, from one-directional impact to reflexive interaction for readjustment of organizational characteristics to changes in context, for the benefit of organizational performance (Donaldson, 2001).

From a contingency theory perspective, balanced leadership theory indicates that performance is maximized by fitting the leader's characteristics to the situational context in the project. So the relationship, or "fit," between leader and situation is decisive for project performance. Project managers judge the situational fit of potential leader candidates along the following lines:

- *Skill set needed*: the particular technical or other skills that are needed to solve the issue at hand;
- *Personality*: the social and emotional skills required to work with and lead the team, as well as project clients, owners, and other stakeholders;

- *Professionality*: responsibly and professionally conducting the work, business acumen, and experience;
- *Attitude*: willingness to lead, to "go the extra mile," and to add leadership responsibility to the existing workload.

These items are further explained in Chapter 5.

Applying a contingency theory perspective shows that balanced leadership theory differs from traditional leadership theories by taking the timing and contextual dynamics of leadership into account. Given the dynamics of the constant flow of resources and varying temporary employment of skills in projects, the traditional variables for team maturity and team building are balanced out by the situational fit of technical and leadership skills. This does not make the traditional variables obsolete. Their presence still comes as a bonus for the benefit of the project. However, their influence on project performance diminishes in light of the timely and skills-wise optimization of leadership to the situational requirements at every moment in the project.

This leads to the question: how are these dynamics synchronized between project managers and team members? The answer provided in this book is through a socio-cognitive-space (SCS), which is a shared understanding between the project manager and team about:

- *Empowerment*: who is currently empowered to lead and with what level of authority. This provides for unambiguity as to who to follow, and what the leader is allowed to do.
- *Efficacy*: the empowered leader's ability to execute the task to a satisfactory or expected degree, as judged by the person themselves and the team members. This is a piece of important information for team members because it indicates whether the empowered leader is, for example, appointed for training their leadership skills or appointed for solving a major technical issue. It has direct implications for the type of interaction between team members and the empowered leader.
- *Shared mental models of project execution*: the particular skills needed over the project life cycle and the availability of these skills within the project team. This is important information for identification of the times when leaders need to change in the project and for the smoothening of this process.

The frequent synchronization of the three dimensions of the SCS is a requirement for balanced leadership to function well, and thus puts a burden on the project manager to effectively and frequently communicate with the project team. The details of the coordination through the SCS are described in Chapter 9.

The limitations of balanced leadership and its related theory

A theory is only a theory when it can be falsified (Popper, 1959), that is, when we identify circumstances in which the theory does not hold. This is what we do in this section.

Balanced leadership, and to a large extent the theory that explains it, has a number of boundary conditions. We will not provide an exhaustive list, but provide some key criteria. More details can be found in the later chapters in this book.

One of the primary enablers (or disablers) of balanced leadership is the project manager's attitude. In our interviews, we came across a few project managers who told us that they would never (not even temporarily) give up their leadership authority in a project. They wanted to stay in control all the time. These project managers would not allow a team member to step up to their level of authority or subordinate themselves to the (potentially superior) skills of a team member at any point in the project. In these cases, balanced leadership cannot happen, and its related theory cannot be applied. So the attitude of the project manager is a major enabler or disabler for balanced leadership.

Another factor is the national and industry culture. Some national cultures are supportive of balanced leadership, and upper management actively engages with employees far lower in their organizational hierarchy to encourage them to take on leadership assignments. These managers have witnessed the many benefits that come with this level of delegation. In other cultures, the upper managers might not reach that far down and communicate only with their next lower level of managers for them to implement balanced leadership. In these cases, the idea diminishes through the hierarchical layers and is at risk of being stopped entirely by middle managers who do not support the idea. Some industry cultures might also not be supportive of balanced leadership. The case study described in Chapter 11 shows that, for example, some construction projects do not apply balanced leadership because of the traditional perception that the project manager must make all decisions.

Another factor which might be at odds with balanced leadership is agile/scrum projects. Even though it can be argued that it is the extreme form of balanced leadership (with all leadership authority resting with the team and its scrum master), empirical evidence shows that some project teams do not like the underlying assumption of having a vertical leader (i.e., project manager) in the first place. While admitting that (a) a sole internal focus is detrimental to good stakeholder management, and (b) some form of management of the project as such in its context is needed, they object to the idea of vertical leadership. Hence, whether they do balanced leadership or not is an ongoing debate, and the answer most likely in the eyes of the beholder.

Contrarily, product development projects using waterfall or more iterative methodologies are very supportive of balanced leadership. These project teams apply it extensively and argue that it is one of their cornerstones for being successful.

Last but not least, the possibility of applying balanced leadership is influenced by the quality of the synchronization through the SCS and the willingness of team members to step up and take on leadership accountability and responsibility.

Summary

This chapter has described balanced leadership theory. We started by outlining the characteristics of good theories and their interpretation. Then we provided the philosophical and theoretical perspective taken by this theory. This allows the reader to judge the stability and generalizability of the theory. Next we presented the theory in terms of its what, how, why, and limitations. This chapter has served as an overview of the chapters to come. They will provide far more detail about balanced leadership theory.

Acknowledgments

The authors would like to acknowledge the contribution of Anne-Live Vaagaasar of BI Norwegian Business School, Oslo, Norway; Michiel C. Bekker, University of Pretoria, South Africa; and Karuna Jain, National Institute of Industrial Engineering (NITIE), Mumbay, India, as co-researchers in this chapter.

Reflection questions

1. What are the underlying philosophical and theoretical lenses in some of the theories you use at work? How do they impact the stability and credibility of the theory?

2. Reflect on the five events of balanced leadership. Are there other events that you may want to add to the theory? If so, which ones and why?
3. Reflect on the processes in balanced leadership theory. Where do you find them in your daily work?
4. Identify occasions at work when balanced leadership occurs. How does it come about? How did you recognize it as balanced leadership? What situations lend themselves toward the use of balanced leadership?

4
Nomination

Introduction

The balanced leadership theory developed by the authors (Müller et al., 2018b) identified five events that facilitated the movement of leadership between the vertical leader (or project manager) and the horizontal leader (team members/s) during a project. The first event of the cycle is termed *nomination*. This chapter explains the concepts of nomination, how it is currently taking place in projects, and some recommendations on how it could be improved to help a project manager secure the team members that he/she wants.

Müller et al. (2018) define the nomination event as the time when project members are appointed to a project:

> Here the vertical leader aims for influencing the choice of team members in order to build a pool of most suitable resources and potential horizontal leaders for the project. (p. 84)

Figure 4.1 depicts the nomination event within the balanced leadership framework.

The literature on nomination of project team members emphasizes "the importance of selecting" (Pinto & Slevin, 1987, p. 23) competent project team members as a critical success factor in project implementation. We will start this chapter with a discussion on defining a team and its characteristics.

What is a team?

You would have often found that people in organizations work together on some tasks from time to time. Would this make them a team? Or are they just a working group? To find out, we could ask a few questions (see Table 4.1) (Katzenbach & Smith, 2003, p. 113).

We think you are getting an idea by now as to how teams work, as the more boxes you ticked at the left of Table 4.1, the more likely it is that you are observing a team.

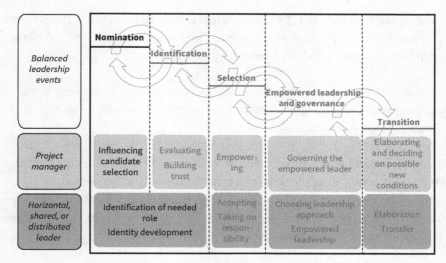

Figure 4.1. Locating the nomination event in the balanced leadership framework.

Table 4.1 Workgroup or Team?

Observation	Tick	Observation	Tick
The leadership of the group appears to be shared within the group.	⊙	There is an identifiable leader who seems to be directing the tasks in a focused way.	⊙
The members of the group appear to be taking mutual accountability for what they are trying to accomplish.	⊙	The work is distributed to individuals in the group, who are then made accountable for their piece of the work.	⊙
The group has developed a purpose for themselves to accomplish it.	⊙	The purpose of the group seems to be just the organization's purpose.	⊙
The product being delivered by the group appears to be a collective effort.	⊙	The product(s) being delivered are work products delivered individually based on assignment.	⊙
The discussions they are having seem to be open, with everyone chipping in while trying to solve problems that they are addressing.	⊙	The meetings they are having seem to be quite formal and run like an efficient office meeting with a clear agenda.	⊙
The group seems to be basing its evaluation on its overall performance on the collective work being produced.	⊙	The evaluations seem to be on the individual work being produced.	⊙
The discussions the group is having seem to be contributing to decisions to carry out real work together.	⊙	The group appears to be discussing and deciding together but then delegating the work in smaller, more manageable bits to individuals to complete.	⊙

Katzenbach and Smith (1993), who wrote a seminal book titled *The Wisdom of Teams: Creating the High-Performance Organization* in the 1990s, differentiated between teams and workgroups by stating:

> A team is a small number of people with complementary skills who are committed to a common purpose, set performance goals, and approach for which they are mutually accountable. (p. 112)

The early definition of Katzenbach and Smith (1993) is still reflected in recent work about teams, their purpose and how they organize themselves.

For example, Thomson (2011, p. 4), who has written a book on teams for managers, offers five salient characteristics that apply to a team and that show similarities to the earlier definition.

- Teams exist to achieve a shared goal.
- Team members are interdependent regarding some common goal.
- Teams are bounded and stable over time.
- Team members have the authority to manage their own work and internal processes.
- Teams operate in a social systems context.

Teams also serve as a mechanism through which an organization learns, improves, and innovates, says Amy Edmondson of the Harvard Business School (Edmondson, 2012). She points to the seminal work of Richard Hackman, who has written a number of books on teams and groups, and points out the importance of designing teams with clear goals, well-thought-out tasks that are conducive to team work, having team members with the right skills and experience to carry out assigned task, and providing adequate resources and access to coaching and support.

All these definitions add up to tell us something about the nature and importance of teams, how they work, what helps them to work together well, and how to empower them in organizations.

An interesting observation made by Edmondson is that the word "team" is often used as a noun that emphasizes its structure and design. However, the work carried out by teams could also be seen as a verb, which she calls "teaming," pointing out the dynamic activity that happens within teams. This is what helps a team to form quickly, as and when needed, and to collaborate effectively (Edmondson, 2012, p. 13).

The term "teaming" is important in the context of project teams, as they are often formed for short durations and are expected to start working effectively in a short time.

This brings us to the question: what is a project team? And how is it different from what we have discussed so far about teams in organizations and their characteristics? For this we refer to a project management standard by the Project Management Institute (PMI), which is a popular body serving project management professionals around the world.

According to PMI (2017, p. 717) a project team "is a set of individuals who support the project manager in performing the work of the project to achieve its objectives." This defines the composition and roles, but does not explain what they do together or how.

Chiocchio, Kelloway, and Hobbs (2015) clarify this by defining project teams with a more extensive definition, by stating that a project team

[. . .] unites people with varied knowledge, expertise and experience who, within the life span of the project but over long work cycles, must acquire and pool large amounts of information in order to define or clarify their purpose, adapt or create the means to progressively elaborate an incrementally or radically new concept, service, product, activity, or more generally, to generate change. (p. 54)

Project teams have also been classified as "core" teams that are part of the project organization for a long time, dedicated to the project to perform an integrative role, and as "component" teams (Chiocchio et al., 2015) that are formed to carry out specialist tasks for shorter durations. A new type of team called "virtual teams" has gained prominence in project work due to such work being performed by teams situated at geographically separated locations. An increase in outsourcing has also seen a rise in project work carried out separated by space and time.

Project teams are expected to perform the tasks allocated to them independently by performing well together. Therefore, they are also expected to possess the characteristics of high-performance teams. We now discuss how high-performance teams are different from normal teams.

Katzenbach and Smith (2003) point out that what sets apart high-performance teams from normal teams

[. . .] is the degree of commitment, particularly how deeply committed the members are to one another. Such commitments go beyond civility and teamwork. Each genuinely helps the others to achieve both personal and professional goals.

Furthermore, such commitments extend beyond company activities and even beyond the life of the team itself. (p. 65)

The concept of high-performance teams grew out of the work of the Tavistock Institute in the United Kingdom in the 1950s and was adopted in the 1980s by major US firms, such as General Electric, Boeing, and Hewlett Packard, that have reportedly achieved significant improvement in results. Although the flavor of high-performance teams faded in the early 1990s, the value that teams bring to organizations has picked up interest again.

Google, which runs its operations like a project-based organization, wanted to find out how its teams succeeded and failed. It commissioned a research project called Project Aristotle and studied "hundreds of Google teams" to figure out how to build a highly productive team (Duhig, 2016). One interesting thing Google found was that a "psychologically safe environment" is essential to bring out the best in teams. Schneider (2017, p. 3) reports that Google's Project Aristotle found five characteristics that contributed to a team's performance:

1. *Dependability*: Teams deliver things on time to meet expectations.
2. *Structure and clarity*: They have clear goals and well-defined roles.
3. *Meaning*: The work being done is considered significant at a personal level.
4. *Impact*: The work being carried out is purposeful and positively contributes to the greater good.
5. *Psychological safety*: Creating a climate where everyone takes risks, is able to voice their opinions, and also is able to ask judgment-free questions, is essential. It is psychological safety that makes people stay at Google, allowing the team to make best use of the diversity and to be successful.

Martinelli, Waddell, and Rahschulte (2017, p. 56), writing about managing virtual teams successfully, add that high-performance teams also exhibit participative leadership, which is an important characteristic relevant in the context of this book.

Teamwork is very important in a project context and is featured as a vital aspect of project management to consider in project management guides and frameworks. For example, PMI (2017, p. 337), in its *Guide to the Project Management Body of Knowledge*, states: "Teamwork is a critical factor for project success, and developing effective projects teams is the primary responsibility of the project manager." This implies that careful attention needs to be paid when nominating project teams to help the project succeed. It is also important in the context of this book that when nominating project team members, one should consider their ability to take on leadership roles. Emphasizing this, Drouin, Müller, Sankaran, and Vaagaasar (2018) suggest that project team members should be selected with a view to assign them leadership roles in the future.

Nominating project team members

The nomination of team members to a project could occur at several points during a project life cycle. In general, the majority of team members may join the project at or soon after it starts. New members could be added as the project moves through its different phases, or when team members leave the project for various reasons. For example, they may leave the organization in which the project is being carried out, or when a contractor in a project is replaced. Sometimes they may be forced to leave due to poor performance or incompatibility with the rest of the team. They could also be replaced by new members as complementary skills become necessary.

We mentioned two types of project teams in the previous section: core and component teams. Chiocchio et al. (2015) add a third category called "integrative teams," who are similar to core teams but have different functions, especially in projects that involve several types of expertise. Although core teams usually have a single goal, integrated teams may be assigned multiple, specific goals. Core teams are homogeneous in terms of knowledge and expertise, while integrated teams would have diverse knowledge and expertise to deal with a variety of goals. An example of such teams in a metro rail project would be:

- *Core team*: Responsible for looking after all the tunneling required for the project;
- *Integrated team*: Responsible for coordination of different types of works, such as civil, mechanical, and electrical works;
- *Component team*: Brought in from time to time to test specific segments of the rail as they are commissioned in stages.

The core team is often recruited from the functional departments when projects are carried out within an organization (Englund & Graham, 1997) so that they can easily liaise with people in the functions where they came from (e.g., business analysts in an IT project). An integrated team can be used to liaise between component teams from different disciplines assigned to a project (Hoegl, Weinkauf, & Gemuenden, 2004). An example of this is when programmers, testers, and developers are brought in from time to time in a large information systems project.

There are four possible scenarios on how teams are nominated to a project:

1. All team members are assigned to a project at the start.
2. Teams are assigned in sequence, with some team members assigned at the start for a long duration during the project, while others are added as the task evolves (Pinto, 2017). This may be due to financial or resource constraints or workload (Tannenbaum, Mathieu, & Cohen, 2012). Another reason why this could happen is when team composition decisions take time, as the required processes and systems are not in place to nominate teams at the project's start (Mathieu, Tannenbaum, Donsbach, & Alliger (2013).
3. Members are selected for a very short duration to carry out a time-critical task. An example is when new systems are added to an existing facility during a maintenance shutdown within a limited time.
4. Nomination by substitution occurs to replace a team member who leaves the team due to personal reasons, incompatibility with the rest of the team, or incompetence.

Characteristics expected of team members

While project team members are often nominated based on their project-related skills and experience, Katzenbach and Smith (2003) suggest that cognitive and social skills may also be taken into consideration. This is echoed by Morgeson, Reider, and Campion (2005), who explain that besides technical skills and personality traits, team members also need social skills and adequate knowledge about teamwork. Other characteristics considered important while nominating team members include the positions held by the team member under consideration in previous projects (Markaki, Salas, & Chadjipantelis, 2011). Prior ties could also help in building trust early among team members (Buvik & Rolfsen, 2015). Thus, technical skills to do the task, social skills to work well together, and knowledge about teamwork—which is strengthened by working in project teams before, as well working again with people with whom they have worked and built trust—are all important in selecting suitable project team members. Let us now examine what processes are used in practice in selecting project team members.

Selection processes

We look at three major tools or frameworks found in the literature and in practice, and discuss a variety of other tools used in practice.

A personality test that is often used in hiring people to an organization, the Myers-Briggs Type Indicator (MBTI), has been used for selecting suitable members of a project team. The indicator was developed based on the personality types proposed by Carl Jung, a Swiss psychiatrist and analyst. Jung's study of personalities was simplified by Isabel Briggs Myers and her mother, Katharine Cook Briggs, into the MBTI instrument that can be used to reveal the preferences and process of decision-making used by people.

There are 16 personality types included in the MBTI indicator (Briggs-Myers, 1987) based on one's preferences. Your preference to focus on the outer or inner world labels you as an introvert (I) or an extrovert (E). The process you use to take in or interpret information classifies you as sensing (S) or intuition (N). The way you make decisions—logically or contextually—explains whether you are a thinking (T) or feeling (F) type. The manner in which you prefer to make decisions is categorized as perceiving (P) or judging (J). MBTI has also been used to gauge one's learning styles.

As an example of the use of MBTI in project team selection, Gorla and Lam (2004) proposed using MBTI types to match roles in teams to personality types to select team leaders, system analysts, and programmers.

The oversimplified categorization used in the MBTI instrument, however, has become the main point of critique of the test, because it leads to poor validity and poor reliability (Grant, 2020). Although people tend to have inborn preferences, it has been observed that people's preferences can also change as they grow or adapt to a situation. Hence, despite its popularity, MBTI is categorized as pseudoscience (Bailey, Madigan, Cope, & Nicholls, 2018; Stein & Swan, 2019).

In a statement provided to the BBC, CPP (the publisher of the MBTI test) president Jeffrey Hayes defended the test's validity (Zurcher, 2014, n.p.):

> It's the world's most popular personality assessment largely because people find it useful and empowering, and much criticism of it stems from misunderstanding regarding its purpose and design [. . .]. It is not, and was never intended to be predictive, and should never be used for hiring, screening or to dictate life decisions.

Meredith Belbin's team roles test (Belbin, 1986) received a much higher level of acceptance and has been used in projects to assemble a team with different talents. Belbin (1986) identified nine generic roles in teams and developed a test to identify personalities that fit these roles. The affinity of a prospective team member for a role can be tested using the Belbin Team Role Self-Perception Inventory. It is recommended that while nominating team members, care be taken that all team roles are represented through individuals (individuals can represent several roles). The roles proposed by Belbin are described in Table 4.2 (Belbin, 1986; Müller & Turner, 2010).

A balance of these personality styles across the team will provide for the required levels of new ideas, drive, and motivation to implement them. One criticism of Belbin's model is that while it focuses on specific characteristics of a role, it ignores social relationships between roles that can assist in overcoming weaknesses of specific roles (Klein, Lim, Saltz, & Mayer, 2004).

Another tool used for selecting project team members is the Motivity-Opportunity-Ability (MOA) framework proposed by Ölander and Thøgersen (1995). According to these authors, *motivity* is "a person's intention to engage in the behavior." It "captures the motivational factors and transforms them into a behavioral disposition" (p. 361). *Ability* represents a person's "ability to carry out his/her intentions" (p. 364), which depends on their habits and knowledge of a task. *Opportunity* represents "objective preconditions for behavior" (p. 365). Ölander and Thøgersen acknowledge that individuals may perceive opportunities differently and hence individuals can be considered subjective as well.

Table 4.2 Belbin's Team Roles

Role	Characteristics
Plant	A creative and imaginative person, needed to solve difficult problems
Monitor-Evaluator	A sober and strategic personality, who oversees all options and accurately judges them
Shaper	A dynamic and challenging personality who enjoys pressure and helps to master obstacles through drive
Coordinator	A mature and confident person who clarifies goals and promotes decision-making
Resource investigator	An enthusiastic and extroverted individual who explores opportunities and develops contacts
Team Worker	A cooperative and tactical person who listens and works, and reduces conflict
Implementer	A disciplined, cooperative, and reliable person who puts ideas into practice
Completer-Finisher	A conscientious and anxious individual who identifies omissions and delivers on time

The MOA framework was used by Hosseini and Akhavan (2017) to select team members in complex engineering projects. The framework has also been used to study "interplay among team members' proactive personalities (abilities), collective efficacy (motivation) and supportive supervision (opportunity) to predict team innovation" (Trost, Skerlavaj, & Anzengruber, 2016, p. 77).

Members of agile project teams are expected to have both social and contextual skills, besides technical skills. Fitsilis, Gerogiannis, and Anthopoulos (2015) propose using a social network system called ONSOCIAL that has profiles of prospective team members and can offer recommendations to help recruit team members. The project manager first inputs the desired characteristics of a team member; the system will then search through the inventory of available team members with those characteristics to find a match. Typical data that are often stored include gender, education level, previous history on a role, type of project worked on, proficiency in a technical skill, competence (technical, social, others), and location. The system expands as more data are collected about team members, resulting in a more granular selection.

Some other methods used to select project team members include interviews, tests based on work to be performed or knowledge required, simulations in the form of post-box in-tray exercises using scenarios to investigate situational judgment, assessment center ratings (McClough & Rogelberg, 2003), and observing how candidates discuss in groups (Markaki et al., 2011). While interviews are the most commonly used selection method, Morgeson et al. (2005) recommend that the questions should be structured to focus on a project's requirements.

Recently, models and mathematical techniques have been proposed, especially in the selection of virtual team members, when face-to-face methods become difficult to administer (Baykasoglu, Dereli, & Das, 2017). Such methods are particularly useful when team members are selected from an available pool of resources (such as in outsourced projects). This could become more prevalent when face-to-face meetings are impossible, as they were in 2020 during the Covid-19 pandemic which interrupted global travel.

From what has been discussed so far, different contexts seem to expect different characteristics from project team members. It is clear that besides technical competencies, social skills and the ability to work in teams, as discussed in the previous section of this chapter, are considered while nominating members in practice.

Difficulties faced in nomination

Although nomination of a suitable team member is critical to a project, several difficulties are faced in practice. To discuss these difficulties it is necessary, first, to understand how organizations function to get things done efficiently, as this has an effect on what a project manager can or cannot do.

Authority and responsibility

Organizations divide the work to be carried out into functions in order to carry out its tasks efficiently. For an organization to function smoothly, authority and responsibility are assigned by top management to carry out tasks by specific functions. Authority gives the right to managers to make certain decisions. Responsibility lays down the performance criteria or obligation of an individual toward the organization.

In a functional organization, a sales manager may have been authorized to make decisions on discounts to be given to customers, while he/she is also responsible to meet sales targets set by the organization's strategy. On the other hand, a project manager could be authorized to reject work that is not up to quality standards, but could be held responsible for delivering a project on time and within cost.

Team members with the required expertise normally work in a functional department which has the authority to release these resources to the project team. This is often the case when projects are set up using a matrix organizational structure, which is commonly used in a functional organization (see Figure 4.2).

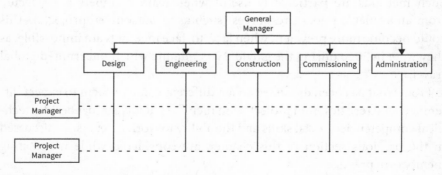

Figure 4.2. The matrix organization.

A major problem faced by project managers in choosing members is lack of authority compared with functional managers in an organization. The functional managers who have the authority are hesitant to release the resources when they are required by a new project if they are otherwise committed to (or currently work in) projects that seemingly have higher priority. This may be due to a protective attitude to their more valuable resources. As a result, projects often end up with people who are available at the time a request is made and who may not meet all the requirements put forward by the project manager (Anantatmula, 2016; Lee & Bohlen, 1997; Stern, 2017). To deal with this situation, project managers need to understand the concepts of organizational politics and power.

Organizational politics

Authority ("the power or right to enforce obedience") and responsibility ("managerial freedom" in executing a task) (*Oxford English Dictionary*, 2008) are often specified through roles and responsibilities. People may not follow these guidelines in an organization, but instead find loopholes to meet their own ends and use their influence to gain personal or functional advantage. However, Ferris and Davidson (2005) argue that while politics (i.e., "activities concerned with seeking power, status, etc." (*Oxford English Dictionary*, 2008) is perceived as having a negative impact on people and the organization, organizations are, by nature, political, due to inherent nature of people. Prominent management scholar Kotter (1985) points out: "[. . .] without political awareness and skill, we face the inevitable prospect of becoming immersed in bureaucratic infighting, parochial politics and destructive power struggles, which greatly retard organizational initiative, innovation, morale, and performance" (p. 44). This is echoed by Horchwarter, Jordan, Ezaj, and Maher (2020), who state that politics can help in achieving compromise in difficult situations at the workplace. Therefore, politics has to be accepted as a way of life in organizations that could have both positive and negative consequences.

Organizational politics could play a role when a functional manager resists his/her valuable people being moved to the core team of a project for long durations. This can result in a conflict between functional managers who own the resources and project managers who need the resources. It may then have to be resolved by management at a higher level than both the functional and project manager.

Power and politics

Politics is closely related to power, which is defined as the ability to influence people, e.g., making a subordinate behave in a certain way through control over resources. Power could affect the thoughts and feelings of a person on whom it is exerted, making them feel intimidated by forcing them to do something that they may not like to do. Although authority is a legitimate right to direct people in an organization, power might not always be legitimate. Therefore, it is important for project managers to understand the various forms of power in an organization to help secure resources for his/her project, as they do have some power that is not directly related to authority. Project managers may then be able to use the power they could wield to secure team members for their projects.

Although there are several models of power in organization studies, we will use French and Raven's (1959) bases of social power model as it has been used by project management scholars who have carried out research on project teams (e.g., Thamhain and Gemmill, 1974; Dunne, Stahl, & Melhart, 1978). French and Raven's (1959, p. 263) bases of social power are illustrated using a few vignettes created by the authors for this chapter. See Boxes 4.1, 4.2, 4.3 and 4.4.

While French and Raven originally proposed five types of power, Raven added a sixth type called *informational power*. Originally, expert power included knowledge and information. But informational power need not always be associated with knowledge.

Box 4.1. Coercive Power

Tom is working in a project organization on a tough project which requires him to put in extra effort to finish the project on time and under budget. His manager Richard understands the importance of the project and also Tom's hard work and offers Tom a bonus, in addition to his pay, if the project is completed successfully. The power Richard is using to influence Tom is legitimate and is known in French and Raven's taxonomy as *reward power*. Of course, Tom needs to see this as a genuine reward, as otherwise it may not work. On the other hand, Richard may resort to another tactic. He could threaten to fire Tom if the project does not show sufficient progress to drive Tom to achieve project objectives. Richard would still be exercising a legitimate source of power, but now the power is characterized as *coercive power*. Of course, this could backfire If Tom quits since there is a lot of demand in the market for someone with his experience.

Box 4.2. Expert Power

Sally is a programmer in an IT project. She is developing a core software program for a bank. Sally is quite proficient, but she is facing a tough challenge in one of the applications and there is no one in her team who is able to help. Sally learns that Susan, who works in another part of the bank, is a highly experienced programmer, and Sally's project manager suggests that she seeks Susan's advice. Sally does not work under Susan, but Susan has knowledge that is required by Sally, and the power that Susan has over Sally is called *expert power*.

Box 4.3. Referent Power

Rajesh works in a hospital as an intern, looking to be confirmed as a doctor after his internship. He wants to purchase a new piece of equipment for his operation theater and wants to call for quotations. He is not so familiar with the suppliers and their record for after-sales service. Rajesh finds out that Gopal, who is the head of maintenance, uses certain preferred suppliers, but he does not know the reasons why. However, Rajesh knows that Gopal and Rajesh's superior, Ram, are good friends and have been working together for several years. Rajesh thinks that if he chooses the equipment from one of Gopal's preferred suppliers, even though it may not be his best choice, he will not err on the wrong side with Ram. The power that Gopal has is called *referent power*.

Box 4.4. Informational Power

Leong is a project manager on a project developing software for a simulator used in operator training. The simulation software programmers have spent more time than what Leong's company estimated due to conflicting information provided by the client's main contractor. However, the contract was awarded to Leong's firm as they are considered experts in providing the software, based on previous experience. Leong wants to submit an extra claim to recover some losses but is unsure about how Tan, the client's project manager who controls the budget and is authorized to sign off on any extra claims, would respond. Leong approaches Cheah, who is a project manager in the client's office. Leong and Cheah were schoolmates. Over a cup of coffee, Leong learns about the percentage of extra claims that Tan has approved in previous projects. This information provides Leong with some idea about the amount he can submit to Tan that has the possibility of being approved. In this situation, Cheah holds *informational power*.

Pinto (2000) explains that the lack of authority that project managers have over line managers often tilts the power balance toward the functional side of an organization, rendering the project manager unable to get the team he/she wants. This is also called an *authority gap*. So how does a project manager close this authority gap by using a source of power he/she has at his/her disposal?

Singh (2009) provides an answer to this by stating that expert and referent power are more effective than coercion in organizational situations. Therefore, project managers, based on their reputation or knowledge, can use expert power to overcome the authority gap. For example, a project manager may be held in high regard within an organization for being very successful with projects he or she has managed. So, he or she may be able to attract people to work in projects assigned to him/her as they may also benefit from being associated with a successful project. This may weaken the power that a functional manager holds over resources he/she controls, as people working for him/her may find ways to overcome their manager's resistance to release them to join the project. The project manager, due to his/her reputation, may also be able to apply pressure on the superiors of functional managers to secure the resources he/she wants. This has been observed by Lovell (1993, p. 77), who states that "the power base of the individual project managers depends on the status of the particular project and his/her reputation and influencing skills." Lovell's argument that the power of a project manager may depend on his/her influencing skills is echoed by Crawford and DaRos (2002), who found that successful project managers can invoke additional power by working through the project sponsors who are more senior in the organization.

This brings us to a discussion of how project managers can use influencing skills based on their power to secure resources they want in an organization.

Why project managers need influencing skills

Project managers, who generally come from technical backgrounds, are often not comfortable getting involved in organizational politics. Pinto (2000) advises that this actually works against their ability to get the team they want. He suggests that they "must also cultivate other methods of influence to secure the resources for their project to succeed as they do not seem to possess power and authority during the assignment process" (p. 86). How do project managers develop influencing skills? To do that, they must understand the types of influence strategies prevalent in organizations and learn to apply those influence skills that are likely to bring results.

What is influence? Keys and Case (1990, p. 38) define influence as "simply the process by which people successfully persuade others to follow their advice, suggestion or order." They suggest that in order to influence, a manager should be able to establish good relationships with people who manage them, people they work with, people they manage, and people outside the organization they have to deal with. Influence can be applied in three directions—upward, downward, and laterally. While upward and downward influence as practiced by managers in functional organizations has been discussed, project managers also may need to apply lateral influence.

Leidecker and Hall (1974, p. 28) point out that "lateral relations are essentially those that a manager has with his peers or other members of the organization with which he does *not* stand in either a superior or subordinate position" (emphasis in original). Sayles (1976, p. 13) adds that such relations are important when managers working in organizations "have separate lines of authority and see the world from separate perspectives." This describes the situation that exists between project managers and functional managers, emphasizing the type of influencing skills that a project manager should focus on.

Influencing tactics

The seminal studies on influence in organizations were carried out by Kipnis and his co-researchers in the 1980s, which are still being used by scholars of organizational behavior (Kipnis, Schmidt, & Wilkinson, 1980; Kipnis, Schmidt, Swaffin-Smith, & Wilkinson, 1984). The work of Kipnis and his co-researchers were tested by Yukl and co-researchers in the 1990s (Yukl & Falbe, 1990; Yukl & Tracey, 1992). We will use the work of these authors to discuss influence strategies in this section.

Seven influence strategies were identified by Kipnis et al. (1984, pp. 59–60) (see Table 4.3) after examining the most commonly used strategies in practice to confirm those that they had proposed in their earlier work (Kipnis et al., 1980).

The original work of Kipnis and his co-researchers is focused mostly on upward and downward strategies. They did not mention lateral strategies, although some of what they found could be used as lateral strategies.

Are you able to identify the type of influencing skills—upward, downward, or lateral—or those that can be used in combination or in a sequence in Table 4.3?

Yukl and his co-researchers, who attempted to replicate the studies of Kipnis et al. (1984), found that managers use "different reasons for influencing subordinates, peers and superiors" (Yukl & Falbe, 1990, p. 139). Thus, they added influencing peers, which is lateral influencing (see Table 4.4).

Imagine a situation where you as a project manager want to apply one of these additional skills. Try to create a script that you would use to ask a person you want to influence. You can use the DESC Script (Table 4.5) as a model to

Table 4.3 Types of Influencing Used in Organizations

Name	Application
Reasoning	Apply influence using facts and data and developing a logical argument to convince
Friendliness	Use friendliness by managing to create a good impression, using flattery and creating goodwill
Coalition	Building up a coalition by mobilizing other people in the organization to strengthen your case
Bargaining	Using trade-offs by negotiating to exchange benefits and favors
Assertiveness	Using a direct approach by using force
Rewards	Using rewards available in organizations or sanctions as a form of punishment

Source: Kipnis et al. (1984).

Table 4.4 Additional Influencing Skills

Name	Application
Inspirational appeal	To evoke emotions using values and ideas to create enthusiasm to persuade
Consulting	Gaining support from others by including them in decision-making on policies, strategies or change
Self-promotion	Creating an appearance of competence or convincing others that you are capable of completing a task well

Sources: Yukl & Falbe (1990); Yukl & Tracey (1992); Jones & Pitman (1982).

Table 4.5 DESC Script

Strategy	Action
Describe	Describe the situation as objectively as possible.
Express	Express clearly how you are thinking and feeling about the situation.
Specify	State what you expect as the outcome or behavior of the other person as a result of your explaining the situation.
Consequences	Tell them about the positive consequences of their action (for both of you and the organization) if the situation is resolved.

prepare a script for when you want to assert yourself in a conflict situation (Smith, 2011).

Work carried out by Higgins, Judge, and Ferris (2003, p. 8) on influencing tactics found that "individuals may not use the same strategy for influencing in any situation." Thus, contextual factors may influence the type of tactic used to influence decisions in organizations.

Project management researchers have also investigated the use of influencing skills by project managers. Sotiriou and Wittmer's research (2001) confirmed that project managers resorted to using their influencing skills to overcome their lack of authority. They concluded that "important factors in overcoming the authority gap included persuasive ability, negotiation and management competence" (p. 18). Studies on influencing tactics used by project managers have also been carried out by Lee and Bohlen (1997) and Lee and Sweeney (2001), who have used the works of Kipnis and Yukl and their associates. They found that "success of influence attempts [by project managers] depends on the methods employed and perceptions of the target people" (Lee & Sweeney, 2001, p. 10). Lee and Sweeney warned, however, that influence tactics used in traditional management settings may not work in a project management context. From their study conducted on influence tactics, Lee and Sweeney (2001, p. 23) concluded:

1. There is no one best tactic or a set of tactics for all situations.
2. Different tactics require different skills to apply, as well as commitment of time.
3. Some interpersonal skills are more useful to pursue some tactics.
4. Influence methods are not based on any logic.
5. Tactics like assertiveness may have a downside.

While Lee and Sweeney differentiate between the terms "influence strategy" and "influence tactics," we do not distinguish between the terms.

It is clear from the discussions so far that project managers would benefit by acquiring influencing skills to overcome the authority gap to get the resources they want. These were also our findings from the case studies conducted to investigate balanced leadership, which we discuss next.

Research study

For one of the balanced leadership studies, we collected data from four case studies in Australia, five in South Africa, and four in Scandinavia. Using 70 interviews, three research questions were examined to investigate the nomination event (Sankaran, Vaagaasar, & Bekker, 2020).

Initially, two questions were asked (pp. 1394–1395):

1. How are project team members nominated in practice and by whom?
2. What do project managers do to have their preferred resources allocated to their project?
3. What influence strategies/tactics are used in practice by project managers to assign team members to their projects? And as a corollary to this question, which of these strategies have proven successful?

From an analysis of the interviews collected from the study, we found the following:

1. *Project managers had the power to nominate the team members they wanted.* In some cases, project managers were able to attract team members to their projects due to their reputation for success, thus demonstrating the value of expert power. In one case, a project manager was able to use the project sponsor's authority to get the team members that the project needed.
2. *Project managers were able to influence team member* nomination. Several influencing tactics were found during the interviews. Some project managers used their social relationship with functional managers to identify "stars," whom they then worked toward nominating to their project. Some project managers used their prior knowledge about a team member who they thought would fit into the project. Other project managers kept track of people who were working in other projects to find out when they could be released to request them to join their project. Sometimes they had conversations with suitable team members to gauge their potential before asking for them.
3. *Project and functional managers had very little say about who was nominated to a project.* In some cases, the allocation of team members was left to the human resources department. This often happened when people were nominated from a resource pool.

The case studies also identified the characteristics of team members favored by project managers when all they could do was to request team members with some specific characteristics. Some of these matched with what was found in the literature.

Technical skills with a high ability to perform was on top of the list. Interpersonal skills were considered important by some project managers. Others wanted to have team players. Some were looking for people with relevant experience. Leadership skills were also mentioned by some project managers.

The case study also highlighted some issues if the right team members were not nominated. Sometimes project managers were not given the type of team members they required and had no authority to refuse those they were given, which created issues. At other times, when team members were outsourced, project managers found that they lacked knowledge about the context in which the project was being implemented.

With regard to practices or methods adopted to select members, it was found that formal selection processes were not used that often. Instead, project managers looked for valued recommendations from senior people. Some organizations did use personality tests and databases in which competency matrices of prospective team members were available. In a project in South Africa, a workshop by external experts was used to find suitable team members.

On comparing with the literature on influencing, four tactics were found to be used in the case studies:

1. Creating an image of competence to attract team members (Jones & Pitman, 1982);
2. Creating coalitions by mobilizing other people (Kipnis et al., 1984);
3. Consultation (Yukl & Falbe, 1990);
4. Reasoning using facts and data (Kipnis et al., 1984).

Two new tactics not mentioned in the literature were also found:

5. Taking a gamble by asking for resources without expectations for success but hoping that it might work;
6. Waiting for the right time by keeping track of resources and trying to get them as soon as they were released from another project. Informal channels were used to implement this strategy.

Summary

Nominating the right team is critical for a project's success. However, project managers often do not get to nominate their own team due to the authority gap in most organizations. Project managers were able to assert themselves to get the resources they wanted in three situations:

1. When a project is critical for the organization;
2. When they have high status in an organization as an expert; and
3. When they can demonstrate that they have been successful.

When they do not enjoy this privilege, they have to work within the politics of the organization and learn to use influencing skills to get the resources they want. Although influencing skills can be used to influence upward and downward in an organization, it was found that lateral influencing skills were more effective with project managers. The use of influencing skills also varied based on the context in which projects were carried out and the ability of the project manager to learn and use those skills effectively.

Acknowledgments

The authors would like to acknowledge the contribution of Anne-Live Vaagaasar of BI Norwegian Business School, Oslo, Norway, and Michiel C. Bekker, University of Pretoria, South Africa, as co-researchers of the case studies included in this chapter.

Further reading

Hackman, J. R. (2002). *Leading teams*. Boston: HBS Press.
ICB4 (2015). *Individual competency baseline for project, programme and portfolio management, Version 4*. Zürich: International Project Management Association.
Markham, S. K. (1998). A longitudinal examination of how champions influence others to support their projects. *Journal of Production and Innovation Management, 15*, 490–504.
Mumford, M. D., Zaccaro, S. J., Harding, F. D., Jacobs, T. O., & Fleishman, E. A. (2000). Leadership skills for a changing world: Solving complex social problems. *Leadership Quarterly, 11*(1), 11–35.
Struber, D. C., & York, K. M. (2007). An exploratory study of the team characteristics model using organizational teams. *Small Group Research, 38*(6), 670–695.

Reflection questions

1. Why do project managers face an authority gap in organizations?
2. Why do project managers need influencing skills to get resources for their project?
3. What type of influencing skills are useful for project managers?
4. How will you as a project manager acquire these skills?

5
Identification

Introduction

The balanced leadership theory developed by the authors (Müller et al., 2018b) identified five events that facilitated the movement of leadership between the vertical leader (or project manager) and an individual or team in a project. The second event was termed *identification* (of a horizontal/team leader).

Identification of leaders to be empowered to take on leadership roles occurs after the nomination event, when the project manager tries to establish a pool of potential leaders from the team who will take on specific tasks assigned to them by the project manager. Once this pool is established, the project manager can then empower the selected candidate by granting them the authority to take on leadership tasks during the execution of the project.

Müller, Sankaran, and Drouin (2018a, p. 98) define the identification event as:

> *Identification of possible candidates for empowerment. It is a two-way activity from both project manager and team members to identify the best possible fit between a situation requiring horizontal leadership and a person executing it.*

Figure 5.1 depicts the identification event within the balanced leadership framework.

How does identification of horizontal/shared/distributed leaders occur in projects? In Chapter 4, where we discussed nomination of team members, we mentioned that while project managers often lack the authority to nominate the team members they want, they may be able to achieve this by using expert power or through applying influencing skills. Therefore, they may be able to identify people with potential leadership skills, who can then be targeted to be appointed as horizontal leaders from the start of the project. But how does this actually happen in projects? Before we discuss that, let us explore how leaders are identified in our everyday experience.

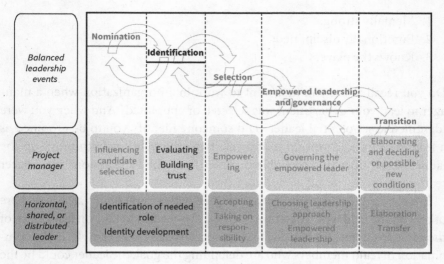

Figure 5.1. Locating the identification event in the balanced leadership framework.

Early experiences of leadership

One of the earliest experiences of leadership could have been when you were aspiring to be the captain of a team at school or college. Let us take the example of a soccer team.

A soccer club suggests the following competencies to look for in a potential captain (Arundel Soccer, 2020):

1. Leads others (motivates, inspires and influences);
2. Extends influence beyond what is simply required;
3. Leads by example as a role model exhibiting high standards;
4. Communicates effectively;
5. Creates a positive climate;
6. Prepares oneself;
7. Develops others;
8. Gets consistent, effective, and ethical results.

The preceding list includes technical (game playing) as well as behavioral competencies (leading people) to be considered to be appointed as a team captain (*Soccer Coach Weekly*, 2020).

The *Soccer Coach Weekly* adds more attributes expected in a team captain:

1. Mentally strong;
2. Emotionally disciplined;
3. Knows the players.

Do you recall when you first went to work in an organization when a manager to lead your department was selected or appointed? And when you were identified as a potential leader? Did someone identify you to be groomed as a leader? What did you do to indicate that you were ready to move up the ladder? How does this resemble or differ from the expectations of a soccer team captain?

In a soccer game, the captain is identified with a band on his arm. Are there others on the field who do not wear the band but seem to take on leadership of the game from time to time due to their special roles? For example, in the combination of team members who are defending the goal, the leader could be the goalkeeper when the ball is close to the goal, or the fullback when the opposite team is advancing rapidly. It could also be the person who is directing how the ball should be maneuvered to be passed to the player most likely to kick the goal. Or the one who takes the lead when the ball reaches him or her.

Thus, you can see that even in a game like soccer, some players are appointed as team captains, while others take on the role depending on the circumstances. It is not much different in organizations carrying out a business. You will also notice that the situation is similar in projects, but the way in which it happens in projects is somewhat different from how it happens in a soccer team or business organization. Let us now consider some competencies of team leaders in an organization that can give us a clue as to how to identify them.

Competencies of team leaders in organizations

In a paper published in *Nature*, Groover and Gotian (2020) offer five power skills to become a team leader. While their recommendation is targeted at scientists who manage research teams, it could apply broadly to technical people who manage teams in organizations. The skills they advocate are as follows:

1. *Knowledge of teamwork*: Able to motivate and utilize the individual strengths of members of the team. Knowledge of teamwork also involves learning to let team members know that you value their contribution and time.

2. *Communication*: This can cause considerable distress if not done well, especially when the team is not co-located or is diverse. It can be improved by being open to different needs and viewpoints. Asking members of the team for their perspective even when it is not offered would help them to overcome their reticence.

3. *Commitment and reliability*: Developing a strong reputation by delivering results that you can promise.

4. *Adaptability*: Being flexible and innovative, staying optimistic but realistic during tough situations in order to focus on the task. Such challenging opportunities should be treated as opportunities for learning. This may require venturing out of one's comfort zone.

5. *Open-mindedness and empathy*: Open to receiving creative, unconventional solutions from the team when difficult situations arise. Ensuring that silent voices are heard by starting the conversation with the most junior person in the team if needed.

A key function of team leaders in organizations is to effectively carry out decisions made by the organization's leadership. A model for team leadership developed by Susan Kogler Hill (2016) is used to illustrate how this can be achieved through internal and external leadership actions taken by team leaders (see Figure 5.2).

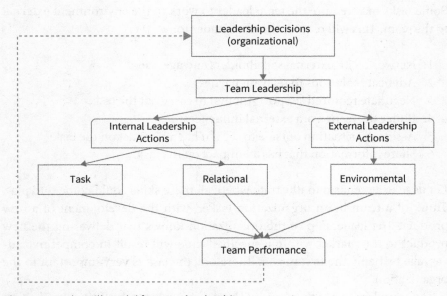

Figure 5.2. The Hill model for team leadership.
Adapted from Northouse (2016, p. 367).

The leader of an organization identifies a problem that has to be solved after appraising the situation and taking into account the constraints faced by the organization in its environment. The leader then assigns a team to solve this problem. The team's leader will then take a number of actions, which could require a variety of skills. The task that a team leader has to undertake may also require actions to be taken outside the organization.

To carry out the task the team leader will need to:

1. Focus on the task;
2. Structure the task to get intended results;
3. Facilitate decisions required in the performance of the task;
4. Train members if additional skills are required;
5. Maintain standards based on good practice.

The team leader will also require relational skills to achieve the task:

1. Coach team members as required to carry out the task;
2. Encourage collaboration in the accomplishment of the task;
3. Manage dysfunctional conflicts;
4. Satisfy the individual needs of the team members;
5. Model behavior.

Some tasks may require the team leader to work in the environment external to the team. This will require the team leader to:

1. Network with external stakeholders and agencies;
2. Advocate solutions to relevant parties;
3. Negotiate required support (inputs) to carry out the task;
4. Buffer the team from external influences;
5. Assess the situation outside to see if it has an impact on the task;
6. Share information that has an impact on the task.

Let us take a scenario to illustrate where all these skills could come into play. Think of a team in an organization tasked with the development of a new product. The leadership of the organization knows that delivering the new product to the market within a specified time will result in competitive advantage by being the first mover. Therefore, the task is very important to the organization.

The team leader has to carry out the development task effectively. The first thing he/she may have to do is to envision the product to get the team to focus on what is to be delivered without darting off in a number of directions. The team leader should then be able to plan how the task will be carried out and to allocate roles and responsibilities. As the team begins to develop the product, the leader will have to provide required information, make decisions, and coordinate the effort of the team. If the team leader finds that the necessary skills are not available due to unfamiliar technologies, he/she may need the team member to be trained in these areas. The team leader will also have to maintain standards of work through quality assurance, safety procedures, and good practices used in product development.

The team leader may find that the team members are not communicating well with each other. This may require coaching by the leader to improve communications. He/she may have to organize meetings where team members would listen to each other's opinions and collaborate on the task. Conflicts may arise due to differing opinions on some unknown aspects of the task, and this may need to be resolved amicably by the team leader so that the teamwork is not stalled. From time to time, the team may be overwhelmed and stressed by the task, and the team leader has to build commitment by motivating the team. There could be stars in the team who may have good ideas but may not come forth with them as they may feel that someone else may claim credit. Therefore, the team leader has to build trust so that everyone shares their ideas. This may require some advocacy. The team leader also needs to demonstrate ethical behavior by demonstrating fairness and ensuring that any ethical issues are brought out in the open and discussed.

To get the task done, the team leader may also have to work outside the team with people in the external environment. For example, there may be a specialist in another part of the organization whose knowledge may be important to the team. The team leader may have to establish a relationship with these specialists, or enable establishing relationships between the specialist with the knowledge and team members who may require specific support. The team's effort may also need to be made visible to the overall organization. To do this, the team leader would have to ensure that the team's work is noticed by keeping top management informed of the progress of the task. The team leader may also need to exert influence upward to gain necessary resources—finance, people, technology, etc. The team leader has a responsibility to protect the team from external demands from across the organization. For example, some members of the team may have been assigned to the team due to their special knowledge, but their managers may still be making demands on them. The leader may also provide assessment support through external agencies who may help ensure that the quality of the work is being maintained. If several teams across the organization are involved in developing new products or services, the team leader may have to act as a bridge, sharing lessons learned as well as the ways in which some challenges are being tackled elsewhere.

From a description of the Hill model and the task expected of a team leader in a scenario, you can appreciate the type of skills a team leader will need to accomplish the task. The skills include those required to carry out the task, maintain relations, and deal with the environment external to the team. An organization's leadership could use the Hill model as a framework to identify team leaders within the organization who possess specific skills required for a task.

Hill's model is based on the two-factor theory of team leadership—concern for production (task) and concern for people (relation). A study carried out by Burke et al. (2006) linking leadership behaviors and team performance outcomes concluded that "task-focused behavior is moderately related to team effectiveness" (p. 288) and "person-focused behaviors were related to perceived team effectiveness, team productivity and team learning" (p. 288), supporting the two-factor theory on which the Hill model is based.

Although the Hill model can help in decision-making, it may not cover all the skills required in a situation for dealing with the environment, coaching and training, and pre-planning (Northouse, 2016, p. 383). Therefore, organizational leaders may have to consider what other skills may be relevant to the particular task that the team has to undertake when identifying team leaders. In the preceding example, it is possible that the product that is being developed requires extensive tests to withstand harsh environments. Therefore, the team leader may be expected to know how these can be carried out and to find the necessary agency or laboratory that can help to undertake these tests.

Although identifying a team leader can be methodically done based on the tasks to be carried out, you may have noticed that leaders also emerge spontaneously when a challenging situation arises. For instance, you might have noticed that when an emergency arises at your home, such as someone having an accident or a fire starting inside the house, some members of the family may be too upset or shocked and may be frozen into inaction. Someone with a cool head who quickly assesses the situation then takes immediate action and gets everyone mobilized behind him/her. Such people have specific qualities that may make them a good team leader.

Box 5.1 shows a vignette experienced by one of the authors that illustrates such a situation (names have been anonymized).

In some organizations, the environment may facilitate the creation of self-managed teams where the leadership may be decided by the team and may even rotate as the team undertakes different tasks. An example of such a team is a community of practice. A community of practice (Wenger & Snyder, 2000,

---

Box 5.1. Team Leadership

A conference dinner is in progress and people are seated around a table, chatting. Drinks have just been served. One of the guests, Shiv, accidentally knocks his glass of wine off the table while gesticulating to make a point, and it shatters on the floor. Shiv is mortified and doesn't know what to do. Professor Vester, who is also seated at the table, promptly gets up and, along with his wife Martha, quickly starts cleaning up the mess. When Shiv gets up to help, Vester stops him, saying: "When someone breaks a plate or a glass at our house all the other family members help out and ask the person who caused the accident to just relax as he or she is already stressed out and feeling guilty." On hearing this, all the other guests seated around the table get up to help out too. This is an example of a spontaneous emergence of team leadership that not only demonstrates a focus on the task, but also takes care of people's feelings.

---

p. 139) may self-organize between "engineers engaged in deep-water drilling, consultants who specialize in strategic marketing, or frontline managers in charge of check processing at a large commercial bank." According to Wenger and Snyder (2000) "people in communities of practice share their experiences and knowledge in free flowing, creative ways that foster new approaches to problems" (p. 139). A real-life example provided by Wenger and Snyder (2000) are the "tech clubs" in DaimlerChrysler that met regularly to discuss product development and delivery with consultants of Hewlett-Packard at monthly teleconferences.

A vignette (Box 5.2) explaining such a self-managed team, in which one of the authors was a team member, shows how it could work (names have been anonymized).

In summary, we can see that teams can be formed in organizations specifically to undertake a task, or they may emerge due to a situation that creates a leader within the team, or they may exist as a self-managed team with rotating leadership. All these situations can also arise in a temporary organization such as a project. Next, we turn to competencies expected of project team leaders.

Competencies of leaders in projects

We start with the competencies of project leaders since they are relevant for all leaders in projects who may manage tasks within a project, which become mini-projects on their own. Pinto (2016), summarizing several studies

---

Box 5.2. Self-Managed Teams

Some years ago, the University of South Australia offered a PhD program for practitioners in Singapore, with supervisors from Australia visiting Singapore yearly to supervise the doctoral candidates. Between supervisory visits, the students communicated with their supervisors through email. Four of the candidates, Richard, Veena, Ram, and Kwan, all managers from different industry sectors—manufacturing, banking, nursing, and engineering—who were supervised by the same pair of supervisors, decided to form a self-managed team to help each other between supervisory visits. The purpose of the team was to learn from each other as well as to stay motivated. The four team members met monthly in one of their homes or offices to learn from each other to work toward completing their doctorate. Each month, one of the student managers would volunteer to lead by preparing a short lecture on a common topic useful to advance their research—a research method or process or a recent literature—and then the others would discuss and see how it could apply to their own research. The team also set itself an ambitious goal to graduate together, which was achieved. Not only that, they were also the first batch of four candidates to graduate successfully from the program. Although they were part-time students and busy managers in industry, they managed to complete their PhD within the time a full-time student was expected to complete such a program due to their focus on the goal they set themselves to achieve.

---

conducted between 1989 and 2005 on project leadership, points to six competencies as being critical to project leaders (p. 145):

1. Proficient project management;
2. Oral communication;
3. Influencing skills (as project leaders face an authority gap);
4. Intellectual capabilities;
5. Ability to handle stress;
6. Diverse management skills (planning, delegation, and decision-making).

Extending this to project teams, Pinto (2016) reports on a study carried out on project team leaders by Einsiedel (1987) and points to five competencies that are associated with project team leaders (p. 145):

1. *Credibility*: Would he/she be taken seriously by the team?
2. *Creative problem-solver*: Can he/she identify and analyze problems well?

3. *Tolerance for ambiguity*: Would he/she be adversely affected by complex and ambiguous situations?
4. *Flexible management style*: Is he/she able to handle rapidly changing situations?
5. *Effective communication skills*: Is he/she able to act as a focal point of communication from a variety of stakeholders?

The two sets of characteristics together can help us identify a team member who can take over as an empowered leader. The common competency between the two sets is the need for good communication skills.

In more recent work on project teams, Anantatmula (2016) adds that in a global economy, in which projects now operate among diverse cultures, it is important for team leaders to be aware of the "context culture and how the messages will be perceived" (p. 40). This may be particularly relevant to virtual teams that work across international cultures.

Anantatmula (2016, p. 55) also proposes a team leadership process in which the key steps advocated are to define roles and processes needed to accomplish the team's task. Once that is done, he suggests two sets of parallel processes to be carried out, as shown in Table 5.1.

How about projects in which agile methods are used? Are expectations from team leaders different in these projects? We mentioned earlier in the chapter that the Hill model is based on the two-factor team leadership model, encompassing task- and relationship-oriented behaviors. This is also confirmed in a study carried out by Srivastava and Jain (2017) on scrum leadership in agile teams. Based on their study of 75 projects in which scrum masters participated, they found that task-oriented behaviors included making decisions, communication, and commitment to tasks, while relationship-oriented behaviors included being people-centric, maintaining cohesion, and being transparent.

In Chapter 4 on nomination, we suggested that project teams have the characteristics of high-performance teams in organizations. In a study on project teams carried out by Ammeter and Dukerich (2002, p. 5) of high-performance

Table 5.1. Team Leadership Process

Task Related	Process Related
Communicate expectations	Employ consistent processes
Build competencies	Facilitate organizational support
Communicate expectations	Manage outcomes

project teams, the team members opined that their primary expectation of team leaders was to communicate the desired goals and values to the team. The team members felt that this helped to create a "tremendous work ethic" and enabled "collegiality and communication" among the team. Their secondary expectation of their leaders was that they kept the team informed about the status of the overall project. Again, communication is found to play a key role. Goal setting is always seen in project-oriented tasks, but the expectation that team values have to be taken into account is an interesting addition to what is expected of team leaders by the people who are led by them.

In summary, project team leaders are expected to have both task-oriented and relationship-oriented competencies. Recently, intercultural knowledge to work with diverse project teams is also becoming important. Leaders also need to understand how the process of team leadership is to be carried out.

How are leaders identified? We start with a discussion on how this is done in organizations, followed by identification processes in project organizations, including findings from a research study.

Identification of potential leaders in organizations

A survey by the Society of Human Resource Management (SHRM) of multinational companies listed in the *Fortune* magazine as excelling in leadership, identified some common processes used in spotting leadership talent relevant for the twenty-first century.

The SHRM report starts with an earlier list of some strategies used by multinational companies to spot high-potential executives (Church & Rotolo, 2013). They were as follows:

1. Multisource ratings (such as 360-degree feedback);
2. Personality inventories;
3. Interviews;
4. Biographical data;
5. Interactive simulations;
6. Cognitive ability;
7. Use of assessment centers;
8. Motivational fit.

Multisource feedback was the most popular assessment, used in 75% of the cases, while self-awareness, motivation, personality, learning ability, and cognitive skills were assessed 50% of the time. The latest report published by the society (Scott, Church, & McLellan, 2017) found that although competencies were still most frequently assessed, some thought leaders believed that outcomes were also very important. For global leaders, performance in assignments at foreign locations was also used as an indicator to gauge their capability to work in intercultural environments. The SHRM report provides examples of strategies used by Eli Lilly, PepsiCo, Luck Companies, Palladium Enterprises, and ANZ Bank.

An article in *Harvard Business Review* on twenty-first-century talent spotting (Fernández-Aráoz, 2014) also found that modern businesses are too volatile and complex. The author argues, based on consulting for organizations across the world over a decade, that focusing only on competencies was not sufficient to hire, spot, and retain talent. He found six ways in which leadership talent was spotted:

1. The first is to hire the right people with the potential to take on senior roles. It was found that Amazon prioritized hiring the best. To spot talent after people join the organization, it is important to find out if they excel in achieving unselfish goals. Other things to look for are curiosity to seek out new experiences; insight in gathering and making sense of information; engagement in being able to use emotion and logic to communicate; connecting with people with a vision to persuade them; and a determination to handle challenging goals, as well as bouncing back from adversity.

2. Once potential talent is gauged, steps must be taken to retain such people. Although monetary rewards are important, it is also crucial to provide them with autonomy to carry out challenging tasks, and to engage them in activities in the pursuit of team, organizational, and societal goals. This was observed in Amazon and the Brazilian mining giant Vale do Rio Doce.

3. The organization also needs to help the identified leaders live up to their potential by offering development opportunities that take them out of their comfort zones. Such practices are adopted by Australia's ANZ Bank and by Japanese organizations.

4. Assess a candidate's intelligence not just by administering IQ tests, but by looking for analytical, verbal, mathematical, and logical abilities. This can be done through a combination of evaluation of the person's educational background and job experiences, and through interviewing.

5. Values such as honesty and integrity are important and can often be gauged through interviews and reference checks. It is important that the candidates also buy into the organizations' values.

6. Evaluate eight leadership abilities: strategic orientation; market insight; results orientation; customer impact; collaboration and influence; organizational development (to improve the company); team leadership; and change leadership. These are evaluated through interviews and by checking references.

Fernández-Aráoz (2014) points to ANZ Bank's experience in spotting and nurturing leadership talent when it went through a rapid expansion in Asia between 2007 and 2010. ANZ Bank refined its leadership development processes by "assessing all its managers for potential and then placing those who rate the highest in business-critical roles" (p. 50). It also used job rotation so that managers could take on different roles in the bank and thus gain corporate and industry knowledge. This was followed by permanent leadership positions, including a mandatory posting to understand the bank's control frameworks. The program commitment is for 15 years, at the end of which the groomed leader is ready to take on a CEO's role in one of the divisions of the bank.

The two preceding examples explain structured processes used in organizations to spot and develop talent.

Lane, Larmaraud, and Yueh (2017) from McKinsey argue that such structured processes may miss finding hidden leaders. To identify such potential leaders it is necessary to "hunt, fish and trawl" for the best talent (p. 1):

Hunting: Seek out people with promise who may not make the short list using assessment processes and cultivate them to take on leadership challenges. An example cited is from an industrial products company which traditionally identified male leaders. Then managers were directed by top management to look for female employees and found some women leaders who had not been spotted before.

Fishing: Using awards for people who demonstrate some unusual skills to root out people who do not make themselves known. An example provided is Adecco's CEO for One Month program, offered as a training opportunity to young people from outside the company to help them become employable, which ended up identifying highly talented individuals. Based on the success of this project in identifying external talent, the company wants to use this process to discover hidden talent internally as well.

Trawling: Digging deep into the work environment to spot people with special talents that cannot be gauged by top-down approaches. This can be done through a snowball approach, asking people to nominate colleagues, or by using social network analysis to get a picture of social networks to identify super connectors.

Although structured processes are discussed in the previous two examples, Loree (2015) argues:

> In some situations, the key success factors that explain current performance might not only be less relevant for future success, they can sometimes work against future promotion and success. Since leadership potential isn't necessarily embedded into many early jobs and roles where it can be easily demonstrated, we need processes to spot the "glimmers" of potential that manifest themselves in less than systematic ways. What do these glimmers look like?

Loree (2015) suggests that talent spotting is an art as well as a science. She uses the example of Bob, who kept talking about product quality and company reputation in a meeting, where everyone else was talking about project deadlines and cost. This behavior "stuck" in the minds of the top management, who recognized that Bob had the talent to be a leader. Recall our previous discussion about looking for team leaders through spontaneous actions.

Now that we have some idea about how permanent organizations identify talent, let us look at what happens in temporary organizations such as projects.

Identifying leaders in projects

In Chapter 4 of this book on the nomination event, we mentioned that project managers, due to lack of authority over resources, face difficulties in looking for team members with potential leadership skills. If this is true, then they will need to set up a process to identify team members who could take over leadership roles after the team members join the project. In practice, they will probably rely on experience or knowledge of the aspect of the project the team member is an expert in (such as software programming). However, these people may not have the best competencies to be a team leader, as we have seen from the discussions about team leaders so far in this chapter. Leaders require a wide variety of competencies, of which knowledge in their area of expertise is only one. Therefore, project managers have to observe team members using multiple lenses to identify potential leaders. They could, for instance, set up interviews and discussions with team members to gain more knowledge about their capabilities or to learn more about prior roles held by team members in previous projects. They could also give them some tasks to see how they tackle them.

As mentioned earlier in this chapter, sometimes leaders emerge during unexpected situations, and project managers would be wise to notice such emergent leaders who may be able to take on a critical task and lead it. Project managers could also be on the lookout for self-managing teams that may form in the projects to tackle specific issues. The guilds that are encouraged to be formed in agile projects are an example of self-managing teams.

The Project Management Institutes' talent triangle (PMI, 2015) includes technical project management, strategic and business management, and leadership skills. Examples of capabilities required of leaders from this triangle could be useful to identify project as well as team leaders. These are:

1. Generating new ideas (brainstorming);
2. Coaching and mentoring;
3. Conflict management;
4. Emotional intelligence;
5. Influencing;
6. Interpersonal skills;
7. Listening;
8. Negotiation;
9. Problem-solving;
10. Team-building.

Although examples of talent spotting for project leaders is not common in project organizations, Lane, Larmaraud, and Yueh (2015) found that Google, a project-based organization, uses data collected in the organization to evaluate leader and team performance and uses the analysis to develop capable leaders.

During the balanced leadership research project, a study on identification of temporary horizontal leaders was carried out in China using five case studies by researchers from China and Norway. During these case studies, 28 interviews were conducted to theorize the phenomenon. This was followed by five more in-depth interviews to validate the findings from the first set of interviews (Müller et al., 2018a).

From this study, three criteria emerged for identifying leaders: professionality, personality, and attitude.

In the context of the study, professionality includes professional skills, teamworking skills, and experience of the team member. In order to qualify as a temporary leader, a team member must have a minimum amount of professional skills to carry out the task. Once this threshold is reached, the ability to apply the professional expertise within the team becomes important. Although it is natural to expect that a more experienced team member will be preferred as a temporary leader, the study showed that younger members were often preferred because the project manager himself or herself felt threatened by the presence of more experienced people who may compete with them to take over their role. It was also found that professionality was often evaluated based on knowledge of past performance of team members.

Personality was gauged as a combination of social and emotional skills. Social skills refer to recognizing emotions of others in order to interact positively and work well with them. Emotional skills were identified as the team member being able to recognize their own emotions and adjust their behavior accordingly. Emotional intelligence in project leadership is discussed in more depth in Chapter 6 on empowerment. A further factor was the perceived fit between the requirements of the leadership situation and the chosen temporary leader. In other words, is the temporary leader fit to carry out the challenges required by the task, such as being able to negotiate with difficult clients, or to motivate a disappointed team?

Attitude presented itself in two ways. It included the team member's intention to take on the team leader's task and his/her attitude toward the task itself. The former is the willingness to "go the extra mile" and add some leadership responsibility plus the related extra workload to the existing workload. Attitude includes the mental disposition to act as a leader, and hence, to feel comfortable in directing others, deciding, taking risks, or, more generally, leaving one's comfort zone when needed.

From the study it appeared that two parallel processes take place, one executed by the project manager and the other by team members. The project manager's process consists of three steps, while four steps are executed by the team member to culminate in the identification event.

The three steps taken by the project managers were the following:

1. *Preliminary evaluation*: Screening potential candidates and creating a pool of members who can take on a leadership role.
2. *Development*: Undertaking measures to actively develop the team members in the eligible pool to take on the leadership role when it arises. This could include training or giving team members additional tasks to develop their skills.
3. *Assessment*: Evaluating the candidate to ensure that the team member is ready to take on the role of a team leader before assigning it to him/her.

Box 5.3. Identifying and Training Team Leaders

A project manager, Heng, noticed that a document control engineer, Tan, in the project was eager to learn. Heng then had a conversation with Tan and expressed his opinion that she may be wasting her time in document control based on her qualifications and inquired about her interest in taking on a planning role in the project. Tan showed an interest in taking on the challenge and Heng then decided to send her to attend courses to gain proficiency in planning tasks so that she could be ready to undertake a project independently.

The vignette in Box 5.3 shows an example of the steps used by project managers in the study to identify and train team leaders (names have been anonymized).

The research also identified a reciprocal process adopted by team members to put up their hand to be team leaders. These were the following:

1. *Preliminary evaluation*: The team members evaluated the project manager's ways of working in anticipation of collaborating with him/her to look for opportunities for horizontal leadership. This includes a "what's in it for me" evaluation by the team member
2. *Competition*: Team members try to identify a role or a skills gap that they can fill to become visible and to make themselves known that they are available for a leadership role. They hoped that this would build trust with the project manager.
3. *Development*: During this stage they developed their capability to lead with the help of the project manager.
4. *Guidance and encouragement*: Once they felt prepared for a leadership role, the team members looked to the project manager for guidance and encouragement.

The vignette in Box 5.4 illustrates a situation in which a team member actively promoted himself to be identified as a horizontal leader (names have been anonymized).

The research concluded that the processes identified through the study resembled a generative dance between actors in the situation (Cook & Brown, 1999) on how they acted and reacted during the identification process. The research teams also recognized that the findings from the research echoed what was found from leader-member exchange (LMX) theory where the leader classifies followers as being *in-group* or *out-group*.

Box 5.4. Self-Promotion to Horizontal Leader

Chan felt that his project leader, Heng, considered him to be a reliable person, and he often sought Heng's help when he faced a difficult situation. Heng kept encouraging and praising Chan, which made him feel confident of his work. Heng would ask Chan to do some basic work before assigning him a more important task. Based on the result from the basic work and Heng's attitude toward him after completing the task, Chan will know if he has caught the attention of Heng to be a potential horizontal leader in the project.

In-group in this context were members who were showing signs of willingness to take on more responsibility and negotiating to expand their roles and responsibilities, whereas *out-group* refers to those who limited themselves to their contractual roles and responsibilities within the project. Leaders were observed to vary their supervision style based on whether the team members were in-group or out-group. The research concluded that "LMX explains the process of identification as one of an invitation by the vertical leader to build high quality LMX relationships" (Müller et al., 2018a, p. 104). This indicates that identification of team leaders is a dialectical process arising out of a strategic alliance between project managers (vertical leaders) and prospective team members (potential empowered leaders).

This is echoed in a recent paper by Graen and Schiemann (2013), which extends the original work on LMX theory by Graen and Uhl-Bien (1995) discussing leadership development, and states that forming "unique strategic alliances with team members may increase the inclusion of these [millennial] generational members, and help them to tackle common organizational problems" (p. 452). This is relevant to project management situations as more and more millennials enter the workforce, to help bridge the intergenerational gap.

Figure 5.3 shows the processes and criteria for the identification of horizontal leaders from the study reported in this chapter.

Summary

We started this chapter by exploring team leadership in organizations. This was important, as it gave us an idea about what to look for in potential leaders in projects so that we can identify and develop them to take on leadership tasks in our projects when the need arises. Then we looked at how leadership

Figure 5.3. Process and criteria for identification of temporary leaders.
Adapted from Müller et al. (2018a).

talent is spotted in organizations that value leadership, so that we can understand processes used to identify leaders, which may be relevant to project organizations. We then considered some ways in which project leaders could identify temporary leaders and looked at a study that concluded that project managers and prospective leaders used different steps to help with the identification event, using professionality, personality, and attitude as signs to look for. We also saw how project managers tended to work with prospective team members to help them take on leadership roles through mentoring and guidance. Leadership is critical to project performance and therefore project managers should learn how to select or identify team members who can take on leadership roles from time to time to support the project manager to complete the project successfully. This chapter has given you some ideas on how identification of temporary leaders can be carried out in practice. Project-based organizations can also learn from how multinational companies spot leadership talent and grow leaders, which has been explained in this chapter. In the next chapter we will discuss how leaders are selected and empowered to take on leadership roles.

Acknowledgments

The authors would like to acknowledge the contribution of Fangwei Zhu, Xiuxia Sun, Linzhuo Wang, and Miao Yu from Dalian University of Technology, China, to this chapter through their research on the identification of temporary horizontal leaders.

Further reading

Cobb, A. T. (2012). *Leading project teams: The basics of project management and team leadership* (2nd ed.). Thousand Oaks, CA: Sage.

Ferguson, A. (2015). *Leading: Lessons in leadership from the legendary Manchester United manager*. London: Hodder & Stroughton.

Hackman, J. R. (2002). *Leading teams: Setting the stage for great performances*. Boston, MA: HBS Press.

Lencioni, P. (2002). *The five dysfunctions of a team: A leadership fable*. San Francisco, CA: Jossey-Bass.

Müller, R., & Turner, J. R. (2010). *Project-oriented leadership*. Surrey, UK: Gower.

Pellerin, C. (2009). *How NASA builds teams: Mission critical soft skills for scientists, engineers, and project teams*. Hoboken, NJ: John Wiley & Sons.

Soccer Coach Weekly (2020). Six attributes to look for in a team captain. Available at https://www.soccercoachweekly.net/soccer-coaching/tips-advice/six-attributes-to-look-for-in-a-team-captain/.

Tannenbaum, S., & Salas, E. (2021). *Teams that work: The seven drivers of team effectiveness*. New York, NY: Oxford University Press.

Reflection questions

1. Why is it important for projects to have processes in place to identify temporary leaders?
2. Once a team member with leadership potential is identified, what steps can be taken to groom the leader to take on leadership roles?
3. If you were a team member in a project, what would you do to put yourself up for selection as a team leader?

6
Selection and Empowerment

Introduction

The third event in balanced leadership theory is selecting and empowering subteams or individuals to temporarily lead the project to solve an issue at hand or to guide the project through a crisis. Figure 6.1 depicts the location of the event in the balanced leadership framework.

Selection is triggered by a situation that requires leadership by someone other than the project manager. This situation can arise for many different reasons: for example, when the project manager does not possess specific or expert knowledge that is needed for the project; or when the project manager allows a team member to train and prepare for future leadership roles; or when a subteam needs to develop a new and innovative solution to solve a problem. When specific or expert skills are required, the project manager will assess the skills needed and map this against the skills identified during the identification event to find the best suited person(s) for empowerment. When individuals are empowered to try out their leadership skills, the project manager has waited until a suitable situation has arisen in which the prospective leader can be appointed without posing a risk for the project. Once the person(s) and the situations match, the project manager selects the individual(s) and then initiates empowerment. During empowerment, an individual or a subgroup of the project team is authorized to lead the team temporarily. We define it as an event when one or several team members are selected and empowered to lead the project. This marks the project manager's transition of leadership authority to the empowered leader(s) and the receiver's acceptance of this authority and its related responsibility. Through this, the project manager becomes a follower of the appointed leader(s), but, at the same time, the project manager also governs the actions of the leader to ensure they are in the best interests of the project.

In the following sections, we first describe the concepts of selection and empowerment in general before discussing how they apply to projects and balanced leadership in projects.

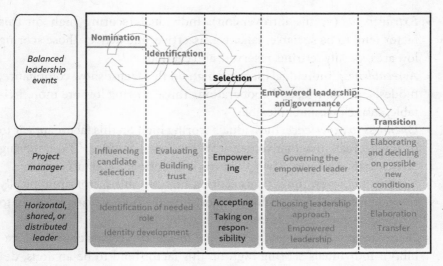

Figure 6.1. Locating the selection and empowerment event in the balanced leadership framework.

Leader selection

Leader selection is the process of mapping situational requirements and needs with individuals' characteristics to select the particular individual(s) to be empowered to lead. As mentioned earlier, the situational requirements in a project can be very diverse. Accordingly, the criteria for selecting the individual(s) as temporary leaders are also diverse. This chapter is not intended to anticipate all the different scenarios in a project and the associated criteria that lead to selecting a possible leader. Instead, we briefly describe some of the approaches described in the literature on leader selection. We start with general management literature and then look into project management–related literature. Again, the described methods cannot consider the situational requirements of a project and are, therefore, only generic.

As outlined in the chapter on nomination of team members, there are many different approaches for selecting leaders. General management literature emphasizes many criteria for leader selection, including personality, leadership style, and person-situation "fit." These criteria are typically based on the assumption that the strength of expression of particular personal traits or their combination allows for predicting performance. A popular model is the five-factor model (or Big Five Personality Factors) (Goldberg, 1993) for profiling individuals. This model comprises the following factors:

- *Extraversion* (versus introversion): Individuals scoring high on this factor tend to be sociable, talkative, assertive, and active. Those scoring low are typically retiring, reserved, and cautious.
- *Agreeableness*: Individuals scoring high on this factor show compliance, modesty, gentleness, and cooperation. Those scoring low are more irritable, suspicious, and inflexible.
- *Openness to experience*: Individuals scoring high on this factor appear to be intellectual, imaginative, sensitive, and open-minded. Those scoring low are typically more down-to-earth, conventional, and insensitive.
- *Conscientiousness*: Individuals scoring high on this factor are typically thorough, careful, responsible, and organized. Those scoring low tend to be irresponsible, disorganized, and unscrupulous.
- *Neuroticism, also known as Emotional Instability* (versus emotional stability): Individuals scoring high on this factor tend to be anxious, depressed, angry, and insecure. Those scoring low are typically calm, poised, and emotionally stable (Roccas, Sagiv, Schwartz, & Knafo, 2002, pp. 792–793).

This model has been used in many studies to predict, among other things, leadership effectiveness and styles. For example, Judge and Bono (2000) showed that extraversion and agreeableness predict a transformational leadership style. Similarly, a meta-analysis by Barrick and Mount (1991) found a correlation between extraversion and managerial success, indicating that extroverted managers are more successful than introverted.

However, both practitioners and academics question the simple formula that extroverted personality leads to managerial success. An example of the former is Susan Cain, a consultant listed as one of the world's top ten influencers. She mentions in the preface of her award-winning book on quiet leaders: "Without introverts we wouldn't have the Apple computer, the theory of relativity or Van Gogh's sunflowers" (Cain, 2013). An example from the academic world is Harvard professor Joseph Badaracco, who showed that some of the world's most successful leaders are clearly introverted. According to Badaracco, they are so successful because (a) their introversion allows them to think through problems and possible solutions at a detailed level, which makes them arrive at well-considered solutions, and (b) they can adjust their presence in front of those they lead to the situation at hand (Badaracco, 2002). Hence they act quite extroverted when needed, but then often use some private time to "recover" from this "performance."

This ability to read others' emotions and then adjust their own style for successfully leading others was taken further by researchers studying the concept of emotional intelligence. Examples include Salovey and Mayer (1990, p. 189), who defined emotional intelligence as "The ability to monitor one's own and others' feelings and emotions, to discriminate among them and to use this information to guide one's thinking and actions." One critical ability for this is empathy—to understand what motivates other people, even if they are from different backgrounds, and being sensitive to their needs (Goleman & Boyatzis, 2008). Hence, successful leadership does not emerge from a single personality trait like extraversion, but from the ability to identify the particular leadership style appropriate in a given situation and the flexibility to adjust the leadership style to these situational needs. Moreover, the writers show that these and other elements that make up emotional intelligence can be learned over time so that individuals can be trained how to become, for example, more empathetic in leadership.

Studies in the realm of project management showed the importance of the awareness of emotions in projects because they influence the project managers' and the team members' decisions and behaviors (Clarke, 2010a). Being aware of the role of emotions and how to manage them from becoming detrimental for the project helps to prevent adverse developments.

Empirical investigations showed that emotional intelligence on the project manager's side could explain up to 43% of project success (Turner & Müller, 2006). This figure is very high when compared with other success factors in projects. Turner and Müller's studies showed that emotional intelligence positively correlates with success in all project types, at all levels of complexity, all industries and geographies, and all project stages. Their research assessed the emotional, intellectual, and managerial competencies of project managers. Through this, they identified "best-fit" constellations between different project types and psychological profiles of project managers. The results indicated the following (Müller & Turner, 2007).

Leaders in engineering and construction projects need a sense of duty and good interpersonal sensitivity, especially in:

- Conscientiousness: a clear commitment to a course of action in the face of challenges; matching "words and deeds" in encouraging others to support the chosen direction;
- Interpersonal sensitivity: being aware of, and taking into account, the needs and perceptions of others in arriving at decisions and proposing solutions to problems and challenges.

Leaders in IT and telecommunication projects should find the right "tone" with others, together with good control over their own feelings and helping project team members take on challenging tasks. They especially need capabilities in:

- Engaging communication: being approachable and accessible, engaging others to win their support through communication tailored for each audience;
- Self-awareness: being aware of their feelings and able to manage them;
- Developing others: encouraging others to take on ever more demanding tasks and roles.

Leaders in business and organizational change projects should actively create the required dynamics for change and accommodate those involved. Of particular importance are their capabilities to:

- Communicate and engage others (as described earlier);
- Motivate others: by showing drive and energy to achieve clear results and make an impact.

More details on these profiles and the methods of developing project managers for the most appropriate leadership in the particular project types in their organization can be found in Müller and Turner (2010a).

The impact of training in emotional intelligence capabilities in the context of projects showed that even a two-day training could lead to a significant increase in emotional intelligence capabilities, with a lasting impact over more extended periods, such as six months (Clarke, 2010b). Studies by Turner and Lloyd-Walker (2008) supported these findings and showed that increased emotional competencies increased both employee satisfaction and project success.

Summing up, the selection of a temporary leader or subgroup in a project is, of course, driven by situational needs, such as the need for specific expert knowledge or the development of future leaders. Nevertheless, project managers consider candidates' personality characteristics for these appointments, as shown in the previous chapter. This section has given a short introduction to the recent developments in the leader selection literature. We now turn to the next step, the empowerment of the selected individual(s).

Empowerment

A *Forbes* report in 2013 quotes Bill Gates as saying, "As we look ahead into the next century, leaders will be those who empower others" (Kruse, 2013), and a quick search on scholar.google.com in the fall of 2020 on the number of academic articles with "empowerment" in their title found more than 132,000 hits. Hence, empowerment is a popular and important topic for both management practitioners and academics.

Empowerment is a management practice whereby decision-making is delegated from higher to lower levels in the organization. With this, individuals at the lower levels gain increased access to information and resources (Spreitzer, 1995). Central to empowerment is the adjustment of efforts to exert control to accomplish goals through participation with others (Zimmermann, 2000). However, for empowerment to happen, several enablers must be in place, such as empowering leadership. In other words, the individual at a higher level of the organization must be willing to temporarily relinquish some of his/her authority to allow the empowered individual to make decisions that are otherwise in the realm of the higher level (Sharma & Kirkman, 2015).

Empowerment literature typically distinguishes between structural empowerment, which sets the context for an individual to be empowered, and psychological empowerment, as a consequence of the structural empowerment (Spreitzer, 2007).

Structural empowerment

Structural empowerment is applying one or more practices for delegation of responsibility to employees to increase their decision-making authority while executing their tasks (Leach, Wall, & Jackson, 2003). Generally speaking, structural empowerment is about setting the conditions within the organization so that empowerment can happen. Among the most often described conditions and practices are the following:

- *Work design* is defined as the autonomy and workload associated with a person's role and the content and structure that frame the tasks and activities of that role. Studies showed that the benefits of empowerment initiatives are often undermined when the tasks of possibly empowered individuals are bundled too much with standardized work processes. Examples include empowerment of individuals to solve a problem but the task execution is firmly prescribed through compliance initiatives, such as those for quality or process compliance (Maynard, Gilson, & Mathieu, 2012). Hence, organizations using empowerment should allow for flexible work design, considering the nature of the tasks and their interdependencies. This flexibility should allow that authority, decision-making, and formal control over resources can be shared when the need arises through empowerment.

- *Empowering Leadership* is "a set of behaviors of the leader who shares power or allocates more responsibilities and autonomy to his or her followers through enhancing the meaningfulness of work, expressing confidence in high performance, promoting participation in decision making, and providing autonomy from bureaucratic constraints" (Cheong, Spain, Yammarino, & Yun, 2016, p. 603). Studies on the characteristics of empowering leadership showed that these leaders have a genuine interest that their followers are motivated and develop autonomous work practices within the constraints of the organization's goals and strategies. They do this through delegation, coordination, information sharing, encouragement, and inspiration. At the same time, they foster capabilities for continuous learning and autonomous work of their followers by being role models and guides (Amundsen & Martinsen, 2014). These characteristics are also typical for transformational leadership styles, such as those described by Bass and Riggio (2006), and coaching styles, such as those found in Goleman, Boyatzis, and McKee (2002). Here, leaders support their empowered individuals by removing barriers, including structural obstacles (Maynard et al., 2012). Studies in balanced leadership in projects showed that empowering could only happen when the project manager has a positive attitude toward empowerment. If the project manager does not like the idea of temporarily relinquishing some leadership authority, empowerment does not occur, and with this, balanced leadership is unlikely to happen.

- *Organizational support*, also known as "sociopolitical support," addresses the overall organizational climate and its support for empowerment. Studies identified three critical dimensions of organizational support: information sharing (i.e., access to potentially sensitive operational information); autonomy across boundaries (i.e., organizational structures and practices that allow for autonomous actions); and team accountability (i.e., empowered teams or individuals possess decision-making authority) (Seibert, Silver, & Randolph, 2004). Other studies showed that this type of support potentially includes aspects like the possibility of an empowered leader to access resources from outside the team or even outside the organization, the organization's support of multi-team cooperation and coordination, the presence of related communication facilities, and an overall culture that fosters collaboration (Maynard et al., 2012).

The preceding list shows the multilevel characteristic of structural empowerment; it spans from the single task and its design, via the leadership of managers, all the way to organizational climate and culture. Empowerment can be fostered or hindered at any of these levels. In the interviews that one of the authors of this book conducted to study empowerment in balanced leadership, he asked a public-sector organization project manager about the criteria that the manager would apply to temporarily give up his leadership authority to a team member to solve a severe problem. The manager's answer was, "I would never give up my leadership authority." This project did not benefit from structural empowerment.

Psychological empowerment

Psychological empowerment is enabled by structural empowerment and is defined as an "increased intrinsic task motivation" stemming from the power given to the individual or team through empowerment. Intrinsic task motivation refers to positively valued experiences through the task, which produces motivation and satisfaction for the individual (Thomas & Velthouse, 1990, p. 666). This refers to the ways individuals or teams experience the state of being empowered.

Among the most popular conceptualizations of this experience is the work by Spreitzer (2007), who identified four dimensions that make up the concept of psychological empowerment:

- *Meaning*: the congruency of the person's beliefs, values, and behaviors with the needs of the person's work role;
- *Competence*: the person's belief in his or her capability to perform the work skillfully;
- *Self-determination*: the autonomy or choice to initiate and regulate activities, behaviors, and processes, including decisions on work methods, efforts, and pace;
- *Impact*: the extent to which the person can influence outcomes at work.

To fully feel psychologically empowered, all four dimensions must be present. If one is missing, the experience will be limited. For example, if the task is meaningful for the individual, but the organization's strict process compliance requirements constrain self-determination in execution, the person will not feel empowered. Individual structural elements (such as work design) can impact specific psychological elements (like self-determination).

There are, of course, individual differences in the level of psychological empowerment that people feel. Studies showed that among those who experience more empowerment are people with stronger self-esteem, higher education levels, and those in higher ranks (Spreitzer, 1995). In terms of situational contingencies, empowerment is especially important in virtual settings, where individuals work independently and with little physical interaction (Spreitzer, 2007).

Pros and cons of empowerment

Outcomes of empowerment have been studied extensively. Besides the impact on motivation and through this on performance and managerial effectiveness, the studies showed that empowered employees report higher levels of job satisfaction and organizational commitment and less job strain and propensity to leave the organization. At a more detailed level, researchers found that the meaning, and, to some extent, the competence, dimensions drive job satisfaction. While these two dimensions also allow predicting career progression, the dimensions for self-determination and impact allow the prediction of organizational commitment (Spreitzer, 2007).

Every coin has two sides, and there are, of course, critical voices when it comes to empowerment. These voices include writers who see empowerment as a ploy by managers to get more out of their employees without increasing their remuneration or authority. Others observe that espousing empowerment increases peer-level monitoring among employees, leading to peer pressures, making the empowered individual perceive themselves as being even more controlled and disempowered. Furthermore, those who are too empowered risk becoming disempowered over time because their supervisors feel threatened by their empowerment level (Spreitzer, 2007).

Spreitzer (2007) suggests three measures to reduce the risk of occurrence of these adverse effects:

1. Let employees know the acceptable levels of empowerment by setting clear limits and boundaries for appropriate empowerment;
2. Reduce employees' self-interested behavior by building trustful relationships with them;

3. Align individual and organizational goals by measuring and rewarding key performance goals.

This section has given a general overview of the concept of empowerment and its dimensions. We have also discussed the enablers and outcomes and some potential adverse effects of empowerment, together with some possible mitigation measures. We now turn to focus on empowerment in projects and project management.

Empowerment in projects

Studies on empowerment in projects and project management typically focus on either the individual's (team member or project manager) or the team's empowerment. As indicated earlier, both are subject to structural and psychological empowerment. This will be described next.

Structural empowerment for individuals is often found in cases of dynamic project environments, where quick and flexible responses to changing circumstances are required (Nauman, Mansur Khan, & Ehsan, 2010). Structural empowerment through appropriate work design, empowering leadership, and organizational support are thereby the means to foster flexibility and pace in project execution. Other contextual criteria that support individuals' empowerment are projects with high task interdependency and highly integrated project teams, both of which require lots of team interaction to complete the task. The empowerment in these settings contrasts with empowerment in projects with high buyer-seller team integration. Here, empowerment is often hampered through overly prescribed work practices by the buying organization, which do not allow individuals from the supplying organization to become empowered. Examples are public-private projects where process compliance or other standardized work practices are prioritized by the public-sector buying organization, which limits the chances of empowerment on the side of the private-sector supplier teams' members (Tuuli, 2018).

Psychological empowerment for individuals is often identified as a mediator between leadership and project success. This mediation presents itself in various ways. For example, Khan, Jaafar, Javed, Mubarak, and Saudagar (2020) showed that leaders who share their resources and authority with team members (i.e., empower them), show recognition and provide feedback to them, and act as a role model contributing positively to the felt psychological empowerment of the team members. This level of felt psychological empowerment correlates with good project results.

Structural empowerment for teams is found more often in dynamic environments (Tuuli, 2018) and is especially of interest in projects with highly educated team members working on tasks with relatively high complexity and uncertainty. These settings are typical for high-tech industries. Parolia, Goodman, Li, and Jiang (2007) showed that empowerment correlates positively with project success in IT projects. Similar results were obtained in studies on NPD (new product development) projects in the electronics, biotechnology, and mechatronics industries. These studies also identified the importance of "media richness" for empowered team members. Media richness refers to the number of information cues that a media can transmit per time unit. Face-to-face communication is often perceived as the "richest" media at one end of the media-richness continuum, as opposed to letters and memos at the other end, and telephone calls and emails somewhere in between. A study by Badir, Büchel, and Tucci (2012) showed that a leader's intensity of communication increases with an increase in their empowerment. The positive effect of empowerment on good project results is mediated by the fit between the media capabilities and the empowered leader's communication intensity. Higher communication intensity after empowerment may require an adjustment of communication media. Hence, communication media may become an element of structural empowerment and, as such, an enabler for psychological empowerment.

Structural empowerment (or empowerment climate) positively influences the effectiveness of project management. This influence is more substantial in virtual settings than in co-located settings. Hence, structural empowerment contributes especially well to good project management in a dynamic context with a virtual team setting (Nauman et al., 2010).

Psychological empowerment for teams is typical in agile projects. Malik, Sarwar, and Orr (2021) showed that psychological empowerment has a strong influence on innovative behavior, which, in turn, has a strong positive influence on project performance. However, they add that it may take some time until the full effect of increased psychological empowerment leads to desired innovation outcomes.

This section has provided a brief summary of the empowerment studies in project management. We now turn to selection and empowerment in balanced leadership.

Selection and empowerment in balanced leadership

In the preceding sections of this chapter, we first introduced the concepts of selection and empowerment from a general management/leadership perspective. Then, we directed our focus on the ways the project management literature addresses these two concepts. Both views provide the basis for a good understanding of the two concepts. Now, we address the different ways that selection and empowerment manifest themselves in the context of balanced leadership.

Earlier in this book, we defined balanced leadership as the dynamic back-and-forth of the transition of leadership authority between a vertical leader (such as a project manager) and horizontal/shared/distributed leader(s) for the realization of desired states in projects (Müller et al., 2018b). "Balanced" here refers to selecting and empowering the best-suited leader in situational contingency at any point in time in the project. Hence, in different situations and at different times in a project, a suitable leader's required characteristics might vary, such as the need for a more creative leader or leader group when an innovative solution is needed to solve a problem, or the need for a more sober, detail-oriented leader to prepare the presentation of the project's final product to the client. Balanced leadership will ensure that the best-suited team member is selected and appointed temporarily for these different situations. The project manager enables the leadership by this team member or a subgroup of team members through empowerment and subsequently governs them for the duration of the temporary appointment of the leader(s). Therefore, horizontal/shared/distributed leadership supplements the vertical leadership from the project manager. Balanced leadership ensures the best possible leadership at any point in time in the project.

A team of researchers from Dalian University of Technology in China and BI Norwegian Business School performed a detailed investigation of the selection and empowerment event in balanced leadership in projects (Yu, Vaagaasar, Müller, Wang, & Zhu, 2018). They conducted 20 interviews in project-based and project-oriented organizations of different sizes and industries in China. This broad approach to sampling allows for identifying the most generic features of the phenomenon under study. The analysis of the data revealed several insights into the selection and empowerment event.

The empowerment process

The data revealed a three-stage process of pre-empowerment, empowerment, and post-empowerment.

During *pre-empowerment*, the project manager goes through two steps. The first is called empowerment orientation, where the project manager analyzes the project's situation and the conditions in the team, often through interaction with team members to derive at a selection decision. The selected candidate(s) are hereby prepared for their specific task, including clarifying formal and informal requirements for their role, the task's scope, and other details. The second step is the formalization of the decision. Formalization can range from a very informal to very formal process. A formal process, for example, is when specific certifications (such as for safety in construction projects) are required for the role, and/or when the temporary leader needs to be authorized by the client. Depending on the requirements of the leader's role, this step may go unnoticed when almost no formalization is needed (e.g., when the deputy project manager takes over frequently) or may require a substantial preparation time (e.g., when formal approval from the client needs to be obtained).

The end of the formalization marks the transition into the *empowerment stage*. This stage consists of three steps:

1. *Decision announcement*: At this first step, the project team is officially or sometimes unofficially informed of the selection decision and the empowerment of the individual(s).
2. *Execution and control*: During this step, the empowered leader or team accepts and executes the role, while the project manager follows the empowered leader(s) and controls or regulates the fulfillment of the task within the formal and informal requirements discussed at the pre-empowerment stage.
3. *Empowerment termination*: This marks the point in time when empowerment ends, and the project manager assumes leadership authority again.

The third stage is *post-empowerment*; at this stage, the empowered leader(s) and the project manager evaluate the performance and task fulfillment and its impact on possible further empowerment decisions or career ambitions. This is further described in Chapter 8 on leadership transition.

Dimensions of empowerment

The preceding process reveals five dimensions that make up the selection and empowerment event. The content of these dimensions varies substantially across projects, and their combinations reveal certain patterns. The dimensions are: the leader's announcement, leader's acceptance, leader's autonomy, control of the leader, and future of the leader (see also Table 6.1).

Leader announcement is the way the project manager announces the empowerment decision. Differences in the announcement develop from differences in the legitimacy of particular ways to announce a leader in different situations. Announcements can be categorized into:

- *Simple or no announcement*: typical for situations where the announcement would be a greater effort than the announced task. Examples include very short appointments to solve an issue through a relatively small task. Other examples include weakly integrated teams, where team members do not know each other and their roles very well and feel obligated to react to anyone contacting them.
- *Official announcement*: typical for situations that require communication of information about the legitimacy of the candidate, his or her degree of authorization, and role clarification for those impacted by the decision. It is a significant enabler for the psychological empowerment of the candidate. This announcement can be made orally in project team meetings, but may also happen through formal letters to team and management, clients, or other stakeholders.
- *Official announcement with assistance*: typical for situations where the official announcement is supported by the project manager through informal discussion with team members (or other stakeholders). This can happen when particular team members are frustrated because they were not chosen for the temporary leader role, or when team members foresee particular tensions or issues when working under the empowered candidate's leadership.

Leader acceptance is about the degree to which the project team accepts the empowered leader and his or her decisions. Acceptance includes cognitive and behavioral elements, which typically manifest themselves in the feedback and interaction between the appointed leader and the team members. The study identified three categories of acceptance:

- *Easy acceptance*: The team members show their acceptance of the leader through related behavior and interaction, for example, through willing cooperation.
- *Gradual acceptance*: The team members have some initial difficulties with the decisions or behavior of the leader but become comfortable with it over time.
- *Indifference*: The team members do not rate the leader's decisions or behavior sufficiently severely to cause noticeable uncollaborative behavior. Harmony is prioritized over a short-term disagreement with the leader.

Leader autonomy refers to the authority and scope of the leadership task. The project manager grants this autonomy to the empowered leader. The granted autonomy ranges from very limited to very wide in four categories:

- *Autonomy in work*: the freedom to act as a leader. As long as the leader is aligned with the values of the task or project, they are typically given higher levels of autonomy by the project manager. Conversely, if the leader indicates discrepancies in values and actions, the project manager typically limits the level of autonomy.
- *Autonomy in decision-making* refers to the types of decisions the leader is authorized to make. These limitations are linked to the kind of issue the leader is supposed to solve. For example, the leader might only be allowed to make technical decisions because the issue at hand is technical. Costs or delivery time implications stemming from the technical solution may need approval from the project manager.
- *Limited autonomy* describes circumstances in which the leader has little to no freedom to decide and mainly has to follow orders and needs to get approval for most of the decisions.
- *Limited autonomy with voice behavior* refers to circumstances where the appointed leader also has very little freedom to decide himself or herself, but the project manager encourages feedback on the orders given.

Leader control describes the ways the project manager initially controls the empowered leader. The type of control may be adjusted over time based on situational dependency (see next chapter). Four categories of control were identified:

- *Outcome control*: The project manager checks the accomplishment of previously agreed work outcomes regularly.

- *Pro-active outcome control*: The project manager and the leader agree on outcomes and their measures. The project manager controls the progress toward these outcomes frequently, for example, in daily formal meetings.
- *Mentoring and outcome control*: The project manager and the leader agree on outcomes and their measures. The project manager mentors the leader through the process of outcome development.
- *Outcome and behavior control*: The project manager and the leader agree on outcomes, as well as the process (which prescribes behavior) to accomplish the agreed-upon outcomes. The project manager controls both outcomes and process compliance regularly, such as weekly.

Future of the leader describes the longer-term intention that underpins the appointment of a temporary leader. Three categories were identified:

- *Back to the previous role in the project team*: This refers to situations in which a temporary leader is appointed solely to lead the project through a particular issue or crisis.
- *Move to a leader position*: The temporary leader is appointed to be trained in his or her leadership skills or shows the potential for leadership development. If the leader performs well, it increases the possibility of becoming a formal project manager in the future.
- *Move to a higher position*: The temporary leader is appointed to be trained in management skills. The intention is to promote him or her to a line management position.

Table 6.1 summarizes the preceding dimensions. The table implies a timely sequence from left to right, which is merely conceptual. Some of the dimensions can overlap in time, or aspects of later dimensions can influence earlier

Table 6.1 The Dimensions of Empowerment

Leader Announcement	Leader Acceptance	Leader Autonomy	Leader Control	Future of the Leader
• Simple or no announcement • Official announcement • Official announcement with assistance	• Easy acceptance • Gradual acceptance • Indifference	• Autonomy in work • Autonomy in decision-making • Limited autonomy • Limited autonomy with voice behavior	• Outcome control • Proactive outcome control • Mentoring and outcome control • Outcome and behavior control	• Back to the previous role • Move to a leader position • Move to a higher position

dimensions. These questions are further discussed in the remainder of this chapter.

Practices of empowering

The five dimensions of empowering and their particular combinations play a key role in the motivation and intention in selecting and empowering individuals. This leads us to the reasons for selecting and empowering.

The study identified several reasons for selecting and empowering the individual(s). In analyzing these reasons, two major distinctions were seen:

a. The decision was either related to a task or a person; that is, the goal of empowerment is either in executing a task, such as solving an issue, or developing an individual as a leader.

b. The legitimacy of the selection and, with it, the justification of the selected individuals(s) as either being high or low. In the highly legitimized (i.e., highly justifiable) case, the decision to empower an individual is easy for the project team to comprehend, such as empowering the deputy project manager to lead the project during the project manager's vacation. In the case of low legitimacy, the decision is often enforced through situational circumstances, for example, when empowering a team member who is not fully qualified for the task because no better-qualified resource is available.

Figure 6.2 shows these two distinctions as the respective horizontal and vertical axis. This results in four types of empowerment decisions: bench player and project manager deputy as task-oriented empowerments, as well as oysters and future stars as people-oriented decisions. The four different types show distinct patterns of expression of the five dimensions of empowerment. The following describes the four types and their patterns.

Deputies: high legitimacy and task-orientation: This type of empowerment relates to situations where deputies, such as those for the project manager, are empowered to perform particular tasks. Their legitimacy is high as they already have the status of a deputy. Hence the team is prepared for them as a leader. Their task can include standing in for the project manager because of the latter's unavailability, solving an issue using the deputy's specialist skills, or arriving at an innovative solution with a subteam led by the deputy. The empowered individuals are typically acknowledged and are easily accepted

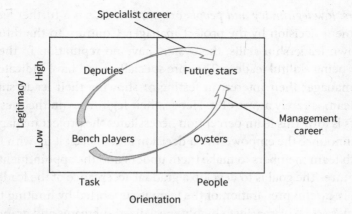

Figure 6.2. Potential career developments through empowerment.

by the team for their competence through their status as deputy. This perception by the team contributes positively to the selected individual's psychological empowerment. Therefore, the required announcement is simple or sometimes not even necessary. Deputies typically possess autonomy for executing their work. The project manager typically controls them in terms of pre-agreed outcomes (e.g., solution of a problem, specific deliverables, or project results). At the end of their appointment period, they usually move back to their prior role in the team.

Future stars: high legitimacy and people-orientation: This type of empowerment decision addresses the leadership development of an individual. Hence, it is not predominantly for executing a specific task, but for training, developing, and/or cultivating a team member's leadership skills. Future stars are already known within the project team as leaders because they have shown their leadership skills at earlier occasions in the same project or elsewhere with the team members. Hence, they are perceived as highly legitimate for the role. Accordingly, the team accepts them easily as temporary leaders. The appointment is often made in an official way to avoid misunderstandings about the empowerment decision's motivation and goals. All this contributes positively to their psychological empowerment. During the execution of their role, they are typically granted a wider autonomy than deputies by having decision-making authority, which, in turn, is proactively controlled by the project manager, who also controls the accomplishments of agreed-upon outcomes of the project. At the end of their appointment, future stars either go back to their prior role in the team and become project managers in a later project, or soon move on to lead another project.

Oysters: low legitimacy and people orientation: This is a further leadership development decision by the project manager. Contrary to the future stars' well-known leadership skills, the oysters have no reputation in the project team for being skillful leaders. They are specialists and have indicated to the project manager their interest in testing or showing their leadership skills, but the team is rarely aware of it. Hence, their legitimacy in the eyes of team members is low. This team perception necessitates the project manager to officially announce the empowerment decision and to back it up with informal talks with team members to make them understand the appointment's developing nature. The goal is to develop a gradual acceptance of the leader by the team. This careful preparation of the team is supported by limiting the leadership role's scope primarily to highly specialized subteams and granting limited autonomy in work and decision-making, but allowing the candidate to voice his/her opinions and give feedback to the project manager. The project manager mentors the candidate and controls carefully the accomplishment of agreed-upon project outcomes. At the end of their appointment period, the candidate often moves back to the prior role in the team and waits for further opportunities to develop leadership skills to gradually become a future star. Alternatively, the candidate may take over specialist teams in a line organization outside of the project.

Bench players: low legitimacy and task orientation: This empowerment decision is based on an immediate or urgent need to lead the project through a specific task, such as emergencies or other circumstances when timely action takes priority over the quality of the action. Hence, it is a task-oriented appointment of an immediately available but not necessarily best-qualified resource for the task. This questionable fit of situation and resource qualifications lowers the individual's perceived legitimacy by the team for the execution of the task. This low level of legitimacy leads to indifference in the acceptance of the leader. Team members may follow the empowered leader because of the short nature of the appointment or lack of alternative leaders, even though they do not buy in to the leader's appointment or decisions. Driven by the low legitimacy, the project managers announce the leader officially and back it up with informal talks with team members, discussing the short-term nature and decision criteria of the assignment. To keep potential risks as low as possible, project managers grant only limited authority to the leader and control them tightly both in terms of project outcomes and process compliance. Bench players typically return to their prior roles in the team at the end of their appointment period.

Table 6.2 summarizes the preceding discussion and shows the empowerment dimensions' particular profiles for each empowerment type.

The preceding discussion on the leader's future implies a career development, which is depicted in Figure 6.2. As a bench player, a potential future leader is given the first opportunity to show leader capabilities and develop leadership skills. Building on this experience, the candidate may decide to become a (project) manager in the long run, typically by becoming a future star first. To get there, the candidate has a choice of two different career routes.

Route 1: Specialist career: The bench player continues to build primarily on the professional skills by honing them while taking on occasional empowerments as a temporary leader. By building a reputation, the candidate may move into the role of a deputy project manager. Through repetitive assignments as a temporary leader, the candidate builds a reputation as a leader and becomes a future star. From there, he or she moves into other leadership or management roles.

Route 2: Management career: The bench player's first experience with leadership assignments triggers the ambition to become a manager. The bench player works with the project manager to look for more opportunities to develop leadership skills, which moves him or her into the oyster quadrant and, through frequent repetition of leadership assignments, into the future stars quadrant. From there, he or she may move into other leadership or management roles.

Table 6.2 Empowerment Types and Related Empowerment Dimension Profiles

Empowerment Dimension	Empowerment Type			
	Deputies	Future stars	Oysters	Bench players
Leader announcement	Simple or no announcement	Official announcement	Official announcement with assistance	Official announcement with assistance
Leader acceptance	Easy acceptance	Easy acceptance	Gradual acceptance	Indifferent
Leader autonomy	Autonomy in work	Autonomy in decision-making	Limited autonomy with voice behavior	Limited authority
Leader control	Outcome control	Proactive outcome control	Outcome control plus mentoring	Outcome and behavior control
Future of the leader	Back to prior role	Move to a leader position	Move to a leader position	Back to prior position

Individuals starting in the deputies or oysters quadrant follow their particular route. Here, a deputy should develop people skills by taking on training opportunities for becoming a future star to qualify for a full project manager role. Accordingly, individuals in the oysters quadrant who want to become project managers should assess their task-level experience and the degree this is needed in the projects they would like to manage. If they need more task experience, they may try to move into a bench player or deputy quadrant first, before they engage in becoming a future star. With their task-level skills developed to the extent needed in their projects, they can grow into a future star by frequently taking on people-oriented tasks to build the skills and experience needed for a future star.

This chapter has introduced the selection and empowerment literature, both from general management and project management perspective. Then the empowerment practices in projects were discussed, leading to four distinct empowerment types distinguished by five empowerment dimensions. Together, the types and dimensions explain the legitimacy and the task or role orientation of an empowerment decision and collectively provide a career framework for future leaders.

Acknowledgments

The authors would like to acknowledge the contribution of Miao Yu, Anne Live Vaagaasar, Linzhuo Wang, and Fangwei Zhu. Their studies provided invaluable insights into the selection and empowerment event in balanced leadership.

Further reading

Kirkman, B. L., & Rosen, B. (1999). Beyond self-management: Antecedents and consequences of team empowerment. *Academy of Management Journal*, *42*(1), 58–74. https://doi.org/10.5465/256874.

Reflection questions

1. What are the elements of structural empowerment, and how do they emerge in projects?

2. What are the characteristics of psychological empowerment, and how do they manifest in projects?
3. What are the differences between the four empowerment types, and how do the empowerment dimensions influence them?
4. Which career options in management open up through empowerment?

7

Empowered Leadership and
Its Governance

Introduction

The present chapter addresses leadership execution by empowered leader(s) and its governance by the project manager. Empowered leader(s) can be individuals performing horizontal leadership or subteams of the project team performing shared or distributed leadership. We define this as the event when the empowered leader(s) accept their role and lead the project while being governed by the project manager. Figure 7.1 depicts the event within the balanced leadership framework.

One underlying assumption of this chapter is that the project manager empowers in situational contingency either:

- an individual to temporarily lead the project, which leads to horizontal leadership (see Chapter 2);
- a subteam led by one subteam member, which leads to shared leadership (see Chapter 1); or
- a subteam with no leader, where leadership develops through distributed leadership (see Chapter 1).

Horizontal, shared, and distributed leadership are discussed in Chapters 1 and 2 and are therefore not repeated here. Instead, we discuss the importance of empowered leadership for organizations and projects and the project manager's role in governing the empowered leader(s).

Empowered leaders

In Chapter 6, we showed that the reasons leading to empowerment could vary substantially and, along with this, the empowered candidate's perceived legitimacy. Hence, one of the main differences between long-term, formal leaders

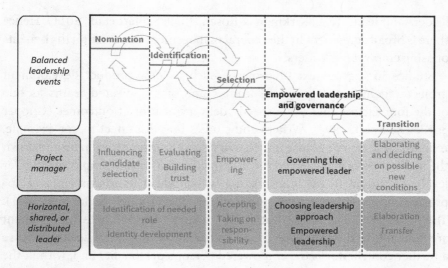

Figure 7.1. Locating the empowerment and its governance event in the balanced leadership framework.

and temporary leaders in horizontal, shared, or distributed leadership could be their perceived legitimacy for the leader role. An empowered leader might lack legitimacy compared with a formally appointed leader (Zhu, Wang, Sun, Sun, & Müller, 2019). Other contextual characteristics that differ between these two leader roles might be related to the assignment's duration, the individual's perceived seniority in the profession, the perceived managerial leadership capabilities, and so forth. Therefore, the circumstances for empowered leaders can vary substantially from those for formal leaders, such as project managers. These uncertainties raise the question of whether temporarily empowered leaders are just as successful as longer-term or more formal leaders.

Numerous studies identified empowered leaders as a critical factor for better achievement of organizational goals, such as performance results and climate. Results-related investigations addressed generic as well as more focused views of the organization. The former included studies that empirically show higher productivity, proactiveness, and better customer service through empowered leaders and teams (e.g., Kirkman & Rosen, 1999; Seibert, Wang, & Coutyright, 2011). The more focused studies showed, for example, the benefits of empowerment in continuous improvement initiatives for more ambidexterity in organizations (van Assen, 2020). Studies on better organizational climate emphasized higher levels of job satisfaction, organizational and team commitment, and fewer turnover intentions through empowered leaders and teams (e.g., Kirkman & Rosen, 1999; Seibert et al., 2011). Hence there is broad agreement in the general management literature on the benefits of using empowered leaders.

Studies in the context of projects, such as new product development projects, identified empowered leaders and/or empowered teams as one of the four factors that drive speedy delivery of project outcomes (Cooper & Kleinschmidt, 1994). Writers and studies link this effect to, for example, reduced cycle times because unnecessary email communication up and down the hierarchies is avoided (Peters, 1988), and leaders' and employees' higher level of freedom in decision-making, which shortens discussion and approval times and access times to resources (McDonough & Barczak, 1991). This could be read as if organizational performance and climate improvement are reducible to the empowered leader's role alone. It is not that easy because a further contributor is the empowered person's personality and, with it, the person's leadership. For example, Wegner (2004) showed that the more frequently empowered employees engaged in either transactional or transformational leadership, thereby reducing their laissez-faire leadership, the higher their organization's performance.

Moreover, once employees are empowered, the organization's formal managers' influence on organizational results lessens. This influence change indicates that empowered leaders take over large parts of the impact on organizational or project results when they accept their role as leaders and show their leadership style. We discuss this further in the context of balanced leadership in Chapter 10.

So far, we have portrayed empowered leadership as beneficial because it enhances self-efficacy, autonomy, and performance. However, there are also unfavorable effects of having empowered leaders in an organization. Among them are the so-called burdening processes, which describe that empowering leaders may increase their followers' perceived job-induced tension, which can adversely affect their followers' performance. Hence there are two sides to the empowered leader coin: (a) enabling, through self-efficacy and autonomy to higher performance, and (b) burdening, through higher job-related tensions resulting in adverse effects on performance (Cheong, Spain, Yammarino, & Yun, 2016).

Leadership styles of empowered leaders

In the introductory chapter, we said that this book is not about leadership styles, such as transactional and transformational styles. Nevertheless, we should address to some extent the leadership style of empowered leaders. We do this because their situation differs from that of more formally appointed and often longer-term leaders.

Studies on personality traits, especially prestige and dominance motivations, found correlations with the ways empowered leaders fulfill their roles. Prestige motivation refers to "a desire for respect and admiration, and an orientation for seeking the freely conferred, voluntary respect of subordinates." In this study, the highly psychologically empowered leaders with high prestige motivation tend to show increasing support of their followers and their autonomy. The followers respond to this with respect and deference (Lee, Hays, & Johnson, 2020, p. 2). Dominance motivation, which is "the desire for authority over others, and an orientation for maintaining subordination through control," induces a different leadership approach. Empowered leaders with this trait tend to increase authority and control in line with their level of psychological empowerment (Lee, Hays, & Johnson, 2020, p. 2).

There are, of course, many other factors that impact leadership by empowered leaders, such as industry culture, national culture, expectations from the project manager, etc. There is no one-size-fits-all style that works in all circumstances, and there is no formula to calculate which style is used by whom. Moreover, individual leadership styles can change, as we discussed in Chapter 6. The best leaders are those who can adjust their style to the requirements of the situation. Our studies in balanced leadership contexts showed some patterns in relation to industries and cultures. As described in Chapter 2, case studies in construction projects in English-speaking countries revealed a preference for a mixture of autocratic and democratic styles, while in IT projects in Scandinavia, the democratic style dominated (Drouin, Müller, Sankaran, & Vaagaasar, 2018). Although it is unclear whether this preference is mainly influenced by national or industry culture, we can assume that the styles are appropriate for the type of project in which they are used. If that was not the case, the project manager would have terminated the leader's empowerment, as we shall see in Chapter 8.

Role identity of empowered leaders

The question addressed here is how empowered leaders feel in their role. Does their understanding of the role match that of the project team and others? And what are the consequences thereof? To answer these questions, we take the perspective of identity theory (Stets & Burke, 2000, p. 225):

In identity theory, the core of an identity is the categorization of the self as an occupant of a role, and the incorporation, into the self, of the meanings and expectations associated with that role and its performance.

Applying this concept to the roles in an organization or a project leads to *role identity*, which is defined as a person's "imaginative view of himself as he likes to think of himself being and acting as an occupant" (McCall & Simmons, 1978, p. 65). Central to role identity theory is "the match between the individual meanings of occupying a particular role and the behaviors that a person enacts in that role while interacting with others" (Stets & Burke, 2000, p. 227). By taking on a role identity, such as a leader in a project, the person adopts role-related self-meanings and expectations in relation to other roles in the group. When fulfilling the role, the person acts to represent and preserve these meanings and expectations (Stets & Burke, 2000). Role identity influences people's behavior. Stronger role identity makes people behave more according to their view of the assigned role in order to verify their identity (Zhu et al., 2019). However, if roles and identities do not match, people tend to become less satisfied with their roles and potentially leave the group or role (Riley & Burke, 1995). For example, an empowered leader's behavior may be driven by the person's self-meanings and expectations of "how a leader should behave in projects" that might or might not be congruent with the project team's expected behavior in that role. In the case of congruency, the leader will validate the group's and their own expectations and develop a strong identity. In contrast, in case of a discrepancy between the group's expectations of the role and the leader's understanding of it, the role identity will diminish.

Past studies used role identity theory to understand various phenomena in projects, for example, by studying the implications stemming from assigning projects an identity as being innovative. This identity allows the project to be purposefully positioned differently within various stakeholder groups, depending on the groups' particular expectations (Sergeeva, 2017), or by studying the relationship between project managers' career satisfaction and their professional identity. Results indicate that project managers with a high level of professional identification (that is, a strong role identity as project manager) mainly validate their role understanding through external project networks and reduce the need for internal validation within the organization (McKevitt, Carbery, & Lyons, 2017).

Researchers from Dalian University of Technology in China and BI Norwegian Business School investigated horizontal leaders' role identity in balanced leadership. The study was motivated by the need to understand the drivers for horizontal leaders' role identity, in the context of possibly low legitimacy of the appointed leaders, stemming from the short duration of their appointments (Zhu et al., 2019). The study identified the necessary conditions for high and low role identity of horizontal leaders in balanced leadership. The most common way to build a strong horizontal leader role identity is by formal empowerment by the project manager and informally communicated expectations from the team. Team expectations (in terms of the team expecting someone who can fix the problem, take the lead, and is qualified) plays a key role. Its absence is the only necessary condition for low role identity. Hence, the presence of team expectations serves as a hygiene factor for developing a role identity.

Four distinct factors were identified as being necessary for strong role identity:

- *Intrinsic rewards*: a satisfaction that stems from the work as a horizontal leader; high intrinsic rewards emerge through feelings of "being good," "moving work forward," "delivering high-quality work," and so forth;
- *Self-efficacy*: the horizontal leader's belief in being able to master the task by mobilizing their motivation, cognitive resources, and courses of action required for horizontal leadership;
- *Personal expectations*: the leader's expectations on their performance and image outcomes from the assignment;
- *High job complexity*: the difficulty and complexity of the tasks during the assignment. A certain level of complexity is needed for the horizontal leader to develop an identity for the role.

Apart from these necessary conditions, there are differences between junior ($\leq$ 10 years of experience) and senior (>10 years of experience) horizontal leaders.

For junior horizontal leaders, the appointment is essential to build a strong role identity, as it carries extra meaning for them, including the chance for more empowerment opportunities and possible career advancement. Thus, the intrinsic reward stemming from empowerment is key and should be used by project managers to build and maintain a strong role identity. However, this should be supported by assignments with higher job complexity, extrinsic rewards, and training opportunities. Generally, junior horizontal leaders' role identity is more resilient than that of their senior counterparts, as only the absence of several of the preceding factors will lower their role identity.

For senior horizontal leaders, "not losing face" is important. They tend to have a strong role identity as long as they receive feedback regarding team expectations. The absence thereof reduces the strength of the role identity.

Hence, to maintain senior horizontal leaders' role identity, project managers should carefully manage the team's horizontal leaders' support in the form of feedback and communication of expectations.

This section has outlined the concept and importance of role identity during the appointment of the empowered leader(s). Particular focus was given to horizontal leaders, as their role is not as extensively described as that of other empowered leaders in the literature. Tips were provided on how project managers can manage horizontal leaders' role identity both generally and for different seniority levels in particular.

This allows us to turn now to some of the other tasks of the project manager during the assignment of empowered leaders, that is, to govern their leadership.

Governance versus leadership

In Chapter 6 we said that once a temporary leader is empowered, the project manager starts to follow this leader while simultaneously governing the leader's actions. In this section, we examine this issue, starting with a definition of terms and their relationship to each other; we then describe governance in detail.

We address three different activities: (project) management, leadership, and governance. How are they defined, what is the difference between them, and how do they relate to each other? To answer these questions, we take a sociological perspective. Many sociologists agree on two basic concepts underlying societies and therefore also organizations or projects. These are *structures* and *human agency* (Archer, 2004). From a sociological perspective, all phenomena in societies are reducible to these two concepts.

Structures refer to the stable arrangement of the human and nonhuman elements that make up an organization (Britannica, 2020). Examples include organizational structures, which outline the relationship between positions and their occupants; or job descriptions, which outline the role and responsibilities of these positions; or policies, which are guidelines for executing work. Other structures may include processes that describe the timely flow of activities; or the project managers' ideas on how team members should perform their tasks. Structures are essentially the factors determining or limiting people and their decisions in organizations (Archer, 1995; Britannica, 2020).

Human agency refers to the actions of people within these structures. That means people are supposed to work within limits set by the structures. However, people may or may not behave in accordance with the formal and informal limits, including the spoken and unspoken expectations that are associated with a role in a structure.

Therefore, structure and human agency relate to each other in one way or another. However, they build on different ontological assumptions; for example, human agents possess self-reflective capabilities that structures lack. Therefore, implementations of structural demands are mediated by human agency (Archer, 2007). A leading sociologist, Margaret Archer (2010), describes the two as inseparable and mutually constitutive and proposes an analytical dualism when attempting to understand the relationship between structures and human agency. Doing this, we accept that the two concepts are interdependent so that they influence each other, but neither dominates the other. Each can only be understood in relation to the other.

We can apply this perspective of structure and agency to define the differences between management, leadership, governance, and, as we will see, governmentality (Müller, 2019) (see also Table 6.1 in Chapter 6).

- *Management* is concerned with "getting things done" through planning, executing, and controlling. This implies a task orientation in the pursuance of planned goals. Thus, it provides the structure to perform tasks to conduct, accomplish, or bring about something. It is objective by nature, as it is typically numbers-driven and rational (Bennis & Nanus, 1985). Hence, management provides the structural means for the execution of tasks. It is a goal-oriented activity to accomplish (project) objectives.

- *Leadership* is an interpersonal, person-oriented, social influence (Endres & Weibler, 2017), which guides direction, course, action, and opinion (Bennis & Nanus, 1985). It includes people-oriented concepts, such as motivation, charisma, resonance, etc., making it subjective by nature. It complements management, as it reflects the human-agency perspective to execute tasks (or projects). To that end, it is a people-oriented activity to accomplish (project) objectives.

- *Governance,* which is often called "the management of management" (Too & Weaver, 2014), is the structural framework to steer managers to execute their roles (OECD, 2004). Hence, it defines and sets the limits for managers' roles, often through policies, processes, etc. By its nature, it is objective and a structural means to steer management. To that end, it is a framework for managers to do their work and to be held accountable for it. Thus, governance relates to management, as both are structures.

- *Governmentality* is associated with leadership, as both are human-agency-related activities. Governmentality describes how those in governance positions (such as steering committee members, project owners,

Table 7.1 Mutual Positioning of Management, Leadership, Governance, and Governmentality

	Structure	Human Agency
Steering	**Governance:** Framework for managers to do their tasks; the way mangers are held accountable—the structures, policies, processes, etc.	**Governmentality:** Ways governors interact with those they govern; mentalities, rationalities, ways of interaction, chosen by those in governance roles to implement, maintain, and change the governance structure
Executing	**Management:** Goal-oriented activity to accomplish project objectives	**Leadership:** People-oriented activity to accomplish project objectives

Source: Adapted from Müller (2019).

etc.) interact with those they govern (i.e., project managers or temporarily appointed leaders for the project). In other words, governmentality describes human behavior, the human agency, of those who steer leaders. Thus, governmentality is the governors' chosen way of interaction with those they govern.

The preceding list implies that governance and management provide structure, and governmentality and leadership provide for human agency. Management and leadership work at the management execution level, whereas governance and governmentality work at the steering level. Table 7.1 depicts these relations.

Governance

Governance is a long-standing concept applied at various levels in societies. It describes the ways to steer self-managing entities—and, with that, the managers of these entities. It is probably most obvious in the United Nations' governance work in their attempt to steer the community of sovereign states on earth. Other examples include corporate governance, which addresses the many semi-sovereign business units in a corporation by steering their managers. Thus, governance institutionalizes the interaction between players, such as between managers, shareholders, and the board of directors in a corporation. With the many levels at which governance applies comes a wide variety of definitions of the term *governance*. Some define governance as procedures and processes (OECD, 2001), others as a control system (Larcker & Tayan,

2011), others as the relationships between stakeholders (Monks & Minow, 1995), and yet others as an ethical phenomenon, in place to hold the balance between economic and social goals and between individual and communal goals (Cadbury, 2002). Generally speaking, the higher up we look at the hierarchy, the more general the definition. Country-level governance is often defined as "the process of steering society and the economy through collective action and in accordance with common goals" (Ansell & Torfing, 2016, p. 4). Corporate governance is often defined as per the Organisation for Economic Co-operation and Development (OECD, 2004, p. 11):

> [It is] a set of relationships between a company's management, its board, its shareholders and other stakeholders. Corporate governance also provides the structure through which the objectives of the company are set, and the means of attaining those objectives and monitoring performance are determined.

At the project level, the related *project governance* applies these principles to projects for ensuring consistent and predictable project delivery. Project governance is a subset of corporate governance or its agreed-upon subset in contracts with external parties. It provides responsibilities, processes, and policies, and other means to ensure that projects are managed in the best interest of the stakeholders, including the project owner. Underneath these "visible" objects are the mechanisms through which governance is exercised. The two most often identified governance mechanisms are trust and control (Das & Teng, 1998).

Trust is the "willingness of a party to be vulnerable to the actions of another party based on the expectation that the other will perform a particular action important to the trustor, irrespective of the ability to monitor or control that other party" (Schoorman, Mayer, & Davis, 2007, p. 712). Trust-based governance systems rely on minimum levels of control and thereby reduce transaction costs (i.e., the administrative costs for searching, bargaining, policing, and enforcing control structures, such as a contract in a project). However, this increases the risk for opportunism, especially in temporary endeavors such as projects, because it may remain unnoticed until the end of the project (Müller, 2017; Nooteboom, 1996).

Control is a measurable and rational mechanism in project governance. It is often described as the complement of the more subjective trust mechanism. It is the primary mechanism in many traditional definitions that see governance as a collection of control mechanisms (Cadbury, 1992; Larcker & Tayan, 2011). Seeing governance predominantly as a control function leads to governance structures (i.e., policies, processes, institutions, etc.) that aim to reduce the risks of hazards (Williamson, 1991). Examples include frequent and detailed reporting of the project manager to the steering committee (Turner & Müller, 2004), or "behavior control" through enforcement of process compliance (Ouchi, 1980). Relying too much on control can lead to being caught in a Weberian "iron cage of bureaucracy," which perpetually increases formalism and from which it becomes increasingly difficult to escape (Müller & Kvalnes, 2017).

Trust and control, the two governance mechanisms, are in a complex relationship. The OECD defines governance as both a control function and a relationship between stakeholders and managers, which implies a trust component (OECD, 2004). They see governance as not mutually exclusive or reducible to only one of the two mechanisms, but as two mechanisms in a complex and nonlinear relationship (Clases, Bachmann, & Wehner, 2003; Pinto, Slevin, & English, 2009). Both mechanisms are present in every governance structure. However, a closer look at the governance structures, policies, etc., and their enforcement helps identify whether a governance system is built predominantly from a trust or a control perspective.

Thus, governance is a structure to steer managers, based either more on trust or more on control. However, to be successful, a governance structure must be tailored to the specific circumstances of the unit to be governed. In complex organizational settings, such as the United Nations, European Union, or corporations, we find several different governance approaches simultaneously. This is referred to as multilevel governance (MLG). This concept distinguishes between two complementary types of governance (Bache, Bartle, & Flinders, 2016; Hooghe & Marks, 2003):

Type I governance takes a system-wide perspective and steers the different autonomous and non-overlapping units (such as countries, business units, or projects in a portfolio) to avoid clashes between them and provide a decision-board that can act on behalf of the constituting members. The objective is to achieve system efficiency. An example could be a board of directors in a corporation. In the realm of projects, Type I is known as the *governance of projects,* that is, the governance of groups of projects or even the entirety of all projects in an organization. Examples include a portfolio of IT projects in a financial services corporation. All projects in the portfolio share the same characteristic; they are IT-related. Still, they are sovereign entities because they do not overlap in the functions they provide or the solutions they generate. This system of projects is governed through Type I governance, ensuring that at the portfolio (or system) level, the right management objectives, resources, and processes are in place to identify, select, and execute those projects in the best interest of the organization's strategy. Even though the individual projects in the portfolio are sovereign entities, the governance of projects ensures that projects' commonalities are treated equally within the portfolio system. Examples include similar criteria for selecting similar projects, just a few defined and tested project management methodologies to run these projects, standardized reporting across projects to allow comparing their performance, and so forth. Studies have shown that this is a major contribution to organizational success (Müller, Martinsuo, & Blomquist, 2008).

Type II governance takes a task perspective and steers individual endeavors or the solution of particular issues. It centers around technical proficiency and application of knowledge across different sovereign units. The objective is to achieve Pareto optimality, an economic state where the particular use of resources achieves maximum benefit for all parties. An example could be a department of project managers within a corporation. Type II governance is often embedded in Type I governance. In the world of projects, Type II governance is known as *project governance*, which is the individual project's governance within a portfolio of projects. This governance is project-oriented and often deals with technical solutions. Governance focuses here on the project's particularities, such as tailoring planning and control processes to meet the project objectives in the best possible way, or the particular skills, resources, and timing needed to deliver the project outcome within the limits of time, cost, and quality requirements. Although the projects in the portfolio are sovereign, autonomous, and non-overlapping entities, the resources working in these projects move across projects to apply their skills when needed. Hence, the resources cross the boundaries between the projects. From a corporate perspective, the resource usage across projects is Pareto optimized for the benefit of the organization and its stakeholders. Hence, project governance (Type II governance) is embedded in the governance of the portfolio (Type I governance).

Project managers applying balanced leadership mainly perform Type II governance, that is, governing the pool of possible temporary leaders in situational contingency to achieve the most beneficial combination of leadership resources over time for the project and its objectives. Through the formal and informal expectations project managers convey to the temporary leader(s) upon empowerment, they provide the structure within which the leader(s) perform their task. The ways these expectations are conveyed from the project manager to the empowered leader(s) are a matter of human agency, and thus of governmentality.

Governmentality

Governmentality is a combination of the words *governance* and *mentality* (i.e., the particular way of thinking about someone or something). It was coined by the French semiologist Roland Barthes in 1957 in his classic work *Mythologies* (Barthes, 2013), and became popular through Michel Foucault's work on power (e.g., Foucault, 1991). Governmentality describes the attitude (i.e., mentality) of those in governance positions toward those they steer, and how this manifests itself in their interaction. More recent work by Dean (2010) categorizes governmentality into three different types of interactions:

- *Authoritarian governmentality* is characterized by clear and unambiguous directions from the governor (e.g., the project manager to the empowered leader(s)). This is often paired with organizational structures that reflect centralized decision-making, significant power distance, and few choices in governance approaches (Burchell, 1991). Authoritarian approaches "seek to operate through obedient rather than free subjects, or, at a minimum, endeavor to neutralize any opposition to authority" (Dean, 2010, p. 155). Examples include projects with clear and strictly enforced directives by the steering committee. This may include major public investment projects, where process compliance is enforced within rigid governance structures to legitimize the spending of taxpayers' money (Miller & Hobbs, 2005).
- *Liberal governmentality* is characterized by the heterogeneity of governance approaches (Burchell, 1991). Here, the governed persons are treated as rational, self-thinking, and self-deciding individuals. Governors do not enforce particular behavior, but provide choices and incentives that influence the governed individuals' decisions and behavior. The incentives are typically framed by anticipating economic and market rationality on the side of the governed individual(s), so that the individual still has a choice, but the decision is influenced by the incentives (Dean, 2010). In projects, this is often found in steering groups controlling and incentivizing their project managers by the accomplishment of agreed-upon outcomes (instead of process compliance). These flexible governance structures are often found in customer delivery projects (Dinsmore & Rocha, 2012).
- *Neoliberal governmentality* is characterized by influencing the societal context of the governed person(s), and through this, steering their decisions and behavior (Lemke, 2001). This type of governmentality addresses peoples' self-governance in a societal context, building on

their collective interest and their willingness to consent. By voluntarily obeying their societal context, the individual's behavior is shaped, but not necessarily determined (Clegg, Pitsis, Rura-Polley, & Marosszeky, 2002). In other words, neoliberal governmentality is similar to a culture. It provides a value system for individuals to steer their behavior (Clegg, 2019). This form of governmentality is found, for example, in projects that foster self-control within basic governance structures, such as community-governed open source development projects (Franck & Jungwirth, 2003).

Authoritarian and liberal approaches operate through direct person-to-person interaction. Neoliberal governmentality works indirectly through the context and its value system. As indicated earlier, governmentality approaches differ by context. Studies on the impact of governance and governmentality on project results showed that all governmentality approaches correlate with project performance. However, the impact is mediated by the governance structure. Trust-based governance structures support the strong impact of governmentality on project performance, while control-based structures reduce this impact. Especially influential is neoliberal governmentality. The stronger it is expressed in the organization, the better the results of the projects. This effect is seen in all types of organizations but is especially strong in organizations with few governance institutions, such as steering committees and project management offices, where there is little authoritarian and liberal governmentality (Müller, Zhai, & Wang, 2017).

Governance of empowered leaders

During the appointment of one or a group of temporary leaders, the project manager wears "two hats," or in other words, performs two roles.

One is to follow the appointed leader(s). This is a salient characteristic of balanced leadership because it goes beyond just delegating a task to a team member. By just delegating a task, for example, to solve a technical problem, the project manager would still be the project leader. The person with the delegated task would perform the task without the project manager being "another pair of hands" in the project. Thus, the leadership would stay with the project manager, and the person with the delegated task will lack the authority that comes with the empowerment to lead. Hence, in balanced leadership, the project manager admits that there is momentarily a better leader for the project than himself/herself. Because of this, the project manager subordinates himself/herself to the appointed leader to give this person full leadership authority, to ensure that the team follows the empowered leader.

However, there is no leadership without limitations, and these are set by governance. The project manager plays a second role, that is, to make sure the appointed leader acts in the project's best interests and objectives. For that, the project manager observes and steers the empowered leader's task fulfillment to ensure compliance with the expectations that led to the empowerment. In the case of congruency of the project manager's expectations and the empowered leader's behavior, it is highly likely that the empowered leader can fulfill the task until completion. However, if the expectations in the leader's role are severely violated, it is likely that the project manager will terminate the appointment and either take on the task himself/herself or appoint another temporary leader. More details about these decisions are discussed in the next chapter.

A study by ISM University in Lithuania and BI Norwegian Business School investigated the particularities of the governance of empowered leaders in balanced leadership. In this study, the governance of empowered leaders is defined as "a process of interaction, unfolding through mechanisms, structures and methods established in a project team formally or informally in order to achieve project goals" (Pilkienė, Alonderienė, Chmieliauskas, Šimkonis, & Müller, 2018, p. 915). *Mechanisms* were described as the particular mix of trust or control when executing governance. *Structures* were described as the stable arrangements of the human and nonhuman elements of the organization, such as institutions, policies, roles, responsibilities, etc. *Methods* refer to the particular way governance is carried out, for example, by monthly meetings with Earned Value as a progress-control technique.

The particular way of governing empowered leaders is determined by:

- *The governance context*: This includes projects' external and internal factors, as well as project-manager-specific and empowered-leader-specific factors. External factors include organizational culture and structure, corporate governance, and governance of projects. Internal factors center around different types of risk. Project-manager-specific factors include their own leadership style and role perception and the characteristics of the empowered leader and his/her situational fit. Special emphasis is placed on the empowered leader's integrity and benevolence. Integrity refers to the empowered leader's adherence to a set of principles as judged by the project manager, for example, the congruency of words and behavior. Benevolence refers to the extent to which the empowered leader is believed to want to do good for the project (Mayer, Davis, & Schoorman, 1995).

- *The governance mechanisms*: The particular mix of trust and control is largely influenced by the socio-cognitive space, which is explained in Chapter 9 in this volume. Of special interest is the team's shared understanding of the empowered leader's qualifications for mastering the task. This perceived qualification is a major driver for the level of trust granted to the leader. Control comes in various forms, such as diagnostic control by measuring progress against timetables, interactive control by observing the leader, and belief control by checking the value system of the leader and its congruency with that of the project.
- *Governance practices*: This refers to how governance unfolds in terms of organizational structures, methods, and roles. Structures can be formal or informal, and the more trust prevails, the more informal they tend to be. Methods to build trust include regular physical meetings with the team in addition to communication by emails, calls, or virtually.
- *Governance process*: This refers to the project manager balancing the right mix of trust and control. This mix depends on the preceding criteria, the particular status of the project, and the changes to them. Thus, the mix of trust and control is steadily adjusted to the situation.

Overall, two governance patterns were identified. One is trust-based governance, where the project manager shows more supportive attitudes, develops empowered leaders, and gives them more freedom in execution. The other is control-based governance, with a stronger focus on controlling the leader's role fulfillment, including their behavior, decisions, and the accomplishment of project objectives.

The particular mix of trust and control is mainly driven by three factors:

1. *Professionality*: The lower the empowered leader's perceived professionality, the more control is applied by the project manager. Conversely, the higher the perceived professionality, the more trust is applied.
2. *Personality*: The less the empowered leader is perceived to be a good fit for the leadership situation, the more control is applied. The more the leader is seen as a good fit, the more trust is applied.
3. *Benevolence*: The more the leader's benevolence is regarded as low, the more control prevails. The more it is regarded as high, the more trust is applied.

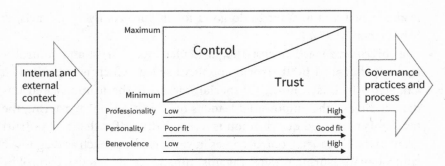

Figure 7.2. A model for the governance of empowered leaders.

The overall level of trust versus control is influenced by the situation-dependent importance assigned to these three dimensions. The related model is shown in Figure 7.2.

Figure 7.2 summarizes the preceding discussion on governance of empowered leaders. Reading it from left to right, it shows that external and internal context factors set the initial stage. From there, the particular balance of trust and control is chosen, influenced by the context factors and the perception of professionality, personality, and benevolence of the empowered leader. This informs the governance practices and processes applied by the project manager. The model is dynamic as the factors can steadily vary and, with them, the balance of trust and control and the associated governance practices and processes.

Summary

This chapter started by addressing empowered leaders and their positive impact on organizational results. Then we discussed the factors that positively and negatively influence the role identity of these leaders. Subsequently, we turned the perspective toward project managers and discussed how they govern the empowered leaders during their assignment. For this, we presented the concepts of governance and governmentality and how they relate to concepts such as management and leadership. Finally, we integrated the chapter's content into a model for the governance of empowered leaders. The next chapter will address the transition of empowered leaders after their assignment.

Acknowledgments

The authors would like to acknowledge the contribution of Fangwei Zhu, Linzhuo Wang, Mouxuan Sun, and Xiuxia Sun from Dalian University of Technology, China; as well as Margarita Pilkienė, Raimonda Alonderienė, Alfredas Chmieliauskas, and Saulius Šimkonis from ISM University of Management and Economics in Lithuania.

Further reading

Müller, R. (Ed.) (2017). *Governance and governmentality for projects: Enablers, practices and consequences*. New York, NY: Routledge.

Reflection questions

1. How does empowering in balanced leadership differ from delegating a task?
2. Why does an empowered leader need to be governed?
3. How can we distinguish between management, leadership, governance, and governmentality?
4. Is the governance in your organization (or sports club, etc.) more trust-based or more control-based? What are the indicators for this?

8
Leadership Transition

Introduction

This chapter describes the last event in the balanced leadership framework; that is, leadership transition. We define this event as the end of the empowered leader's temporary assignment when the transfer of leadership authority occurs, and the elaboration of possible changes to the conditions for future appointments of distributed/shared/horizontal leaders. Figure 8.1 depicts the event in the framework for balanced leadership.

There are two main actors in this event, the empowered leader and the project manager. The latter acted as the governor during the leader's assignment, and now that the assignment comes to its end (or is prematurely terminated by the project manager), decisions must be made on: (a) whether the criteria for choosing the empowered leader were appropriate or need to be updated; (b) how the empowered leader performed during the assignment; and (c) who will continue in the leadership role.

We address how these decisions are made. For this, we start from the broad perspective of transition and transition theory. Then we narrow the perspective to the morphogenetic cycle and its relevance for the transition event. From here, we address the particularities of transition in projects by reporting on a study that developed a model for transition in balanced leadership. The chapter finishes with an example showing how the model works in practice.

Transition and transition theory

Transition is defined as the "process or a period of changing from one state or condition to another" (Oxford English Dictionary, 2021). While originally referring to the change of substance stage, such as from liquid to gas, the concept entered many different disciplines over time. These include government and law (Voß, Smith, & Grin, 2009), economics (Loorbach, 2010), and management (Stephens & Graham, 2010), and is typically used to describe the change from one qualitative state to another. The concept entered political

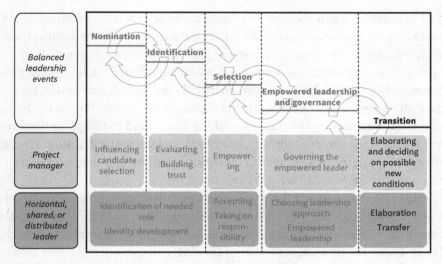

Figure 8.1. Locating the transition event in the balanced leadership framework.

and management science through studies on change in societies and organizations. Previous studies often integrate findings from various disciplines, such as complexity science, sociology, or political science, to understand the systemic nature of the transition actors, variables, and processes. An emerging field of research in this discipline is transition management, which aims to understand societal, organizational, and practical phenomena by looking at them as complex and adaptive systems where the change results from co-evolution of different processes (such as demographic and governance processes) (Loorbach, Frantzeskaki, & Lijnis Huffenreuter, 2015).

Studies of transitions in management and organization science address movements within, for example, organizations or projects, and how to manage them. Examples include the research on the transition of project management offices (PMOs) over time, and its contingency on internal and external factors. PMOs are organizational units for the improvement of project results in a firm or enterprise. They transition because their charter frequently changes in terms of the problem they have to solve, such as improving project portfolio management or standardizing project management practices, and the different skill sets needed to work on these problems. Hence, PMOs are often organizations in constant transition. Once they have resolved one problem, they are chartered with solving a new one, potentially requiring very different skills and therefore a change of specialists in the PMO. Hence, a transition is triggered by a change in mandate and an associated change in skills. A series of studies identified the variety of internal and external factors that lead to these frequent changes in mandates, which then lead to transitions. Moreover, these studies identified particular transition patterns, such as those to change the level of standardization of project management practices in the firm, with each level of standardization requiring different skill sets and processes within the PMO. Other patterns include the growth and contraction of the PMO in terms of scope of work and staffing levels, depending on the firm's economic situation, or the transition of the PMO (and the organization) toward more agile ways of working, requiring upskilling and training. Hence, all of these patterns require a PMO transition from one qualitative state to another (Aubry, Hobbs, Müller, & Blomquist, 2010).

Transition management theory proposes that these transitions unfold at different levels and through processes, actors, outcomes, and reflections. Levels refer to the echelon of strategic, tactical, and operational levels (Loorbach, 2010). Using the previous example of the PMO transition, the board of directors and the upper management team (as actors) would define the desired outcomes at a strategic level, such as the firm's overall scope in terms of project work. This would address questions like how much work is done through projects, the need for a PMO in the organization, or the vision and initial mandate for this PMO. Then they would draft the process for implementing this transition to establish a PMO, reflect on the progress and accomplishments, and potentially adjust their goals and processes. Transitions at this level take the longest time to implement.

At the tactical level, transitions address the institutions, structures, and rules required for daily work. The PMO manager and his/her supervisor (as actors) would reflect on the mandate and determine the desired outcomes in terms of quantity and depth of skill needs for the PMO. This is complemented by processes, policies, methodologies, and other guidelines for the execution of work. Again, the reflections of the stakeholders and actors will guide and adjust the implementation.

At the operational level, the transitions would address the content of the PMO work. As actors, PMO members will pursue their new objectives, such as moving from consulting project managers in the use of agile methodologies to working with portfolio managers on a new process and the criteria to select "the best" projects for the company. Transition processes are developed and reflectively implemented for this as part of the firm's operation.

The preceding example shows that transitions happen at various levels in the organization, independent of the number of actors at the operational level. Transitions in balanced leadership involve two main actors: the project manager and the empowered leader(s) at the operational level. However, these transitions are framed by the decisions at the strategic and tactical levels, as discussed in Chapter 3. In the following sections, we will exemplify some of these dependencies using two different scenarios.

Scenario 1 is a mid-sized engineering company that develops and manufactures equipment for the automobile industry. The company's customers increasingly require a wider variety of functions and technologies in their products. Therefore, upper management decided that, in the future, development projects will be executed through dedicated temporary organizations, following existing project management standards. Contrarily, manufacturing will remain a continuous process, following operations management principles. Upper management, as a strategic actor, aims to maintain a high level of skills diversity and devises processes and objectives that middle management (as a tactical actor) can use for combining the different skill sets of their employees (i.e., the operational actors) contingent on the requirements of individual projects. Hence, the strategic level paves the way for middle managers to use skill sets flexibly. This flexibility is taken further in projects, where managers implement this strategy through balanced leadership. Here, the best possible leader at any point in time is appointed to solve, for example, technical problems. Table 8.1 shows the actors, outcomes, and processes, as well as the principal reflections that drive this transition at each level.

In this example, the transition event in balanced leadership takes place at the operational level. Framed by the need to have technical specialists leading

Table 8.1 Transition Management: Scenario 1

Levels	Actors	Outcomes	Processes	Reflections
Strategic	Upper management	Meet the diversity in customer requirements	Devise high-level processes that provide for flexibility in structures and work assignments	Are we implementing the right culture and structure to support skills diversity?
Tactical	Middle management	Meet the diversity in project skills requirements	Hiring and training processes that emphasize flexibility in collaboration and integration in different teams	Do we provide for sufficient flexibility in combining skill sets for projects?
Operational	Project management	Have specialists as leaders to solve the diverse set of technical issues	Empower temporary leaders to solve technical issues	Do we identify and use best possible skill sets at any point in time?

the project through a period to resolve technical issues—as devised by upper management's strategy—the project manager is concerned with the following:

a. The empowered leader(s)' performance in terms of meeting the conditional requirements of the appointment for the best interests of the project;
b. The "fit" of the empowered leader(s)' personality with the leadership situation when leading the project team during this period.

Overall, the goal of leader appointment (and the basis for its evaluation at the end) is to solve a technical issue successfully. However, in Chapter 6, when we discussed the selection and empowerment of leaders, we outlined various reasons for leaders to be selected. Technical skills were only one of them. Others included the development of future higher-level leaders. This is addressed in scenario 2.

Scenario 2 is a global IT company that is growing rapidly and needs to expand its sales, training, development, and manufacturing capabilities. To address the need for managers who can steer this growth, they implemented an annual trainee program for future managers, from which they aim to identify two to three "high-potential" candidates for accelerated development into higher-level management positions. The long-term objective is to transition this company into a larger market player, using a young, flexible, and internally developed cadre of dynamic managers. Table 8.2 shows the related levels and their actors, outcomes, processes, and respective reflections.

Also, in this scenario, the transition event in balanced leadership takes place at the operational level. However, this time it is framed by the need to develop future managers and leaders for the organization—as devised by upper management's strategy. The project manager is once again concerned with the empowered leader's performance regarding the conditional requirements and the "fit" of personality to lead the team. However, these criteria are balanced by the objective of developing future leaders by giving them a training ground to understand the organization's business and customers. Overall, the appointment's goal and the basis for evaluation are the type and level of leadership skills obtained during the assignment.

By comparing the two scenarios, we see that the evaluation criteria differ with the purpose of the assignment. In scenario 1, a slight mistake in the leadership of the team while solving a major technical issue will most likely not result in a negative evaluation of the assignment. Conversely, a slight technical mistake in scenario 2, together with effective leadership of the team, might not lead to a negative evaluation of the assignment either.

Table 8.2 Transition Management: Scenario 2

Levels	Actors	Outcomes	Processes	Reflections
Strategic	Upper management	An extended cadre of managers with in-depth knowledge of the organization's business	Develop and implement trainee and qualification program for "high potentials"	Is the culture and structure appropriate to support management identification and development?
Tactical	Middle management	Identify and develop future leaders	Hiring and training processes for identifying, training, and practicing of candidates	Are the selection criteria and training programs appropriate to meet future demands?
Operational	Project management	Provide a training ground for future leaders to learn about the organization's business and customers	Empower "future stars" to give them an opportunity to gain leadership experiences	Is the project situation appropriate for empowering a "future star"?

So far, this chapter has discussed the nature of transitions and transition theory. It showed that transitions happen at several levels, where upper levels frame the decisions in transitions of lower levels. This framing provides for different interpretations of transition content and the evaluations thereof. We now look at the operational level with its projects. Here we focus on the different evaluations of the empowered leader(s)' assignments and their outcomes. For this, we start with the morphogenetic cycle as our theoretical lens.

The morphogenetic cycle in the transition event

In Chapter 3 we outlined realist social theory and its morphogenetic cycle. The latter describes a three-step process (Archer, 1995):

- *Conditioning*: the influences, both structural and human, that frame the situation of delegation. This includes the formal conditions, such as those given through policies, contracts, etc., and informal conditions, such as the articulated or unarticulated expectations of the delegating institution or manager.

- *Agency*: the interaction of the empowered leader with the imposed conditions. This interaction leads to four possible outcomes: (i) *necessary complementarity* (i.e., conditions and agency are in sync, leading to protection of the status quo); (ii) *necessary incompatibility* (i.e., systemic differences between agent and institution, leading to compromises); (iii) *contingent incompatibility* (i.e., extreme differences between agent and institutions, leading to the elimination of one party); and (iv) *contingent compatibility* (i.e., the construction of compatibilities for mutual benefit, leading to opportunism).
- *Elaboration*: evaluation and possible changes that occur as a result of agency. Elaboration addresses two levels: (a) the empowered leader (i.e., the agent) and his/her chances to be empowered again in the future; and (b) the criteria to select an empowered leader in similar situations (i.e., the structure) and the need to retain or change these criteria.

The evaluation during elaboration has typically one of two outcomes—either *morphostasis*, where the current form, organization, or structure is preserved or maintained, or *morphogenetics*, where the current form, organization, or structure is changed (Archer, 1995).

The relationship between the four (in)compatibilities of agency and a possible morphostasis or morphogenetic outcome at the elaboration stage is discussed in the following.

In *necessary complementarity* the conditions and the agency are in sync. That means for balanced leadership that the currently empowered leader is considered again when future balanced/shared/horizontal leadership situations arise. The processes and criteria to empower a temporary leader remain unchanged; hence, a morphostatic outcome.

In *necessary incompatibility* a partial incompatibility prevails, which is often overcome through compromises. Here the empowered leader may not be reconsidered on future occasions; hence a morphogenetic outcome.

Contingent incompatibility is marked by extreme differences between the conditions and agency. Here the leadership assignment will most likely be prematurely terminated, and the person not considered for empowerment again. The selection criteria might be changed, too; hence an outcome of morphogenesis.

In *contingent compatibility*, a partial incompatibility prevails, which can be overcome by one or both parties adjusting their perspectives to allow for a compromise that benefits all parties. This is known as *opportunism* and can lead to either morphostatic or morphogenetic results.

The preceding discussion has shown the steps of the morphogenetic cycle, with conditioning, agency, and elaboration. We then discussed the principles applied during the elaboration step to derive a morphostatic or morphogenetic outcome. With this theoretical background, we can now start to understand the practices and particularities of transitions in projects and in balanced leadership.

Study of transition

A research team with members from ISM University of Management and Economics in Lithuania and BI Norwegian Business School investigated the nature of the transition event in balanced leadership in projects, its variables, and their impact on transition outcomes (Alonderienė, Müller, Pilkienė, Šimkonis, & Chmieliauskas, 2020). They conducted 30 interviews in eight large engineering organizations of different sizes and industries, including biotechnology, IT, and civil engineering, in the public and private sectors.

In this study, they identified the variables that determine the outcomes in terms of morphostasis and morphogenetics. These are described in the following (see also Table 8.3).

Transition mechanisms: this refers to the eventual transition of the empowered leader. Three possible mechanisms are identified: compatibility, partial incompatibility, and extreme incompatibility between conditions and agency. Compatibility indicates a match between the conditions and the empowered leader's work, typically leading to morphostasis. Partial incompatibility can lead to either morphostatic or morphogenetic results, whereby the final decision is often influenced by external factors (e.g., no substitute available for the empowered leader, resulting in morphostasis). Extreme incompatibility often results in the premature termination of the leader's appointment.

Actors: this refers to the empowered leader and the project manager. Three dimensions make up this variable, which is measured during the time of the empowered leader's assignment:

- The empowered leader's *performance* during the assignment and the *level of knowledge* required to fulfill the role, as perceived by the project manager: This ranges from low in cases of extreme and partial incompatibility to high in cases of compatibility.
- The project manager's perception of the presence and strength of a *leadership and management style* by the empowered leader: It ranges from no

leadership or acceptance of leadership responsibility in cases of extreme incompatibility, to lacking ownership, initiative, and general passiveness in cases of partial incompatibility, to inspirational, motivational, and transformative leadership in cases of compatibility. Hence, it is measured from not visibly expressed to strongly expressed.

- The empowered leader's psychological characteristics and human relations: It is the project manager's perception of the presence of crucial personality characteristics on the side of the empowered leader. This ranges from lack of learning capabilities, lack of taking responsibility, or even hostile leadership in cases of partial and extreme incompatibility, to benevolence and motivation in cases of compatibility.

Conditions: this refers to the empowered leader's fulfillment of the formal and informal expectations and the resulting communication style between the project manager and the empowered leader. Two dimensions make up this variable:

- The project manager's perception of the empowered leader's *quality of work* with respect to the imposed conditions: It ranges from unacceptable levels of required explanations and repetitive failure in fulfilling the role in cases of extreme incompatibility, to missing role fulfillment due to lack of benevolence in partial incompatibility, to outstanding quality and value generation in cases of compatibility.
- The adjustment of *communication style* between project manager and empowered leader, following the quality of work over time: This is also an expression of the trust by the project manager. It ranges from high formality paired with increased use of control elements in cases of extreme incompatibility to a decrease in formality in cases of compatibility and partial compatibility.

Transition criteria: this refers to the underlying mix of trust and control in the relationship between project manager and empowered leader. It ranges from deteriorating trust and increasing control in cases of extreme incompatibility, to some level of control but generally "warmer relationships" in cases of partial incompatibility, to increasing trust over time in cases of compatibility.

Transition context: this is related to the contextual influences and includes factors like resource availability, project external factors, and project internal factors. The variable is made up of three dimensions:

- The availability of an *alternative person* as a possible leader: This ranges from availability, on the one hand, in cases of partial (situational logic 3, described in the following) and extreme incompatibility leading to morphogenesis; and continues to unavailability, on the other hand, in cases of partial incompatibility (situational logic 2, described in the following), and compatibility, leading to morphostasis.
- The stability of the *external context* in terms of the frequency of changes: This addresses instabilities that are caused, for example, through changes in the organization's strategy or structure. It ranges from unstable in cases of morphogenesis to stable in cases of morphostasis.
- The stability of the *internal context* in terms of the frequency of changes: This addresses instability within the project, such as scope or budget changes. It ranges from unstable in cases of morphogenesis to stable in cases of morphostasis.

Now that we have discussed the transition event's variables and their measurement, we can identify the particular patterns of variables that are associated with morphostatic and morphogenetic outcomes. Four different situational logics are identified. Table 8.3 shows their relation to the two possible outcomes. The four situational logics are described in the following.

Situational logic 1: Compatibility with conditions leading to morphostasis

This situational logic is characterized by high-performing and knowledgeable actors (i.e., empowered leaders) who strongly express their leadership and management styles, and show benevolence and motivation. They fulfill the conditions well through the high quality of their work. Their project managers tend to develop more informal communication practices with them over time, as their relationship is mainly based on trust. The internal and external contexts tend to be stable, while at times, morphostasis is enforced due to the unavailability of an alternate person as leader.

Situational logic 2: Partial incompatibility leading to morphostasis

This situational logic is associated with morphostatic outcomes. Here the project manager decides to stay with the empowered leader and existing selection criteria, even though the conditions were not met in the best possible way. Reasons for morphostasis include the desire to avoid turbulence in the team due to a new leader or to give the empowered leader another chance to learn and grow in the role. The relationship and communication are generally trust-based and rather informal, but still more formal than in situational logic 1. A further reason for morphostasis might be the lack of alternative leaders. The context is relatively stable in this situational logic.

Situational logic 3: Partial incompatibility leading to morphogenesis

In this situational logic, amendments lead to some level of morphogenesis. Characteristics for this situational logic are shortcomings such as in the empowered leader's performance and/or knowledge, or the lack of leadership and/or management surfacing through passiveness or hostility. Other indicators are incompatibility between conditions and quality of work, typically paired with higher levels of control and formal communication. Morphogenesis may also be triggered by unstable contexts, requiring a change to the task and its leader or the availability of a better-suited leader. The outcome of the preceding measures is typically the replacement of the empowered leader. However, morphogenesis can also be triggered differently in this situational logic. Context changes, such as in scope, budget, strategy, etc., in the context of otherwise acceptable performance, may render the empowered leader's task obsolete but leave the selection criteria intact. Conversely, the empowered leader may stay in the role, but the task is adjusted to his/her capabilities and performance. Hence the conditions are changed, but not the leader. Many combinations are possible.

Situational logic 4: Extreme incompatibility leading to morphogenesis

In this situational logic, the empowered leader's assignment is terminated. Patterns in this logic include low performance and knowledge, invisible leadership, lack of willingness to take on responsibility, and outright failure to meet the conditions on the empowered leader's part. This often goes with formal communication and high levels of control exercised by the project manager. Further factors might include unstable contexts that enforce the termination, or the availability of a substitute for the empowered leader. Lessons

Table 8.3 Relationship between Transition Variables and Outcomes

Transition Outcome	Morphostasis		Morphogenesis	
Situational logic	I	II	III	IV
Transition mechanisms	Compatibility	Partial incompatibility		Extreme incompatibility
Actors (empowered leader):				
• Performance and knowledge	• High			• Low
• Leadership and management style	• Strongly expressed			• Not visible
• Psychological and human relations factors	• Benevolence, motivation			• Lack of responsibility and ownership
Conditions:				
• Quality of work	• Outstanding, value creation			• Repetitive failure
• Communication style adaptation	• Decreasing formality			• Increasing formality
Transition criteria	• Trust			• Control
Transition context:				
• Replacement available	• No			• Yes
• Stability of external context	• Stable			• Unstable
• Stability of internal context	• Stable			• Unstable

Source: after Alonderienė et al. (2020).

learned from this situational logic often lead to a change in conditions and criteria for the selection of future leaders.

A model of the transition event

After introducing the variables that make up the transfer event, their measures, and their relationship to particular outcomes, we can now present a theory in the form of a model that describes the transition event. Figure 8.2 depicts the model.

The timely flow in the transition event starts with the empowered leader as a human *actor*, with his/her specific performance, leadership, and psychological factors, working within the structural *conditions* through the quality of work and communication style with the project manager. The measures of both actor and condition variables are the input to the *mechanisms* variable,

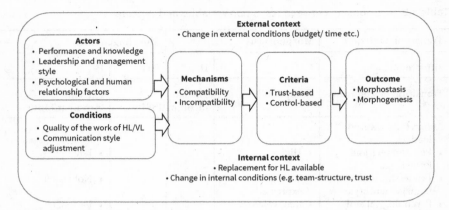

Figure 8.2. A model for the transfer event.
Note: HL = Horizontal leader, VL = Vertical leader

where the project manager and empowered leader engage in a reflection on the fulfillment of their expectations and interpretations of the conditions. This continues into an evaluation of the level of compatibility or incompatibility of the empowered leader's work with the conditions that structured his/her role. Together with the internal and external context variables, the type of situational logic (1 to 4) is determined. This constitutes the output of the mechanisms variable and is the input to the *criteria* variable. In the criteria variable, the input is evaluated against the existing level (or mix of) trust in or need for control of the empowered leader. The trust and control levels are developed through the interaction between the project manager and empowered leader during the leader's assignment. At this stage, the transition mechanism (compatible, partly (in)compatible), the criteria (trust versus control), and the enabling or disabling factors from the context form the basis for a decision on the outcome being either morphostatic or morphogenetic.

The model applies to the last event in balanced leadership, after empowered leadership and its governance, and before a new cycle with either the same leader or another leader, or the project manager, starts again. It applies equally to individuals having horizontal leadership as to groups with shared or distributed leadership as part of balanced leadership. Enablers for the model include the project manager, who must agree to use balanced leadership, as well as the project types. Projects using waterfall type of methodologies are more likely to use balanced leadership, as in more complex projects, where the specific contribution of individual specialists is a key feature for developing the project's product or service.

We finish this section with an example that applies the model (see Box 8.1).

Box 8.1. Transition Example

Carl, a software engineer, was empowered to lead the project temporarily to navigate it through a severe crisis. This crisis emerged under the project manager's leadership, where the new machine learning module failed to function correctly in the context of the new project portfolio management software. The project manager realized that a specialist like Carl was better suited to lead the project through this issue, as Carl understands the technology and speaks the same language as the stakeholders. Upon his empowerment, Carl was instructed to lead the project but keep the project manager up to date on at least a weekly basis. Also, any activities that might threaten the project's budget and/or schedule had to be approved upfront by the project manager. When Carl took over, he worked with the project team on solving the issues but also consulted several third parties for possible solutions. The project manager found out the latter after the first invoice from a third party arrived. By that time, the issues were mostly solved, partly due to the consulting by the third party. A few days later, the machine learning module worked to the satisfaction of the stakeholders, and Carl's assignment came to an end. However, the next technical issue had already popped up. Even though it was not machine learning related, it was also an issue that Carl could potentially solve. Hence, the project manager had to decide whether to continue with Carl or appoint someone else to solve the new issue.

At the time of transition, the project manager reflected that Carl performed technically well during the assignment, making use of many peoples' knowledge and showed strong leadership skills, together with motivation and benevolence. Carl's quality of work was good, but the caveat was that some of the good quality came from elsewhere, and the costs for this help broke the project's budget. After finding this out, the project manager lost trust in Carl's honesty when it came to his performance. So while the actor (Carl) performed well, compatibility with the conditions was not accomplished due to unofficial support by external parties and associated costs beyond the project's budget. The project manager decided on a partial incompatibility (mechanism) and the need for much stricter control of Carl in future assignments. So the decision criteria changed toward control. Moreover, another specialist was available to solve the new issue. The project manager decided to empower the other person for this assignment and changed the criteria for selecting future leaders, thus resulting in a morphogenetic outcome. Empowered leaders should have a track record of honesty and transparency in their assignments; hence, this case resembles situational logic 3.

Summary

This chapter addressed the final event in balanced leadership, that is, leadership transition. We started the chapter by outlining the nature of transitions and transition theory in organizational settings. Then we discussed the morphogenetic cycle as the theoretical lens for decision-making in the transition event. Finally, we discussed the variables that give rise to situational logics that lead to the decision for morphostasis or morphogenesis at the end of an empowered leader's assignment. We concluded the chapter with an example that illustrates the functioning of the model in a practical setting.

Acknowledgments

The authors would like to acknowledge the contribution of Margarita Pilkienė, Raimonda Alonderienė, Alfredas Chmieliauskas, and Saulius Šimkonis from ISM University of Management and Economics in Lithuania.

Further reading

Archer, M. S. (2010). Morphogenesis versus structuration: On combining structure and action. *British Journal of Sociology*, 61(SUPPL. 1), 225–252.

Reflection questions

1. Think of a transition at the operational level of your organization. What are the potential transitions at the tactical and strategic level that frame it?
2. Reflect on the morphogenetic cycle. Where can you find examples for it in your life? What are some of the indicators for morphogenesis?
3. Think of the relationship between performance, communication, and trust between a project manager and empowered leader. Which examples could you find in your organization that explain this relationship?

9

Coordination through the Socio-Cognitive Space

Introduction

The preceding chapters first outlined a theory for balanced leadership, which identified the five events of nomination, identification, empowerment, empowered leadership and its governance, and leadership transition. Subsequently, we discussed each of these events individually. These discussions provided detailed descriptions of the events based on existing theories, tools, and empirical studies. This allowed us to derive models and theories about each event's internal functioning in terms of its variables and processes. A question that now naturally emerges is that of the role of actors in balanced leadership. How do they coordinate and synchronize their activities across the five events? To answer this question, we first discuss how people make sense of their project reality by applying sense-making theory to project management. This reveals the *interaction* between project actors as a key element for correct interpretation of the situation. We subsequently discuss this interaction in terms of the socio-cognitive space (SCS) as a coordination mechanism between the actors in a project.

Sense-making

The concept of sense-making describes how managers and leaders understand and categorize their reality. It explains how they understand their role and act in it, that is, how they give meaning to their own actions and those of others. It applies especially to situations that can be interpreted in many different ways or that involve several people. As such, sense-making is a predecessor for the development of both the role identity as discussed in Chapter 7, and of SCS as a coordination mechanism in projects.

Definitions of sense-making center around "a process for explanation building." For example, the classic work by Weick and colleagues (Weick,

Sutcliffe, & Obstfeld, 2005, p. 409) defines sense-making as a process of "ongoing retrospective development of plausible images that rationalize what people are doing." Sense-making theory by Weick (1993) theorizes this through a process of *enactment, selection,* and *retention. Enactment* describes what people do and what is done to them. *Selection* describes a person's looking back on previous actions and selecting the particular aspects to focus on, then assigning meaning to the action by taking into account his/her self-view and context. *Retention* is the recall of the assigned meaning and evaluation for guiding future actions in similar situations. Enactments perceived as positive or beneficial are likely to be repeated, while those perceived as unfavorable are most likely be discontinued or changed.

This process guides individuals to plausible but not necessarily accurate interpretations. Weick (1993) shows this through the Mann Gulch Disaster, when an approaching forest fire surrounded a group of firefighters. The foreman yelled at the team to drop their heavy tools, then lit an "escape fire" and instructed his crew to lie down in the area burned by this fire. But the firefighters did not follow his orders. Staying within the burning range was perceived by them as dangerous. They kept their heavy tools and material with them while running uphill toward a ridge, where the 13 firefighters died in the flames.

This example contrasts with the classic story of Xenophon in 400 B.C., who saved thousands of people during a long march to the Black Sea after losing a battle in Greece. Among them were many soldiers who were reluctant to drop their weapons because their enemies were following them. However, carrying their weapons slowed down their pace. Xenophon finally convinced them to drop their arms, which allowed them to march faster than their enemies. This saved their lives. Both examples show that interpretations in sense-making can be accurate or inaccurate, driven by past experiences in different contexts.

Sense-making in project management

Sense-making studies in the context of project management vary by circumstances. A popular study investigated stakeholders' sense-making of project discontinuities and their influence on the management and progress of projects (Alderman, Ivory, McLoughlin, & Vaughan, 2005). The researchers' focus was the role of interpretation in sense-making. Another study focused on cue interpretation in disaster recovery projects (Gacasan & Wiggins, 2017). Yet other studies investigated the impact of cultural sense-making in projects on cross-cultural international alliances (Fellows & Liu, 2016), or sense-making by project participants through lived experiences during organizational change (Lunkka, Pietiläinen, & Suhonen, 2019).

A systematic literature review identified the conceptualization of sense-making in project-related studies as a set of *interactive* and *interpretive* processes. These two processes allow the project manager to put equivocal and ambiguous contextual cues into defined cognitive frameworks to make sense of reality (Bucero & Müller, 2020).

Interaction relates here to the exchange between project managers/leaders and stakeholders, including the project team. It involves bodily resonance, coordination of gestures, facial and vocal expressions, and cultural variations thereof. Project managers or (empowered) leaders adapt their actions to situational contingencies to maintain the link between their own understanding of the project situation and that of the stakeholders.

Interpretation relates to the different ways to understand information, such as mapping them against existing structures, like categories, for clarification and subsequent decisions on actions. Categories can provide maximum information with the least cognitive effort, provided the information received is in line with the known category. For example, someone educated in natural science taxonomies on seeing a red oak tree will identify it as belonging to the family of oak trees, which is part of the tree category. Little cognitive effort is needed to make sense of what this plant is because it fits the cognitive category. For someone not knowing these categories, additional effort is required to understand what this type of tree is and to which plant family it belongs (Roach, 1978).

Projects provide an appropriate context for applying sense-making because projects often allow for different interpretations by different stakeholders. Project managers and leaders need to prioritize information relevant to the situation, often through the help of existing structures and categories, and then decide on ways forward. For this, they manage people (*interaction*), decide on actions (by *interpretation* of facts or past behaviors), manage stakeholders (by *interaction* and *interpretation*), manage conflicts (by *interpretation* and *interaction*), and manage risks (by *interpretation* and *interaction*) (Bucero & Müller, 2020).

The rest of this chapter describes the application of interaction and interpretation as a form of sense-making of project leaders and team members during balanced leadership. This takes place in the socio-cognitive space—a shared mental space between project managers and team members, which allows for synchronized sense-making across individuals.

The socio-cognitive space

Social cognition is an umbrella term for a wide number of distinct and inter-dependent psychological constructs. Generally speaking, it is the "ability to process, understand, and predict other people's behavior as well as to modify one's own behavior based on social signals" (Pertz, Okoniewski, Schlegel, & Thoma, 2020, p. 370).

The concept of socio-cognitive space developed from Fauconnier's Theory of Mental Spaces and Conceptual Blending (Fauconnier, 1994). Here, "mental spaces are real-time constructs created during discourse that provide cognitive structure [. . .] These spaces contain elements and relational connections to other elements that can be incrementally added while the spaces dynamically adjust and adapt as the discourse progresses" (Birdsell, 2014, p. 73). The theory builds on the notion that people's mental spaces in their working memory contain knowledge about a subject, which, when established, enters the long-term memory as a frame. This frame can be used in short-term memory when needed. Several mental spaces with related content in short-term memory might lead to blending: the development of a generic mental space. The structure of the generic space derives through a process of composition (the cross-mapping of spaces), completion (adding additional structures depending on time, background knowledge, and discourse context), and elaboration (the blending of elements from separate existing spaces) (Fauconnier & Turner, 1998).

Peverelli (2000) transferred the notion of mental space, together with Weick's sense-making theory, into the realm of organization theory and added the socio-cognitive element. Space constitutes a group of actors with common cognitive and social structures who come together at a certain time and place. These structures have consequences for the behaviors of those actors. He gives the example of a group of people meeting every day at the same bus stop to drive to work. They all share the same expectation—that the bus will arrive at the time stated in the timetable—which constitutes the cognitive aspect. They are also waiting collectively at the same place, which constitutes the social aspect. Under certain circumstances, such as when the bus is repeatedly late, they may start to discuss a joint formal complaint, which constitutes a possible behavioral aspect. During their interaction, they agree on rules that prescribe the ways they act. These rules confine and give meaning to their actions. In summary, the SCS consists of the cognitive and social dimensions, with the possibility of an emerging behavioral dimension resulting from the first two. Within a given SCS, the cognitive element is stronger than the social element (Peverelli, 2000).

The socio-cognitive space in balanced leadership

The SCS in balanced leadership was investigated through a series of studies. A first conceptual study by Müller, Vaagaasar, Nikolova, Sankaran, and Drouin (2015) started from the notion that "people create social systems and their lives are, in turn, influenced by them" (Cullen & Leavy, 2017, p. 53), thereby crediting the dynamic interplay between personal and social structural influences within social settings. Their study revealed some of the cornerstones for coordination in balanced leadership:

- Horizontal/shared/distributed leadership is enabled by the project manager. Only when the project manager accepts these forms of leadership in his/her project, can such coordination emerge.
- If it is allowed to emerge, the coordination among the project participants happens through the SCS.
- For coordination to function, the SCS must consist of three elements that are shared across the project participants. These are knowledge about (a) the shared mental model for project execution (i.e., skill needs, ways to collaborate, and the understanding of the context of the project); (b) the currently empowered leader; and (c) the level of efficacy of the empowered leader.
- The nature of the SCS is influenced by the personality of the project manager, the types of projects, and factors influencing the selection of team members.

Subsequent empirical studies confirmed these hypotheses; for example, the first bullet point was validated in Müller et al. (2018b), and the others in Müller, Sankaran, and Drouin (2018). In the following section, we discuss the three elements listed in the third bullet:

- *The shared mental model for project execution* refers to the team members' knowledge about the availability of particular skill needs and skills in the project, the ways the team members collaborate for project execution, and the shared understanding of the project context's peculiarity. Knowing this allows sensing when a transfer of leadership among team members needs to occur and the extent to which the empowered person satisfies this need. This knowledge develops efficacy perceptions among the team members, which may influence the nature of the interaction with the empowered leader. Synchronization of this knowledge is important in order to make sense of appointments of empowered leaders, which in turn influences the work-harmony in the team. From a mental-space theory perspective, this constitutes the cognitive dimension, as it requires cognitive effort to oversee the skill needs over the project's life cycle, and the way this can be satisfied over the course of the project.

- *The currently empowered leader* information entails two components: (a) the name of the individual or team currently empowered to lead; and (b) the level of empowerment for this person or team. For project managers, empowering leaders means sharing power and decision-making authority. It also entails additional responsibilities for the project managers, such as following and simultaneously governing the empowered leader. Many of the implications of empowering are discussed in Chapters 6 and 7. Empowerment can be granted to individuals, as in horizontal leadership, or groups, as in shared and distributed leadership. It is granted either directly or indirectly. The former is done when the project manager names an individual or team. The latter occurs when particular individuals are identified through existing documents, such as the project plan. Hence, this element of the SCS should remove ambiguities by clarifying whom to follow for the time being and what the level of authority of the leader is. The latter refers to limitations, such as empowerment for solving technical issues only, using resources from the existing team, or empowerment to contract external parties to overcome particular issues in the project, etc. From a mental space theory perspective, this element constitutes the social dimension by identifying the particular individual(s) granted *primus inter pares* (first among equals) status in the social group, which in this case is a project team.

- *Efficacy* refers to the empowered leader's ability to execute the task to a satisfactory or expected degree. It is a combination of (a) the person's self-efficacy shown to others (i.e., the person's visible self-perception of his/her ability to master the task); and (b) the team members' perceived efficacy of the empowered leader. Both are interpreted in the context of the reason for empowerment. As discussed in Chapter 6, there are many possible reasons for temporarily empowering individual(s), ranging from solving problems through technical expertise to providing leadership training opportunities for future higher-level managers. The combination of (self-)efficacy and empowerment motivation steers the interaction between the empowered leader and the team. As shown in Chapter 7, team members of an empowered leader who is on a training assignment will most likely behave more supportively and empathetically than team members following directions from a technical expert. Hence, this element constitutes the behavioral dimension of the mental space, as it triggers certain behaviors, simulated by the social and cognitive dimensions.

The information cues required to develop a shared understanding of these three elements emerge in various situations. Most obvious are the regular project meetings, where upcoming tasks and issues (including the need for particular temporary leaders) are discussed. Other occasions are informal discussions during work execution, breaks, or personal observations. Transparency by the project manager and team members is critical for building and maintaining a functioning SCS across the project manager and the team.

Leadership approaches and their SCS content in different types of projects

In a continuation of the study by Drouin et al. (2017), the authors of this book conducted a series of four case studies with 21 interviews in organizations of different sizes, industries, and geographies to identify how the content of the SCS relates to different project types and leadership approaches.

Project types were defined in accordance with the project management methodology used. Four types of methodologies were distinguished:

- *Traditional methodologies* are chosen when the project deliverables are specifiable, predictable, and possible to plan at the outset of the project. Examples include the popular PRINCE2 methodology (Prince2.com, 2020). These methodologies are often tailored to the specifics of a project. However, they still retain their basic characteristic that allows them to "plan the project upfront." These methodologies are often found, for example, in construction projects.
- *Waterfall methodologies* also aim for being able to plan a project completely upfront, but also allow for iterative steps in the life cycle, like repeated requirements analysis, prototyping, or proof of concept. These methodologies are popular for new product or technology development projects (PMI, 2017).
- *Agile methodologies* comprise a family of methodologies to incrementally develop products through small teams, following the principle of continuously improving design and testing based on immediate feedback and change (Serrador & Pinto, 2015). Agile methods use iterative cycles to develop project deliverables, which minimize documentation requirements

and maximize flexibility for changes through frequent communication among team members (van Oorschot, Sengupta, & Wassenhove, 2018).

• *Agile/scrum* is a specific type of agile methodology based on a single-team process framework that consists of roles, events, artifacts, and rules. It fosters flexibility and adaptiveness through incremental deliverables paired with team interaction and learning, as well as co-creation through constant interaction with project stakeholders to ensure meeting their requirements (Scrumguides.org, 2020).

We will now discuss the impact of leadership approaches and their associated SCS content. Table 9.1 summarizes our discussions.

Projects using traditional methodologies in construction show strong vertical leadership approaches by the project manager. Balanced and horizontal leadership is rarely exercised, because all decisions are required to be formally made by the project manager. However, a covert type of horizontal leadership exists. In this case, the project manager informally asks a team member for advice and then officially announces this advice as the project manager's decision. Hence, the project manager's vertical leadership is highly expressed, while balanced and horizontal leadership is low. The SCS element for shared mental model for project execution is synchronized across the team members by referring to the project plan. The upfront planning, stemming from the traditional methodology, allows identifying the required skills for any point in time during the project life cycle. Empowerment is indirect and covert, as discussed earlier. When present, it targets individuals, typically those identified from the project plan. Efficacy is judged in light of the motivation for the empowerment, with reference to the role that the project manager assigns to the empowered individual. This is typically done by assigning roles to selected persons early on at the planning stage to allow them to prepare for their roles and to develop their self-efficacy. Altogether, the three SCS elements are expressed at a low level in these projects, as the project plan dominates over team members' opinions.

Projects using waterfall methodologies for product development show a strong preference for balanced leadership. This stems from the need to continuously adjust structures and plans to solve newly arising issues during development, which are addressed by empowering the best suitable expert to solve technical problems, but also making use of the project manager to structure and organize these dynamics in the project. This process ensures smooth processing and continuation of the identification, empowerment, governance, and transition events. Leadership authority frequently shifts among team members and project managers when different specialists are appointed as horizontal leaders to solve issues in their particular area of expertise. Hence, balanced leadership is strong, while both vertical leadership by the project manager and horizontal leadership by team members are at a medium level. The SCS element for shared mental model for project execution is mainly informed by the project plan, which is frequently updated to reflect reality. Empowerment is typically done by the project manager directly naming individuals who are temporarily empowered as horizontal leaders. Judgment on their efficacy builds on their past performance and their reputation. Hence, the project plan is the common reference for decision-making and synchronization.

Projects using agile methods, such as IT systems development, show leadership shared between project managers and horizontal leaders. Collaborative work culture and agile processes allow for the distribution of problems across teams and the project manager. Technical issues are addressed by horizontal leaders. Process, structural, and stakeholder-related issues are addressed by project managers, leading to a strong expression of both balanced and horizontal leadership in these projects. The project manager's vertical leadership is reduced to a medium level to keep the project moving without too much "steering" by a manager. In terms of SCS elements, the information needed to build a shared mental model for project execution is identified interactively within the team, typically by reference to records that help identify particular specialists, information from the particular community of practice, or other word-of-mouth measures. Empowerment is typically at the level of teams or subteams, which are named directly, for everyone to understand who is in charge of solving issues. Judgment on the empowered leaders' efficacy is based on the individuals' in-project performance and through informal means, such as joint breaks and leisure-time activities. Skill shortcomings in empowered teams and individuals are addressed through dedicated training, support, and mentoring activities within the project. In these projects, the common reference point for the SCS is the team itself, with its existing skills and experiences in working together, which might be extended to known specialists in the community of practice.

Projects using agile/scrum methodologies show a dominance of horizontal leadership, paired with medium levels of balanced leadership and low levels of vertical leadership. Hence, the majority of the leadership is technical leadership by specialists, which is dynamically coordinated across the different specialists using balanced leadership. Vertical leadership is rudimentary and often confined to some initial structuring during the early stages of the project, and subsequently replaced by balanced leadership through the team. The situation within the project informs the SCS element of shared mental model

Table 9.1 Leadership Approaches and Socio-Cognitive Space in Different Types of Projects

Project Type	Leadership			SCS		
	Balanced Leadership	Vertical Leadership	Horizontal Leadership	Shared mental models of project execution	Empowerment	Efficacy
Traditional (Construction)	Low	High	Low	Known experts and project plan	Indirect for individuals	Roles assigned by the project manager
Waterfall (IT)	High	Medium	Medium	Based on the project plan	Direct for individuals	Past performance, reputation
Agile	High	Medium	High	Experts are identified through records, communities of practice, and by word of mouth.	Direct for teams	Boosted through training, buddying, mentoring
Agile/ Scrum	Medium	Low	High	Based on the project as it unfolds	Direct for teams	Performance of team and individuals therein

for project execution. It dynamically changes with developments in the project in terms of required skills, the ways for information gathering and interaction to address issues, and the availability of skills through existing team members. Empowerment is strong and direct by naming empowered (sub-) teams as leaders, or even self-empowerment of some subteams. Judgments on efficacy draw from the performance and contributions of subteams and their individuals in the currently ongoing project. This process renders the project and its resources as the common reference point for the SCS.

Table 9.1 shows that the elements in projects using traditional and waterfall methodologies typically refer to the project plan, indirect empowerment of individuals through identification in the project plan, and efficacy judgments based on past performance; that is, the combination of formal documents and individuals' reputations governs the SCS and, with it, the choice of leadership.

Agile and agile/scrum-driven projects show different patterns. The baseline for identifying the skills required are the existing project and its team. Accordingly, skill needs are identified when the need for them arises, using either existing team members (and training them if needed), records, and

Table 9.2 SCS Content in Different Project Ontologies

	Socio-Cognitive Space		
Ontology	Skill needs	Empowerment	Efficacy
Being	Project plan	Individual	Past performance
Becoming	Team's perception of the project	Teams and subteams	In project performance

word-of-mouth suggestions from the community of practice. Empowerment is at the level of teams or subteams, whose efficacy is judged based on the in-project performance. Hence, the dynamics within the project and the existing team members combine into governing the choice of leadership for the project.

This difference between traditional/waterfall- and agile-driven projects indicates two very different worldviews or ontologies (see Chapter 3 for a discussion on ontology). SCSs in traditional/waterfall-driven projects refer to a relatively stable reality, which is outside the individual's mind and can be measured and objectively observed. This is known as a "being ontology," that is, an understanding of (project) reality as being made of existing objects that others can acknowledge as existing, such as plans and records of past performance. Contrarily, SCSs in agile and agile/scrum-driven projects indicate a "becoming ontology," which refers to a dynamically changing reality that continuously goes on and comes about and is typically perceived subjectively by individuals (Jing & Van De Ven, 2016). Table 9.2 summarizes the differences between the two worldviews.

The relationship between horizontal leadership, SCS, and project success

So far, this chapter has addressed SCS in terms of its theoretical foundation, that is, sense-making theory, and the components of the SCS. Then we discussed the content of SCS components in various types of projects, which showed the essential philosophical differences between projects run by traditional or agile methodologies.

This discussion naturally leads to the question: does it matter? In other words, do horizontal leadership and the SCS have an impact on projects and their success? A quantitative study by the authors of this book addressed these questions (Müller, Sankaran, & Drouin, 2018a).

Existing literature indicated that leadership influences project success. Many existing studies showed the impact of vertical, shared, and distributed leadership on project success. However, no study had yet tested the impact of horizontal leadership on project success. Accordingly, our study's first hypothesis proposed that horizontal leadership impacts project success. Existing literature on sense-making and mental spaces indicated an indirect relationship with success measures, especially a mediating relationship between leadership and success. A mediation effect happens when an independent variable impacts a second variable which, in turn, impacts a dependent variable. The variable in the middle of this chain is the mediator variable, which "mediates" the relationship between the first and last variable in this sequence. An example of such a relationship is the number of people at the beach (i.e., the dependent variable) being impacted by the outside temperature (the independent variable). The higher the temperature, the more people are seen at the beach. However, there is a mediating variable, which is rain. If there is no rain, there is a strong correlation between high temperature and many people at the beach. However, when the rain pours down, the effect of warm temperature is absorbed by the mediating variable (rain) and is not passed on to the dependent variable. Accordingly, few people are seen at the beach. The former case indicates no mediation, whereas the latter case indicates full mediation by the mediating variable. Statistical tests identify the average level of mediation.

Hence, the model tested by the study hypothesized horizontal leadership (as defined in Chapter 2) as the independent variable, which impacts project success as the dependent variable, and this relationship as being mediated by the SCS. Existing measurement constructs from earlier studies were used for measuring the variables. A worldwide online questionnaire to project managers and team members yielded 174 responses, which were analyzed using Partial Least Squares–Structural Equation Modeling (PLS-SEM).

The results showed that horizontal leadership significantly impacts project success and that this relationship is partly mediated by the self-efficacy of the appointed leader and the shared mental model.

Measuring the direct impact of horizontal leadership on project success, that is, without a mediating variable, showed that about 23% of project success can be attributed to horizontal leadership. This is typically known as practical significance (or R-square). Cohen (1988) informs us that values above 12% are of high practical significance in behavioral science: hence, being approximately twice as high as the threshold, the effect of horizontal leadership on project success is very strong. But how strong is the influence of the SCS? Measuring the impact of the SCS alone (without horizontal leadership) on

Table 9.3 Impact of Horizontal Leadership on Project Success and Its Mediation through the SCS

Variable	Impact on Project Success	Mediation
Horizontal leadership	23%	
SCS	38%	
Horizontal leadership + SCS	40%	30%

project success showed that about 38% of project success can be attributed to the SCS. Finally, the joint impact of horizontal leadership and SCS on project success showed that 40% of project success can be attributed to the combination of horizontal leadership as the independent variable and SCS as the mediator variable. Table 9.3 summarizes the findings.

Project success was measured by an existing construct that balances "hard" measures, such as time, cost, and quality, with "soft" factors, such as stakeholder satisfaction and project team satisfaction, as well as short-term measures, such as meeting user requirements, and long-term measures, such as reoccurring business (Turner & Müller, 2006).

Horizontal leadership measured the horizontal leader's leadership style's appropriateness, the level of authority to lead both team and task, and being respected by the team. Higher levels of these measures correlated with higher levels of project success. SCS was measured along its three components. Examples for questions included the following:

- Shared mental model:
  - o Context-related (SMM-context): creating an environment for safe and open discussions, communication and listening, team's knowledge of contextual constraints (e.g., skills), experience and skills available in the team;
  - o Work-related (SMM-work): knowledge of processes and tasks and their relations, understanding of information sources to fulfill these tasks, team collaborations and commitment;
- Empowerment: clarity of horizontal leader and his/her empowerment, impact of the empowered leader;
- Self-efficacy:
  - o General self-efficacy (SEF-general): achievements of goals, perseverance, failure handling;
  - o New tasks efficacy (SEF-new): attitude toward new tasks, perseverance in learning new things and in face of difficulties.

Mediation effects are classified into *no mediation* (less than 20% effect by the mediator variable), *partial mediation* (20%–80% mediation), and *full mediation* (>80%).

SMM-context, that is, the team's situational understanding and attitude, has the strongest mediation effect, absorbing 42% of horizontal leadership's impact on project success. Hence, it partly mediates the impact of horizontal leadership on success. Positive attitudes toward the tasks at hand, the willingness to interact for problem-solving, and the awareness of constraints in terms of quality and quantity of experts impact project results positively. This absorbs the direct effect from horizontal leadership to project success to a large extent, but not completely. By absorbing almost half of the leadership, this shared mental model can "make or break" the success of a project, adding to the need to carefully foster and maintain this shared mental model in project settings. Similar results are indicated by studies on mental models in shared leadership, which showed that compatible mental models across team members allow them to work under a common set of assumptions and therefore more efficiently (Pearce & Conger, 2003).

SEF-general partly mediates the horizontal leadership–project success relationship. With 21% mediation, it is just above the threshold for no mediation and is of a much smaller extent than SMM-context. However, it still has a mediation effect that should not be ignored. Higher levels of SEF-general measures correlate with higher levels of project success. This finding is supported by Blomquist, Farashah, and Thomas (2016). They confirmed self-efficacy as a good predictor of project performance.

SMM-work, at 19%, is at the borderline between no and partial mediation. This construct measures the team's knowledge of work processes, tasks, information sources, and other items related to the execution of the team's charter. Greater knowledge about these items correlates with higher project success. This is supported by other studies that show the importance of these "knowledge" items for successful collaboration in teams (Johnson, Lee, Khalil, & Huang, 2007).

The variables for SEF-new and empowerment were not correlated with project success. Figure 9.1 depicts the mediation model.

Process-wise, an update of the SCS follows the horizontal leader's announcement and empowerment. This triggers observation by the team and sensitivity for the horizontal leader's self-efficacy and the team's perception of his/her efficacy. Once horizontal leadership sets in, the SCS starts to mediate its impact on project success through the shared mental models and the general self-efficacy.

The preceding results are indicative of both horizontal leadership and the SCS being success factors for projects. The strength of success factors

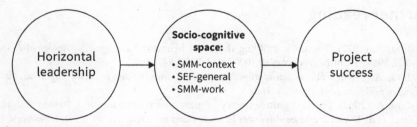

Figure 9.1. The mediation model for horizontal leadership and shared mental models on project success.

identified in previous publications varies. For example, Pinto and Slevin's (1988) popular 10 success factors jointly explain about 66% of project success, that is, about 7% per factor. Müller and Turner's (2007) study on the impact of the project manager's personality in terms of intellectual, emotional, and managerial competences (IQ, EQ, MQ) on project success showed an impact between 9% and 43%, depending on the project type. Together, these studies contribute to answering the long-standing question: are we mainly managing people or tasks in projects? While earlier studies focused mainly on task-related factors, such as having a project plan, and having management support (e.g., Pinto & Slevin, 1988), more recent studies emphasized the soft factors, such as personality (e.g., Turner & Müller, 2006), attitudes (e.g., Müller & Turner, 2010b), and leadership (Müller, Sankaran, & Drouin, 2018), and shifted the balance toward the relatively higher importance of soft factors for project accomplishments.

Summary

This chapter has addressed the coordination among and between actors and events in balanced leadership. We started the chapter by outlining sense-making theory as the theoretical lens and then discussed the SCS as the means to perform the sense-making activities of interaction and interpretation. Subsequently, we discussed the components of the SCS and their different content in different types of projects. Finally, we identified the role and quantified the impact of horizontal leadership and the SCS on project results.

Acknowledgments

The authors would like to acknowledge the contribution of Anne Live Vaagaasar of BI Norwegian Business School.

Further reading

Bandura, A. (1977). Toward a unifying theory of behavioral change. *Psychological Review*, *84*(2), 191–215. https://doi.org/10.1037/0033-295X.84.2.191.

Bandura, A. (1986). *Social foundations of thought and action: a social cognitive theory.* Englewood Cliffs, NJ: Prentice-Hall.

Bandura, A. (2002). Social cognitive theory of mass communication. In J. Bryant and M. B. Oliver (Eds.), *Media effects: Advances in theory and research* (pp. 94–124). New York, NY: Routledge.

Reflection questions

1. Why is sense-making important for coordination in balanced leadership?
2. What types of projects are you involved in, and what are the indicators of their underlying ontology?
3. Have you observed horizontal leadership in the projects you are involved in? If so, how did you recognize it?
4. What are the indicators of a well synchronized shared mental model within a project?

10

Balanced Leadership Case Study

Transport for New South Wales, Australia

Introduction

Throughout this book, we have discussed that balanced leadership occurs "when the vertical leader temporarily enables and allows horizontal leadership to happen in some situations, for example for a team member to take the lead on a problem for which he or she is an expert and it seems as advantageous for the project" (Müller, Packendorff, & Sankaran, 2017, p. 187). The transition between vertical and horizontal leadership takes place as five events: *nomination* (Chapter 4), when resources are nominated as project team members; *identification* (Chapter 5), when potential horizontal leaders are identified by the project manager; *selection* (Chapter 6), when a team member is empowered as a horizontal leader; *horizontal leadership and its governance* (Chapter 7), how leadership is exercised by the horizontal leader and how the project manager governs the horizontal leader during this assignment; and *transition* (Chapter 8), the termination of the horizontal leader's assignment.

The dynamic nature of these events helps to use the skills and attributes of the team member to deliver better project results. As discussed in Chapter 9, the coordination of this dynamic is supported by the creation of a socio-cognitive space (SCS), shown in Figure 10.3 later in the chapter, which is a shared understanding among project manager and team members about (a) *empowerment* (i.e., who is empowered to lead); (b) *efficacy* (i.e., the extent to which the empowered leader possesses the skills and competencies to lead); and (c) *shared mental models* (i.e., which skills are available and when in the team) (Müller, Vaagaasar, Nikolova, Sankaran, & Drouin, 2015).

Background

This case study reports on the application of balanced leadership in programs and projects carried out at Transport for New South Wales (NSW) in Australia (hereafter referred to as Transport). Transport's role is to lead the development of a safe, efficient, integrated transport system that keeps people and goods moving, connects communities, and shapes the future of the cities, centers, and regions. It is responsible for strategy, planning, policy, regulation, funding allocation, and other non-service delivery functions for all modes of transport in NSW including road, rail, ferry, light rail, point to point, regional air, cycling, and walking. Aviation is out of the scope of Transport and is handled by a different government authority.

For this case study, a program manager (vertical leader) and a subject matter expert working in the program team (horizontal leader) were interviewed.

A questionnaire used in the original case studies conducted for the balanced leadership study was used for the interviews. The questions covered decision-making processes, events occurring during the balanced leadership process, and socio-cognitive space.

The program manager we interviewed for the case study, Sandeep Mathur, manages programs to support Transport operations. His designation is director of Active Transport Program, Insights, and GIS. The team member interviewed was Daniel Yu, who is a senior domain architect. The responsibility of the program management unit (PMU) is to aggregate and curate the data generated by all modes of transport and publish it through various channels for use by Transport and operators to create value from the data. Once there is a request to develop a solution from a client department, the program management team begins to develop how it could be delivered. As an example, a program called "dangerous intersections" was trialed using data sent from vehicles at a rate of 25 records per second to detect crash blackspots by applying machine learning (Henry, 2020).

Mathur was able to discuss the role of senior management and that of the program manager in Transport during the interview, as he has a dual responsibility.

Transport's key responsibility is to deliver infrastructure to ease congestion in a crowded metropolis whose population is increasing. Sydney's population is projected to rise from 4.9 million in 2020 to 6.6 million in 2036. Recent examples of successfully delivered infrastructure by Transport include the first phase of Sydney Metro Rail to deliver a high-frequency metro network across greater Sydney, and Light Rail running through Sydney's Central Business District (CBD), called the CBD & South East Light Rail. These systems are major investments, costing more than US$1 billion and can be classified as megaprojects (Flyvbjerg, 2014). There are several other rail projects in the pipeline, such as the Paramatta Light Rail in the western part of Sydney, for a suburb touted as the second CBD. One of the major strategies for Transport is to connect different parts of the city for fast and efficient movement of people. Sydney Metro is also driverless, which is likely to be followed by the automation of the entire rail network. Sydney has a Future Transport Strategy developed for 2056 (Future Transport 2056, 2020).

Sydney is expected to grow into three cities: the current main city, or Eastern Harbour City; the rapidly growing area around Paramatta in the west, or the Central River City (the Paramatta River has ferry services running to Sydney CBD); and a new city in the far west supported by the development of the new Badgerys Creek Airport and Aerotropolis, to be called the Western Parkland City.

Data are very important for Transport to support the implementation of its future strategy. The PMU provides strategic support for developing new initiatives, with data underpinning the future strategy. As Mathur explained PMU's role for the rest of the organization, "Look, we have all the data for you. Come and use it."

The PMU also acts as a key repository for data. The operators of transport systems in Sydney have a need to use the same operational data. So, PMU's role is strategic in onboarding data, which includes curating the data (treating it to make it more useful for processing), publishing it, and sharing it.

In the next section we focus on decision-making practices in Transport, as making good and timely decisions is an important role of leadership in organizations (Useem, 2010).

Decision-making

In our study on balanced leadership, we were interested in how decisions are made within projects at different hierarchical levels. We were particularly interested in how strategic and tactical decisions regarding projects were made in organizations we studied. So, we had also added senior management to our interviews, as they would have an overview of how decision-making happens in organizations and what effect this had on projects being implemented by the organization. Studying how strategic decisions are made in organizations is important for successful project delivery, as they may impact the project goals. According to Bourgault, Drouin, Daoudi, and Hamel (2008), these decisions have an impact on how resources are allocated to projects, as well as on overall project effectiveness. In one of the publications from our balanced leadership case study (Drouin, Müller, Sankaran, & Vaagaasar, 2018), we studied differences in decision-making in projects carried out in Canada,

Australia, and Scandinavia. In our comparative study of these cases, we examined how decisions were made in projects while solving a problem, choosing between options, or developing a solution (Bourgault et al., 2008). We explain our findings in the following.

Figure 10.1 shows the hierarchy of decision-making in organizations related to programs and projects. In general, strategic decisions in organizations are usually made by senior management or the board; tactical decisions resulting in management control are made by middle management; and operational decisions are made by employees who are likely to be without management responsibilities. Translated to projects, the decision-making could be represented as shown in Figure 10.1.

In organizations where the organizational strategy is linked to projects, strategic decisions would normally be made by senior management. Decisions regarding the execution of projects would be made by the project manager, and a team leader will make decisions about specific tasks delegated to the team he/she is leading. In some organizations there would be other decision-making entities between the top management and the project manager. For instance, in project-based organizations (where most of the work is carried out through projects) or project-oriented organizations (where projects are also considered very important to be managed well), portfolio managers could be involved in making decisions regarding selection, prioritization, balancing, and optimization of projects in alignment with the organization's strategy. Program managers may be involved in making decisions regarding the coordination of projects within a program. Steering committees set up for governing projects and project sponsors who have a stake in the project may make decisions that may have an impact on the project. A more comprehensive discussion about the various types of organizations and their working can be found in a book by the present authors on Organizational Project Management, which includes case studies illustrating the implementation

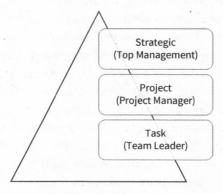

Figure 10.1. Decision-making in organizations.

of sophisticated ways in which an organization's philosophy and strategy are linked to projects (Müller, Drouin, & Sankaran, 2019). Next, we discuss what we found in a sample of case studies that resulted in the development of Balanced Leadership Theory.

Our study of decision-making in Canadian, Australian, and Scandinavian projects found that 83% of the decisions delegated to horizontal leaders were of a technical nature, whereas vertical leaders were in charge of 79% of business management decisions, and 21% of strategic and political decisions were handled by senior management. The type of decisions made by vertical leaders were found to be administration and contract related (55%), human resource management related (45%), and related to structural and governance aspects of projects (41%). Horizontal leaders were involved mostly with technical decisions (37%) and daily tasks in projects (33%), with moderate involvement in stakeholder-related decisions (18%). Next, we discuss what we found with Transport.

We found that decision-making related to projects happens at various levels within Transport. Portfolio-level decisions are made by senior management and the minister. Once the portfolio strategy authorizes programs by deciding "what to do," the program and project teams focus on the "how to do," to deliver these portfolios. Delivery decisions such as which technology to adopt and which vendors to use are made by the team responsible for program delivery. Thus decision-making in Transport is essentially tiered.

To make decisions at the program/project and team level, different teams working in the program, as well as specialists from the functional departments, are involved. To develop the required solutions, the program management team works with a team of architects, such as domain and enterprise architects. This is how design decisions are made. A governance forum is also organized to ratify selected key decisions due to their strategic nature.

Once the solution design is firmed up, a procurement process is triggered to determine suitable vendors to deliver the solution with PMU. The program and project managers discuss and decide to "get the right vendor to invite for a bid to deliver." Programs are generally delivered using a combination of internal resources and competent vendors. A short list of qualified vendors has been developed by Transport, and the formality of the procurement process for each project depends on the size of the contract.

The PMU relies on the architects for advice on solutions; however, decisions regarding delivery rests with the PMU. Further, the monetary value of the decision determines the level at which the delivery decision will be authorized—program director, program manager, or project manager, or by a governance forum. These delegations to make decisions are included in the program management plans. Although Transport is part of the public sector, Mathur believes that the decision-making is fast. Mathur had spent many years in the private sector before joining Transport and is knowledgeable about decision-making speed in the private sector.

Once a vendor is selected, adopting procurement procedures established in Transport, the program and project managers develop a schedule with the vendors based on the project scope. Once this is agreed upon, approval is sought from senior management. When this approval is obtained, the scope of work, work breakdown structure, and schedule are discussed with the project team.

Mathur explained that the solution and design decisions resided with the team because the program or project managers lacked the depth of technical knowledge required to make these decisions on their own. The program manager can ask questions of the specialists to understand why one decision is superior to another, but is not in a position to challenge the decision. As a way of encouraging the team, the program manager often says: "Look, team, you are there because you bring that skill. Let's use your skills." This was confirmed by team member Daniel Yu, who stated, "So, I pretty much have the authority to make the technology decision." Yu added, however, that he would consult with the vendor who delivers the project. This is where the next level of decision-making takes place. "For example, we are using lots of public cloud technology. So, I would sit down with people from Microsoft or from Amazon; the industry experts."

When decisions were more complicated, group discussions would be held within Transport using workshops: "But sometimes the decision can impact lots of other people as well. So, in that scenario, we'll have a group discussion using solution workshops."

The division of responsibility in decision-making in Transport is in line with the findings from the case studies of the balanced leadership studies (Drouin et al., 2018; Agarwal, Dixit, Nikolova, Jain, & Sankaran, 2021). From the interviews conducted for the case study, it was learned that more strategic decisions are made at senior management level (portfolio decision) and program management level (sourcing decisions), while technical decisions (solutions design) are left to the specialist team members such as architects.

Next, we clarify how the five events proposed by the balanced leadership theory (Müller et al., 2018b) took place in programs delivered by PMU.

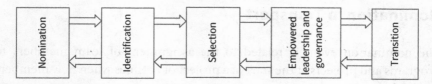

Figure 10.2. Balanced leadership events.

Events associated with balanced leadership

The balanced leadership theory proposes that the shifting of leadership between vertical and horizontal leaders takes place as five events (Chapter 3).

Figure 10.2 shows the five events, which are explained further.

Nomination refers to when project members join a project. Depending on the context, project managers may be able exert their influence on who will be assigned to their project and may look out for people who may be able to take on horizontal leadership roles when needed.

The *identification* of a horizontal leader could occur in two ways. The project manager (or vertical leader) may identify a horizontal leader, or a proactive team member may self-nominate for the role. This process could occur through subtle interactions once the project teams are in place (Müller, Zhu, Sun, Wang, & Yu, 2018).

Selection occurs when a project manager empowers team members to take on the role of a horizontal leader and is enabled by the interactions between elements of a socio-cognitive space (Drouin et al., 2017).

Horizontal leadership and governance refer to the process used by the vertical leader, based on trust established during selection, to steer the horizontal leader without interfering too much with the actual task but adjusting the control he/she has to govern the work based on the capability of the horizontal leader.

Transition occurs when the task handed over to the horizontal leader by the vertical leader is completed, or when the vertical leader makes a decision to do so mid-task and either takes the task back or assigns another member of the team to take over the role. The way transition occurs could have an impact on the role of the horizontal leader in the future.

Next, we explain how these five events took place in Transport based on the interviews.

Nomination in Transport

The nomination event is related to the assignment of team members to programs and projects at the start of a project or at times when new members are needed.

The teams in Transport are generally regarded as high-performing teams and capable of undertaking the role assigned to them. From what was learned from the interviews, nomination did not seem to be a major issue in projects within Transport, as the capability of people in the PMU is well known to the program manager. The program manager generally knew who was available and requested the member to be assigned to the program. Once a team member was assigned, their role within the program or project was also clearly defined by the program and project managers. As explained by Mathur, he would say to them: "You are a test lead. You make a call on how you want to test the system." Thus, people with leadership potential appear to be known prior to their being nominated, with an expectation that they will take up leadership roles when it is required of them.

The issues faced in some cases in balanced leadership, where functional managers have authority over staff assigned to projects (Sankaran, Vaagaasar, & Bekker, 2020), did not appear to cause problems in Transport.

As pointed out earlier in this chapter, technology solutions in Transport are often delivered by vendors. So, there is another layer of leadership distribution where vendors are responsible for delivering comprehensive solutions as part of projects within a program. In such situations, the specialist looking after the solution within the program has the responsibility to ensure that appropriate members are selected to carry out the project. Yu offered the following explanation on how team members from vendors are nominated:

> They [vendors] need to provide [details of] their previous relevant project as well as the team member they're going to allocate to us, with their full employment history and resume [. . .] So that's the first gate [where] we basically validate whether this particular vendor as well as their people working with us have the right capability.

Identification in Transport

Identification of possible horizontal leaders in Transport takes place mostly at nomination itself. However, some leaders are also identified after the project starts when a need arises for someone to lead a task. To do this, first it is ascertained whether the identified member is trustworthy. This situation is discussed further under selection and empowerment.

Selection and empowerment in Transport

The selection event was also observed in Transport, as leaders had to be selected when their capability was not completely known at nomination. In such a situation, a team member is identified as a trustworthy leader based on an evaluation of their capability. The program/project manager would then assign the leadership of the task to the selected team member, explaining the task and demonstrating an outcome-based control approach: "This is what needs to be done. I'll let you go and deliver that outcome."

Empowerment of horizontal leaders when selected to lead tasks took place in several ways. While subject matter experts who are given decision-making responsibilities are generally capable of handling technical decisions, they may require advice from other subject matter experts within Transport when the task seems to have a greater impact across operations. In this case, the program or project manager assists them to contact those experts so that they are assured that they are on the right track.

Empowered leadership and governance in Transport

Governance mechanisms are also established at various levels to assist horizontal leaders to carry out tasks handed over to them. Such governance can take place at project, program, or technology levels. Technology governance can take place in a variety of ways to include decisions that span solutioning and enterprise architecture.

Mathur emphasized that members of the team are empowered, and Transport makes sure they have the right skills so that tasks can be performed efficiently. However, sometimes members of the team may not collaborate well, and this has to be dealt with. Mathur felt that since visibility in the tasks performed is quite high, due to the processes used in Transport, it is easy to detect when someone is not putting in the effort needed.

When the program manager realizes that the empowered leader needs some training, investment is made to develop that capability in the individual.

I did have a situation recently where one of the test leads, who I know is very good, did not have capability on the data analytics side. And I said: "X, do want you to go and learn?"

When it is felt that training may not help, transition plans are made, as explained in the next section.

Transition in Transport

There were instances when the team member was unable to fulfill the tasks assigned to them and the program manager decided that providing support to develop this capability may not help. In such cases, a soft exit from the program is arranged by looking for another role in a different program that was a better match.

In terms of team members from vendors who are unable to deliver, the role of transitioning is left to the specialist in Transport's program overseeing the vendor's work.

Yu explained that he was capable of gauging whether someone could deliver the task assigned to them. Once it is realized that the person who was assigned the task is unable to deliver, action will be taken fast.

But if, in a worst-case scenario, someone is really incapable of doing anything, then we have to go back to the vendor to ask for someone better. But this doesn't really happen [often].

Socio-cognitive space

The balanced leadership theory also proposed that a socio-cognitive space—a psychological construct—plays a role in enabling the five events associated with the balanced leadership theory to occur. Figure 10.3 shows the three elements that occupy the socio-cognitive space.

The socio-cognitive space comprises three elements:

Empowerment: This is related to the vertical leader empowering the horizontal leader once he/she selects a team member to take up the horizontal leadership role. The amount of empowerment required would also need to be taken into consideration.

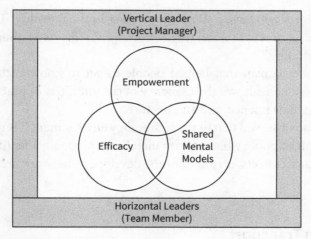

Figure 10.3. Socio-cognitive space.

Shared mental models: This relates to the team's knowledge about the skills existing among the other team members working on the project so that the horizontal leader can access these skills to share his/her leadership role. This knowledge can also enable harmonious work within the team.

Efficacy: This refers to the ability and confidence of the empowered leaders to satisfactorily execute the task he/she is leading.

The following observations are made from data collected from the interviews on the elements of socio-cognitive space identified in the balanced leadership studies.

Empowerment in Transport

Empowerment has already been discussed in detail in a previous section of this chapter.

Shared mental models in Transport

In terms of mental models, the agile project methodology used makes it easy for program and project members in Transport to know each other's capabilities when leadership is transferred to team members.

The daily stand-up meetings ensure regular communication and evaluation of capabilities. A program manager may be managing four or five projects and each project will have a stand-up meeting in the morning. This leads to continuous assessment that can reveal blockages easily. As Mathur explained, "There is no hiding."

Another mechanism that helped people to get to know each other and know whom to consult was the existence of communities of practice in agile management, data science, and architecture.

Mathur also observed that in the technology environment it is usually clear who is capable of doing what, as team members are usually identified as business analysts, architects, scrum masters, developers, network architects, and testers.

Efficacy in Transport

In terms of efficacy, which refers to the empowered leader's ability to carry out the task assigned to him or her effectively, Mathur made an interesting observation about people in Transport:

> I have seen, time and again, it's not the role that matters, but it's the attitude of the people, and anyone can step up at any given point of time.

Summary

The case study of Transport shows that decision-making at different levels followed a tiered approach, similar to what was observed in case studies of the balanced leadership studies. More strategic level decisions were made by top management, decisions related to key project parameters were made at the program or project manager level, and technical decisions were left to the appropriate specialist in the teams. On analyzing events that took place during the execution of programs and projects, examples of each event were found in Transport. Some events provided stronger evidence (e.g., selection) compared with others (e.g., transition). On examining the existence of socio-cognitive space, examples of both empowerment and mental models were found. One difference between case studies in the balanced leadership study and projects in Transport was the presence of an additional project level (solutions by vendors), as a major part of a technology-intensive project was delivered by specialist vendors. So, tasks to be led were also exchanged between the specialist in Transport and the vendor's team. In this context, leadership was shared between the PMU's specialist and the vendor's specialist, rather than following events identified in the balanced leadership theory.

Acknowledgments

The authors would like to thank both Sandeep Mathur, director of Active Transport Program, Insights, and GIS, and Daniel Yu, senior domain architect, both from Transport of New South Wales, Australia, for providing insights on aspects of balanced leadership in practice that contributed to this case study.

Reflection questions

1. What are the types of decisions made in Transport, and who makes them?
2. What events of balanced leadership theory are present in the case study? Which of these are more prominent in the case study?
3. What elements of socio-cognitive space are found in this case study? How does agile methodology support the elements of socio-cognitive space?

11

Balanced Leadership Case Studies

Two Canadian Projects and Their Socio-Cognitive Space

Introduction

Throughout this book, we have maintained that balanced leadership occurs "when the vertical leader temporarily enables and allows horizontal leadership to happen in some situations, for example for a team member to take the lead on a problem for which he or she is an expert and it seems advantageous for the project" (Müller, Packendorff, & Sankaran, 2017, p. 187). The transition between vertical and horizontal leadership takes place as cycles made up of five events, namely, *nomination* (Chapter 4, when resources are nominated as project team members), *identification* (Chapter 5, when potential horizontal leaders are identified by the project manager), *selection* (Chapter 6, when the empowerment of a horizontal leader occurs), *horizontal leadership and its governance* (Chapter 7, when leadership is exercised by the horizontal leader and the project manager governs the horizontal leader during this assignment), and *transition* (Chapter 8, when the termination of the horizontal leader assignment occurs). Figure 11.1 illustrates these events and the need for coordination between them.

This dynamic shifting of leadership makes the best use of the skills and personalities of team leaders and members for better project results. As discussed in Chapter 9, the coordination of this dynamic is supported by a socio-cognitive space (SCS) (see Figure 11.2), which is a shared understanding among project manager and team members about (a) *empowerment* (who is empowered to lead); (b) *efficacy* (the extent to which the empowered leader possesses the skills and competencies to lead); and (c) *shared mental models* (which skills are available and when in the team) (Müller, Vaagaasar, Nikolova, Sankaran, & Drouin, 2015).

The enablement of balanced leadership requires a shared understanding and cognition among team members and the person who is recognized as the leader in certain situations. Thus, balanced leadership needs a space (a) where the linkage and adjustment between vertical and horizontal leadership takes

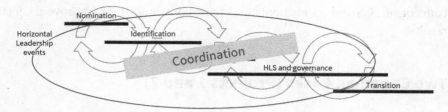

Figure 11.1. Balanced leadership and its five events.
Note: HLS = Horizontal leadership

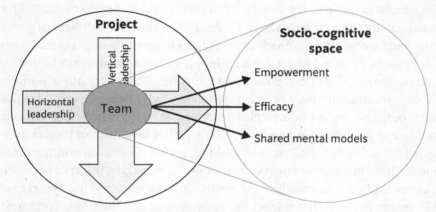

Figure 11.2. Balanced leadership and its SCS.
Adapted from Müller et al. (2015).

place; (b) where team members must be empowered to lead; and (c) where they must have sufficient efficacy to chart the team's way forward. Thus, the SCS, as discussed in Chapter 9, integrates the interaction between the project manager and team members, the feedback received after the behavior, and the conditions supporting the enactment. Figure 11.2 depicts this space as emerging at the junction of vertical and horizontal leadership (left circle). At this junction, coordination is needed, which happens through a shared understanding of who is empowered, the empowered person's efficacy, and the shared mental model for project execution (right circle).

Therefore, the aim of this chapter is to illustrate through two Canadian case studies the role of the SCS and its elements in the collaboration of vertical leaders and project team members in two different types of projects. Project 1 is *the refurbishment of generating and transmission hydroelectricity facilities* and Project 2 is *the construction of a sports stadium*. We hope that the two projects used in this case study will allow readers to better understand the concept of SCS and its elements and their contribution to improve project results.

Two Canadian Cases (Projects 1 and 2)

Project 1: Refurbishment of generating and transmission hydroelectricity facilities

The Canadian company of Project 1 (C1) is a world leader in the field of hydroelectricity (power from water). C1 focuses on the refurbishment of generating and transmission hydroelectric facilities to meet the needs of its clients. The projects managed by C1 are significant, some of them worth billions of dollars. They can last from 6 months to 10 years. To manage these projects, C1 uses multidisciplinary teams of specialists who design, plan, organize, carry out, and supervise complex activities in compliance with rigorous quality and performance standards. C1 also relies on a team of project managers who enjoy the challenges of building power generation and transmission facilities in different environments. For C1, managing this type of project involves leading and coordinating teams working on cost-effective, renewable energy projects that respect the environment and their host communities (C1's website). Well-defined project management practices are used to manage C1's projects. Cost-effectiveness and speed of project execution put real pressure on the team members to deliver projects on cost and in time. However, delays in project delivery do occur and may be related, for instance, to changes in specifications due to climatic conditions (e.g., cold weather). Some delays may be caused by disagreements with stakeholders (e.g., contractual disagreements with contractors). All these project management practices appear to be well understood and applied, not only by the senior managers and project managers, but also by team members.

Project 1 is worth around C$500 million and consists of the rehabilitation of the intake and spillway at a generating station. This undertaking is intended to ensure long-term facility operability. The project lasted 10 years and, at its peak, involved a dozen people from C1 plus external stakeholders such as contractor teams. The project 1 on-site team had a *senior manager*, in charge of a portfolio of five major projects in a specific geographical region, including project 1. This senior manager reported directly to his immediate superior based at the headquarters of the company. The *project manager* was responsible for all project-related activities and reported directly to the senior manager. The *security adviser* was a team member in charge of the construction safety and relations with the contractors. The *on-site engineer* was accountable for all mechanical and technical engineering issues, reported directly to the project manager, and frequently collaborated with the engineering division based at the headquarters. Finally, the *clerk* was mainly in charge of buying equipment to support the management of the teams and the on-site facilities. External stakeholders were mostly contractors (three or four depending on the phase of the project) and the team members of the turbine manufacturer. The senior manager explained how the project was initiated:

> I am the person responsible on site. There is obviously a team based at the head-quarters of C1, which prepared the draft, which began detailed engineering, which began planning. And once the project is approved by the board of directors, my superior at the head office told me, "Well look, we have a new project in [xxx city], which is of the order of $500 million. So, this is the business proposition and here are the plans and specifications. Go to [xxx city] and organize that for us." So, my mandate as on-site senior manager is: I get there, I build temporary facilities to do the work during the project. I make sure to get the resources, both human and technical or material and then I have to organize the whole project. Obviously, for that, I get the people. So, people who will work with me, I make sure to have people who have skills, expertise in the area in which they will work. And it is in this choice of people, that choice is very important if we want to ensure the implementation of the project schedule, in costs, in accordance with safety and environmental regulations. So it is having the right people.

Balanced leadership: The context of project 1 had an influence on the dynamics between horizontal and vertical leaderships. First, the senior manager and most of the team members were engineers and thus shared a common language and similar understanding of issues, which supported a climate of trust in the expertise of everyone to make decisions, especially between engineers, and members of the team. In addition, the leadership expertise was based on one of the following: (i) the credibility of the expert and/or their capability to argue in case of an initial collaboration in the project; (ii) the trust based on proven expertise during previous collaboration; or (iii) a learning capacity by the team member during the project duration. However, due to strong and well-organized project management practices, the flexibility of the team members was limited by a decision-making process that was known and respected by all. Consultation was highly regarded, yet the final decision was basically made by the person who would be held accountable (which was usually the senior manager in the predetermined hierarchical structure). The following quote by the senior manager demonstrates this way of exercising balanced leadership:

> Then finally, year after year, from one year to another, with the experience and knowledge, people were fairly autonomous in making decisions. On the other hand, they knew very well that they must respect the project management practices and methods of C1 and then, we know that there are decisions which cannot be taken by them because it does not fall to them. So, they know to whom to refer for approvals.

In sum, project management processes that were known to the team members seemed to strongly influence the balance between vertical leadership and horizontal leadership. Balanced leadership was based on the recognition that team members had past experiences or had acquired the necessary experience and knowledge through the project to make adequate and credible decisions. It was also grounded on trusting team members who shared a common understanding of key issues to implement the project and a thorough understanding of the internal approval steps.

Vertical leadership: Generally speaking, vertical leadership remained predominant in project 1. The project manager was expected to lead and control all project implementation activities and he reported directly to the senior manager. According to the project manager, "we are in the logic of who does what; most important decision-making is in the hands of the hierarchy." The project manager was also the guardian of project results and success and was recognized as such by team members. As the senior manager said:

> Well, this is to say that everyone who is there is under my direction and all these people are going to be under the project manager. So, it's the project manager who is responsible on site. The staff working on this project fall under his authority.

Horizontal leadership: Horizontal leadership was principally limited to decisions on technical issues and related to daily tasks to conduct the project. According to a team member, "project manager as well as team members use job and role description to share leadership." For instance, engineering decisions were the responsibility of the engineer on site. He was trusted based on his/her technical engineering expertise. The project manager counted on him/her for these types of decisions. This expert also worked closely with engineers based at the headquarters, who were liable for the whole design of the physical structure, to validate and discuss issues. The project manager explained this horizontal leadership situation based on role and responsibilities as follows: "Each team member does their part according to their role and responsibilities [. . .] Each team member plays their role."

Other situations called for horizontal leadership. For example, this could occur during brainstorming sessions where the opinion of team members on specific problem-solving is requested by the project manager. The safety adviser revealed that horizontal leadership occurred in emergency situations on the construction site that required immediate assistance. He described himself as "the eyes and ears of the project on the construction site." Based on this perception, this team member took the freedom to make urgent decisions. Although this initiative to make a decision was appreciated by the project manager and the senior manager, it also caused conflicts with one contractor who tended to escalate the conflict directly to the attention of both the senior manager and the project manager. This was confirmed by the senior manager:

> Or it could be our security adviser who observes an incident, a dangerous situation or an accident. At that time, he immediately calls the contractor to stop the work. He also calls the project manager to tell him, "Hey, there was an accident." The project manager will also implement the required measures provided by our project management practices. Then, of course, they will also inform me. And I take action as long as my actions are required at this time.

The next section presents the key components of the SCS (empowerment, efficacy, and shared mental models) that support the enactment of team members.

Socio-cognitive space components in Canadian case 1

Empowerment: Since the senior manager manages a portfolio of major projects, he had no choice but to delegate some authority and decision-making to the project manager and team members. Empowerment is enabled by the senior manager and the project manager and is often dependent on the team members' competence and within the guidance of the well-established project management methods and practices of C1. For instance, the project manager stated that "my management style is to give them 'latitude' or liberty. I asked my team members to be autonomous." The senior manager also mentioned:

> My management style is to interfere as little as possible, empower people as much as possible, and I ask people to be autonomous. If they cannot do it, it does not matter, we will act accordingly [. . .] Except that the team that I built for project 1, sure they built experience, they follow the directives and methods I gave them. Well, in that case, I try to give my subordinates as much latitude as I can.

In addition, the senior manager gave the following example to reinforce the fact that he was able to empower some team members based on their competence and skills:

> So I'll give you an example. I have a safety adviser I clearly identified because I saw that he is very autonomous and produces quality work. So, well, I went to see him and said, "Look, I put you there, then you'll be our eyes and ears, okay. Then you're gonna act like you're the job's superintendent, yes. Then if you're willing to do it, yes, well go, okay." So, that safety adviser was able to give directives and make decisions that another safety adviser could not do in similar situation.

Finally, the on-site engineer explained empowerment as follows:

> Well, generally, it is like, I would say, all of us here, well, the team, this is not a big team, but I would say that each of us through our responsibilities and scope of action is autonomous. Being autonomous, it does not mean you can do what you want. . . . Sometimes a decision, it is more the responsibility of one team member depending on the kind of decision . . . to let the concerned or appropriate person make decisions, but it is being autonomous within guidelines.

Fostering efficacy: Within clear and specific project management guidelines and practices, the project manager recognizes the individual capabilities of team members, based on their experiences, role, responsibilities, and trust. As explained by the project manager, "We trust our team members based on their respective expertise and roles and responsibilities." By delegating specific tasks to them, the project manager fosters their self-efficacy and develops and supports their self-management. For instance, the team member in charge of the safety on site explained, "I am paid to make these type [*sic*] of decisions." Similarly, the senior manager explained that fostering efficacy is closely connected to the understanding by the team member of C1's project management practices and processes but is limited within these boundaries:

> On the other hand, as part of their work, there are methods to follow. So, it's a bit in that sense that I say that the person is autonomous—he is capable of being responsible, and he is able to deliver the deliverables as part of his duties under which this is required. Then he is also able to provide guidance and recommendations to a contractor, how to do his work to optimize the costs and coordination between different contractors that may be present on site. In sum, I try to make sure that everyone is able to be responsible in his work. So, to have leadership. I guess it's called horizontal leadership.

Finally, the on-site engineer explained fostering efficacy as follows:

> If we look at project 1, well, I think each of us had his background, his past, which perhaps gives confidence to our leader that everyone is capable to be autonomous. Then yes, perhaps each of us had some experience that could be considered.

However, the project manager raised the issue that sometimes some team members tended to go beyond their roles and made decisions that had to be contradicted by the project manager. The project manager explained one such situation:

> Mr. X, did not agree with what a contractor was doing but I understood why he was doing this. So, we [the project manager and the team member] had different views on how to deal with the contractor and I [the project manager] have decided to do it differently.

Shared mental models: Shared mental models are based on knowing the particular skills and accessibility of each team member in order to sense when the transfer of leadership among team members needs to occur (Burke, Fiore, & Salas, 2003). In this case, we could find only one situation where it could have occurred. Team members and the project manager explained that all decisions related to engineering issues are in the hands of the on-site engineer, who reported to the project manager and collaborated with the engineers at the headquarters. The project manager explained this situation as follows: "Well, depending on the subject, for sure, I consulted a lot. In fact, I always consulted engineering when it was technical situations."

Project 2: The construction of a sports stadium

The organization that commissioned this infrastructure project is a municipal government administering an urban city that has over one million inhabitants. With more than 25,000 employees from multiple backgrounds and areas of business, the city's administrative structure is one of the largest employers of the metropolitan area (Municipality's website). The management of the municipality is operated under the authority of a city council and an executive committee. Composed of elected officials, including the mayor, the city council is the primary decision-making body. Reporting directly to the city council, the executive committee is responsible for overseeing the granting of contracts and subsidies, management of human and financial resources, as well as procurement and buildings. In order to conduct the administrative activities and support the implementation of political bodies' decisions, the management of the city's operations and projects is carried out by various departments and offices, including the Sports Department and the Property Planning and Management Department. The former aims to promote an active lifestyle among the citizens. Among its responsibilities, it provides access to sports facilities, offers support to sports competitions, and conducts various other related development programs (Municipality's website). On the other hand, the Property Planning and Management Department is driven by a mission to establish itself as an innovative leader offering efficient and eco-responsible infrastructure solutions that benefit the city's residents. To do this, the division mobilizes a multidisciplinary team that is in charge of planning, managing, and controlling the implementation of projects directed toward the construction, modernization, and renovation of buildings (Municipality's website). Because each department is characterized by a particular set of expertise and skills, it is not uncommon for projects to be conducted in a matrix mode within the organization. Moreover, the political context strongly influences the way projects are accomplished. Indeed, those responsible for the implementation of projects are generally required to operate with limited flexibility because of the importance of respecting decisions made at a higher hierarchical level and the formalities imposed by the strict processes of public service. This particular context also leads to employers working under increased pressure in order to complete projects according to the promised schedules and budgets. Additionally, it directly impacts the way projects are operationalized by dictating how contracts can be granted to external stakeholders and how relationships with the latter are to be managed.

Project 2 involved the construction of a sports stadium at a new location in the city. With an allocated budget of slightly over C$50 million, the stadium had to house both an indoor and an outdoor field. Advocated by some of the city's sports clubs and associations for nearly two decades, the building of a state-of-the-art sports stadium turned out to be an election promise several years prior to its formal authorization. The completion of project 2 subsequently stretched over a period of approximately eight years and involved an architectural contest to select a design that would become a symbol of creativity and innovation. Initially managed by the city's Sports Department, the project was later jointly carried out with the Property Planning and Management Department as it was more experienced in project management and infrastructure construction. Operating under a matrix structure, project 2 was supervised by senior managers from both departments, who were also in charge of other projects and programs simultaneously. Under their authority, two project managers, one from each of the two departments, were assigned full-time to the project. The project manager attached to the Sports Department was mainly in charge of communications, public relations, and fostering relationships with sports associations, while the project manager from the Property Planning and Management Department was assigned to oversee the activities related to the planning and building of the infrastructure. When the construction phase began, an on-site engineer and an on-site assistant junior engineer were added as full-time members of the project team in order to monitor the construction site and ensure compliance with contracts. However, in the second year following the start of construction, both the project manager from the Sports Department and the dedicated on-site engineer permanently left the team. As a result, from that point until the end of project 2, the full-time team was reduced to one project manager and one on-site junior engineer, who consequently became solely responsible for monitoring the activities of the construction site. Additional complementary expertise from other internal departments was solicited on an ad hoc basis during the implementation of the project. As for external stakeholders, the primary parties were the architectural firm, chosen through the design contest, and the building contractor, selected following a call for tender. In addition, a steering committee was formed to facilitate collaboration between the core project team and additional concerned stakeholders, such as representatives from other internal departments, sports associations, municipal regulatory bodies, and energy service providers.

Balanced leadership: The balance between vertical and horizontal leadership was defined by the acknowledgment of the municipal government's formal processes, while recognizing that granting latitude to subordinates is necessary in order to reach the project's goals. At an operational level, senior managers offered relative freedom of action to the project's team members. However, it remained their responsibility to make sure that the work was accomplished appropriately. A senior manager illustrated this dynamic:

> It's important to leave room for maneuver to the project team or the professionals. You know, there must still be leeway, because business needs to advance in that space. That's for sure. But from the top, I have to make sure that my people are well aligned. Basically, do some controlling: "Am I within my budgets? Are things going to be finished on time? If not, why? What can we do to get there?" So, it's alignment with room for maneuver.

Team members were encouraged to develop solutions, then present them for approval to their superior.

Moreover, when a decision required sanction by upper-level management, horizontal leadership enabled experts to share specific knowledge so that formal leaders could make informed decisions. A project manager highlighted this phenomenon:

> I would turn to professionals to enlighten me on questions related to the technical dimension of the project. All technical aspects would come from professionals, then I would compare the information received and sometimes question it. I would seek their expertise because I knew they had the knowledge to inform me about an issue or a cost concern. And then, on the basis of that information, I would make a final decision, or transfer it to a higher hierarchical level for authorization.

It is also noted that formal leaders mobilized their power of influence to defend solutions developed in horizontal leadership settings to higher hierarchical-level representatives. Therefore, the validity of shared decisions appeared to rely upon the support demonstrated by the formal leader. As a project manager recalled:

> One important player, in terms of moving sensitive issues to a higher level of political decision-making, was our director, who had to defend our ideas to an administration that was very concerned about the project. So, in that sense, I would say that he was a very influential person at that level.

Vertical leadership: The type of organization in charge of project 2 and the political context in which it was conducted strongly influenced the practice of leadership. Indeed, pre-established processes dictated the way activities of the municipal government were carried out and specified the hierarchical level authorized to sanction a decision. As a senior manager pointed out:

> So, when you give contracts, well it's super well framed. So in that kind of project there, almost all contracts granting or major expenses went through the executive committee and the city council. And before that, it goes through the hierarchy.

Vertical leadership was also used to overcome challenges faced by the team and stakeholders during the decision-making process. As a senior manager explained:

> The basic principle was simple. [The two project managers] would try to settle things at their level. That was the case also with architects, engineers, and all that. So they would try to figure that at their level. If there were things that they were not

able to solve, well it would go up a level. Then, if I was not able to settle it, it would go up another level. It's interesting to work that way, it makes sure that first we try to fix what we can.

Thus, the decision-making power conferred to an employee depended on the type of decision and its impact on the project. Decisions of a strategic or budgetary nature were the responsibility of the executive committee and the city council. Similarly, if a change requested in the course of the project had a potential to significantly impact costs or scheduling, the city's internal governance mechanisms required that the decision be made by formally appointed senior managers. As a team member illustrated:

Is it going to cost $2 million or is it going to cost $10,000? You know, if it was more than $40,000 of his estimate, I would go straight up to my superior. Because I am not in a position to make that decision.

The project managers were required to plan, lead, and control the project's activities in order to fulfill project 2's end goals. However, day-to-day significant decisions often had to be sanctioned by the senior managers or their directors. Although the project managers had some latitude in accomplishing their tasks, frequent reporting was expected and the implementation of many decisions considered had to be approved by their superior beforehand. This was explained by a team member:

We would always notify our senior manager and the one from the other department. We would prepare briefing summaries to tell them what is happening with the money, where we are on the timeline. Then, for major things, it was they who would say "yes, okay go" or "no, we are not doing this."

Additionally, vertical leadership was observed in problematic situations that could not be solved among concerned parties. Senior managers were expected to decide the outcome when divergent opinions between opposing team members and stakeholders could not be reconciled. As a senior manager recalled:

So, we have a knot there with that unit, it does not advance, or they may not be doing the right thing. So, when the project team was not able to settle the issues, well it would go up to me.

Horizontal leadership: Although the influence of the municipal government's hierarchical structure is omnipresent throughout the life cycle of project 2, emergence of horizontal leadership can also be observed. Consultation of members was highly valued by the team's formal leaders. Therefore, decisions related to project 2 were often developed collectively by project managers, team members, and other solicited contributors. Additionally, horizontal leadership was mobilized to foster cohesion and adherence of all team members to solutions subsequently submitted to superiors. As specified by a project manager:

> If we have a problem, we look at it together, and always in collegiality, with the team and the contractor. So, to me, that was a success. Even if I was making the decisions, they were always shared with the whole team, and then brought to a higher level with, I would say, a consensus. I rarely made a decision that was against other colleagues. We had to agree on the approach.

Moreover, horizontal leadership was strongly related to individuals' specialized expertise. Distribution of leadership was perceived as a way to enhance decision-making and problem-solving processes by encouraging knowledge exchange and ensuring that relevant information was shared. A project manager recalled:

> Basically, we let each expert play their role of expert. What we do is mostly endorse their position. The stadium's structure was extremely complex, so decisions regarding that matter would be up to the experts, such as the architects or engineers. They are the ones who carry the know-how. We might ask, "Are you sure that you have considered all possible options?" but we trust their judgment.

Occasionally, horizontal leadership was also applied as a response to the fast-paced environment in which the project was implemented. Indeed, knowing that inputs from upper hierarchical levels would translate into additional delays, decisions that required immediate actions were taken by the on-site junior engineer. As the latter explained:

> You know, as soon as there is a problem, what is the solution? It was my job to find a solution as soon as possible, with the help of the professionals. You have to think on your feet. Sometimes, it can't be "we will wait three days to take a decision." I think sometimes that's the problem with the city's structure. It takes too much time.

While the preceding remarks highlight a deliberate use of horizontal leadership, it also appears to have been exercised as a result of an unforeseen shortage of staff. Following the departure of the project manager from the Sports Department as well as the on-site engineer, the remaining project manager relied exclusively on one other full-time team member. Therefore, many decision-making responsibilities surrounding the construction site were transferred by default to the junior engineer. In addition, the pair developed a strong bond that resulted in the practice of consulting each other when decisions needed to be made. In this situation, distribution of leadership was unplanned, but became essential in order to accomplish the project's activities on schedule. As the junior engineer shared:

> At some point, it was [the project manager from the Sports Department] who would say "yes." Then she left, so it was [the on-site engineer] who would say "yes, for the construction, that's what we have to do." Then, both of them were gone, so it was me and [the project manager from Property Planning and Management Department] who had to make the decisions. I found it a bit rough [. . .] it was a lot on my shoulders. At the time, I didn't have that much experience on construction sites. But we had to deal with the situation and move forward.

Regardless of the circumstances, the occurrence of horizontal leadership throughout the realization of project 2 was supported by the trust of superiors in their subordinates. Flexibility was thus granted based on the belief that team members were competent and working toward the same goals.

Socio-cognitive space components in Canadian case 2

Empowerment: Subordinates' empowerment was a key component in allowing horizontal leadership to rise. Given the number of projects simultaneously supervised by senior managers and the complexity of project 2, formal leaders were inclined to offer leeway in order for horizontal leadership to come forth and contribute to the achievement of the project's activities. As a senior manager expressed:

> It is favorable to leave room for maneuver to these people because there are so many problems that need to be addressed. So, you know, it makes the project progress.

Similarly, a team member recalled:

[The senior manager] would tell me, "It's alright, do what you think is best, as long as you have it under control." I don't usually manage major contracts like that, but I had been working solely on this project for years now. [The senior manager] has [responsibility for] the whole division [. . .] so he has many other projects to take care of and make decisions for.

Beyond a delegation of authority, empowerment was fostered through helping the subordinates to develop their self-confidence. As the junior engineer recalled:

[The on-site engineer] would tell me, "Come on, put your boots on, you are an engineer, [the construction workers] will respect you. You have to take your place!" So, [the on-site engineer] helped me to take actions and be in charge. To me, that's leadership. Show me how to do it and I will follow, and then I will adapt it to my own style.

Fostering efficacy: In order for horizontal leadership to emerge, team members had to develop self-administering skills. The degree of autonomy granted by formal leaders was related to the trust in subordinates' capacities to manage their assigned responsibilities effectively. As the junior engineer recalled:

I think [the project manager] knew that I was skilled for that. He would tell me, "Go on, make those decisions." I was very autonomous after [the project manager from the Sports Department] and [the on-site engineer] left. He trusted me do to that.

Project managers contributed to enhance their subordinates' efficacy by clarifying team members' expected role and coaching them. A project manager reflected on the matter:

It is my job to make them understand how we are going to work and what their specific role is. But again, in the team, I try not to confine someone's role to something very fixed. I think it's not motivating to always do the same things. So, I try to get people to have different responsibilities. I get them to participate in various meetings. It teaches them at the same time. Because we all have the capacities to do the tasks if we are given the means. So, that's the objective.

Shared mental models: Throughout project 2, shared mental models guided managers and team members to identify the appropriate expertise to solicit depending on the situation. As a senior manager illustrated:

When I had a concern regarding a technical aspect, I would seek information from experts in that field. They would be the most likely to enlighten me.

Likewise, another senior manager explained:

[This employee] was already responsible for [a sport facility], which is a big building in the city. So he knows how to operate this type of center. Well, we figured that the new stadium would be roughly in the same order of size. And therefore, he was the expert we would refer to when we had questions about management of operations.

Summary

Table 11.1 summarizes the results of the two Canadian case studies.

These two Canadian case studies illustrate the perspective of socio-cognitive space to understand how shifting of leadership can be enabled. They show the nature of the dimensions of socio-cognitive space: i.e., empowerment, efficacy, and shared mental models, how these processes evolve and the role they play in supporting the dynamics of the shifting leadership. What we notice in these two cases is that in projects with traditional methodologies, empowerment is enabled indirectly, as it is implied from the project plan and the reputation of the candidate being empowered. Similarly, efficacy sets in and controls the team members (and possible horizontal leaders) contingent on the particular role that the vertical leader assigns to them. Shared mental models are mainly created and maintained through the project plan, and barely exist in Project 1. They also show that projects using traditional methodologies are low in balanced and horizontal leadership, but high in vertical leadership. Here, individuals are empowered based on their past performance and in accordance with a pre-developed project plan, or because the organization lacked resources to conduct the project and the project manager had no choice but to trust and count on their subordinate (project 2), empowered to solve urgent issues that could not wait to go back and forth throughout the hierarchical decision process.

These two Canadian cases have implications for academics and practicing managers. For the former, they contribute to a better understanding of the contextual contingencies for balanced leadership. They emphasize the importance of contextual factors for balanced leadership to happen. In large construction projects, the complexity of subcontractors and large teams, together with legal obligations, prevent such informal and ad hoc transfer as may occur

Table 11.1 Key Results of the Two Canadian Case Studies

Leadership	Canadian Case, Project 1: Refurbishment of Hydroelectricity Facilities	Canadian Case, Project 2: Sports Stadium
Balanced leadership	Recognition that team members have past experiences or acquired experience during Project 1	Recognition that team members acquired experience during Project 2
	Grounded on trusting team members who shared common understanding	Limited within the Municipality's PM practices and processes
	Limited within the company (C1)'s PM practices and processes	
Vertical Leadership	Predominant	Predominant
	Most decisions in the hands of the hierarchy (senior or project managers)	Most decisions need to be validated by the hierarchy (senior managers and executive committee)
	Structured by well-defined PM practices	
Horizontal leadership	Limited to decisions on technical issues	
	Trust based on technical expertise	Leadership from time to time exercised by individual team member (junior engineer)
	Occur in brainstorming sessions	Based on lack of resources to manage Project 2
	On daily task such as specific problem-solving or in case of urgency	Trust based on technical expertise
	In case of urgency	On daily task such as specific problem-solving or in case of urgency
Socio-Cognitive Space Components		
Empowerment	Individuals empowered by VL	Individuals empowered by VL
Efficacy	HL's efficacy is judged on expertise and individual	HL's efficacy is judged on expertise and individual
	Recognized capabilities and skills	
Shared Mental Models	Non-applicable	Experts generally known in the organization

Note: HL = horizontal leadership; PM = project management; VL = vertical leadership.

in more flexible or agile projects. Managerial implications include the deliberate choice of leadership approach, contingent on project methodology.

Reflection questions

1. What events of balanced leadership theory are more prominent in the two Canadian case studies? What can we learn from these case studies with a more predominant vertical leadership approach?
2. What elements of socio-cognitive space are found in these case studies?
3. How do well-defined project management practices support the elements of socio-cognitive space?

12
The Way Ahead

A reflection

In the preface to his book *Creating Leaderful Organizations*, Joe Raelin (2003) emphasizes the need for everyone in (permanent) organizations to serve as leaders at different times. "In the twenty-first-century organization we need to establish communities where everyone shares the experience of leadership of serving as a leader, not sequentially, but concurrently and collectively" (p. xi). These words apply equally well to temporary organizations, as the findings described in this book demonstrate. However, how can this be achieved in practice? That is the focus of this book.

For this, we first defined what we mean by balanced leadership. We showed that task-related decisions are often delegated to horizontal, shared, or distributed leader(s). In contrast, the right to make business-related decisions is retained by the project managers as vertical leaders. Then we outlined a balanced leadership theory and explained its constituent events in the following chapters, with each chapter providing a model of each event's functioning. Subsequently, we presented the socio-cognitive space (SCS) as the coordinating "brain" that synchronizes people, time, and tasks for balanced leadership, and quantified its correlation with project success. Finally, three projects in Canada and Australia showed the interaction of events and SCS in real-life practices.

As a busy project manager, you may ask, shouldn't projects be led by project managers who plan how the projects are to be carried out, and the team members simply follow their instructions? Where is the time to develop team members to take on some leadership roles? While this attitude may work for simple projects where a transactional leadership style is sufficient, it becomes difficult as projects become more complex, for example, by demanding more visionary or transformational approaches than simple directing activities. Balanced leadership takes us a step further by taking into account various leadership approaches and their coordination, to use leadership capabilities present in the project exactly when these capabilities are best for the project. You may find that you are already sharing leadership in your projects. In this case, the book helps you to become more aware of events and processes that support the sharing of leadership, and social and cognitive elements that enable such sharing, thus helping you to make the process you are already using more effective.

While this book can help with project management practice, we hope that project management researchers will also find some inspiration for further studies. Some promising work from research teams other than our own includes the study of balanced leadership by the head coach of the U20 National Football Team in Norway during the World Cup Qualification. Here Aartun and Særsland (2019) show how horizontal leadership helped find the best possible person in the team to do the pep talk before the critical play against Germany, which the Norwegian team subsequently won. Similarly, the head coach selected leading players upfront (as horizontal leaders), which boosted these individuals' motivation.

Contrarily, Kvalnes (2020) showed some of the challenges of horizontal leadership in handling social media accounts in organizations where vertical leaders' insufficient expertise and lack of understanding demand horizontal leadership. The social media experts (as horizontal leaders) tend to ask for more vertical leadership support, so they point to an imbalance where they sense that too much is required from horizontal leadership.

Yet another perspective is revealed by the studies at Tianjin University in China. Here, a team investigated horizontal leadership among co-workers who had never been identified as leaders before, and the effect of their empowerment at different levels of *guanxi*. *Guanxi* are the interpersonal ties, embedded in implicit reciprocal obligations, favors, and other exchanges among individuals in China (Li et al., to appear).

While investigating balanced leadership in projects, we also found, to our surprise, that the attitude of senior management toward balancing of leadership could serve as an enabler to encourage project managers to consider balanced leadership. Thus our studies could also have some human resource implications for organizations to introduce leadership-development capabilities among members of the organization who are assigned to projects, and to develop project managers' capacity to make the best use of balanced leadership features in their own projects.

This raises the question of how to develop these capacities. One way is to find out to what extent projects make use of balanced leadership. We mentioned earlier that there are large differences in the implementation of balanced leadership by industry and project type. In industries and projects with traditional hierarchical views toward leadership, the team members might need to be prepared for these new tasks and to be carefully introduced to balanced leadership before it is used occasionally. This should be done in conjunction with reflective meetings for all participants to learn about the experiences and overcome mistakes that naturally come up when doing things the first time. Over time, it will become a natural way of project leadership.

Organizations that already use balanced leadership might foster a dialogue between the project managers and team members to exchange experiences in the form of "lessons learned" sessions for further refinement of the situations that call for balanced leadership, thus honing the situational fit between circumstances and leadership approach.

A final word

Thank you for your interest in learning more about how leadership can be used more effectively in projects and how projects are led "leaderfully." We hope that reading this book motivated you to think about getting the best leadership in projects by using the leadership capability available as and when appropriate. The next step is the thoughtful application of these insights to your own projects. We wish you every success with this.

References

Aartun, D. B., & Særsland, A. E. (2019). *Daring to dream: Leadership practices in Norway's U20 National Football Team*. BI Norwegian Business School.

Agarwal, U. A., Dixit, V., Nikolova, N., Jain, K., & Sankaran, S. (2021). A psychological contract perspective of vertical and distributed leadership in project-based organizations. *International Journal of Project Management*, online https://doi.org/10.1016/j.ijproman.2020.12.004.

Alderman, N., Ivory, C., McLoughlin, I., & Vaughan, R. (2005). Sense-making as a process within complex service-led projects. *International Journal of Project Management*, *23*(5) 380–385. https://doi.org/10.1016/j.ijproman.2005.01.004.

Alonderienė, R., Müller, R., Pilkienė, M., Šimkonis, S., & Chmieliauskas, A. (2020). Transitions in balanced leadership in projects: The case of horizontal leaders. *IEEE Transactions on Engineering Management*. Online. https://doi.org/10.1109/TEM.2020.3041609.

Ammeter, A. P., & Dukerich, J. M. (2002). Leadership, team building, and team member characteristics in high performance project teams. *Engineering Management Journal*, 14(4), 3–10. doi: 10.1080/10429247.2002.11415178.

Amundsen, S., & Martinsen, Ø. L. (2014). Empowering leadership: Construct clarification, conceptualization, and validation of a new scale. *The Leadership Quarterly*, *25*(3), 487–511.

Anantatmula. V. (2016). *Project teams: A structured development approach*. New York, NY: Business Experts Press.

Angus-Leppan, T., Metcalf, L., & Benn, S. (2010). Leadership styles and CSR practice: An examination of sensemaking, institutional drivers and CSR leadership. *Journal of Business Ethics*, *93*(2), 189–213. https://doi.org/10.1007/s10551-009-0221-y.

Ansell, C., & Torfing, J. (2016). Introduction: theories of governance. In C. Ansell & J. Torfing (Eds.), *Handbook on theories of governance* (pp. 1–17). Cheltenham, UK: Edward Elgar.

Aras, G., & Crowther, D. (2010). Corporate social responsibility: A broader view of corporate governance. In G. Aras & D. Crowther (Eds.), *A handbook of corporate governance and social responsibility* (pp. 265–280). Farnham, UK: Gower.

Archer, M. S. (1995). *Realist social theory: The morphogenetic approach*. Cambridge, UK: Cambridge University Press. https://doi.org/10.2307/2655684.

Archer, M. (2004). *Being human: The problem of agency*. Cambridge, UK: Cambridge University Press.

Archer, M S. (2007). The ontological status of subjectivity: The missing link between structure and agency. In C. Lawson, J. Latsis, & N. Martins (Eds.), *Contributions to social ontology* (pp. 31–45). New York, NY: Routledge.

Archer, M. S. (2010). Morphogenesis versus structuration: On combining structure and action. *British Journal of Sociology*, *61*(SUPPL. 1), 225–252. https://doi.org/10.1111/j.1468-4446.2009.01245.x.

Archer, M. (2020). The morphogenetic approach: Critical realism's explanatory framework approach. In P. Rona & L. Zsolnai (Eds.), *Agency and causal explanation in economics* (pp. 137–150). New York, NY: Springer. https://doi.org/https://doi.org/10.1007/978-3-030-26114-6.

Arundel Soccer. (2020). Soccer coaching and leadership. Available at http://www.arundelsoccer.com/_files/Leadership.pdf.

Aubry, M., Hobbs, B., Müller, R., & Blomquist, T. (2010). Project management offices in transition. *Project Perspectives*, *18*(1), 48–53.

Bache, I., Bartle, I., & Flinders, M. (2016). Multile-level governance. In C. Ansell & J. Torfing (Eds.), *Theories of governance* (pp. 486–498). Cheltenham, UK: Edward Elgar.

Badaracco, J. L. (2002). *Leading quietly: The unorthodox guide to doing the right thing.* Boston, MA: Harvard Business School Press.

Badir, Y. F., Büchel, B., & Tucci, C. L. (2012). A conceptual framework of the impact of NPD project team and leader empowerment on communication and performance: An alliance case context. *International Journal of Project Management, 30*(8), 914–926. https://doi.org/10.1016/j.ijproman.2012.01.013.

Bailey, R. P., Madigan, D. J., Cope, E., & Nicholls, A. R. (2018). The prevalence of pseudoscientific ideas and neuromyths among sports coaches. *Frontiers in Psychology, 9*(May), 1–11. https://doi.org/10.3389/fpsyg.2018.00641.

Barrick, M. R., & Mount, M. K. (1991). The Big Five personality dimensions and job performance: A meta-analysis. *Personnel Psychology, 44*(1), 1–26. https://doi.org/10.1111/j.1744-6570.1991.tb00688.x.

Barthes, R. (2013). *Mythologies.* New York, NY: Hill & Wang.

Bass, B. M. (1990). *Handbook of Leadership: Theory, Research and Applications.* New York: Free Press.

Bass, B. M., & Riggio, R. E. (2006). *Transformational Leadership* (2nd ed.). London, UK: Lawrence Erlbaum Associates.

Baykasoglu, A., Dereli, T., & Das, S. (2017). Project team selection using fuzzy optimization approach. *Cybernetics and Systems: An International Journal, 38*, 155–185.

Belbin, R. M. (1986). *Management teams.* London, UK: Heinemann.

Bennis, W., & Nanus, B. (1985). *Leaders: The strategies for taking charge.* New York, NY: Harper & Row.

Bhaskar, R. (2009). *Scientific realism and human emancipation.* London, UK: Routledge.

Bhatti, N., Maitlo, G. M., Shaikh, N., Hashmi, M. A., & Shaikh, F. M. (2012). The impact of autocratic and democratic leadership style on job satisfaction. *International Business Research, 5*(2), 192.

Blomquist, T., Farashah, A. D., & Thomas, J. (2016). Project management self-efficacy as a predictor of project performance: Constructing and validating a domain-specific scale. *International Journal of Project Management, 34*(8), 1417–1432. https://doi.org/10.1016/j.ijproman.2016.07.010.

Bourgault, M., Drouin, N., Daoudi, J., & Hamel, E. (2008). *Understanding decision-making within distributed project teams.* Upper Darby, PA: PMI Publications.

Briggs Myers, I. (1987). *Introduction to Type: A description of the theory and applications of the Myers-Briggs Type Indicator.* Oxford, UK: Consulting Psychologists Press.

Britannica. (2020). Social structure. Retrieved October 24, 2020, from https://www.britannica.com/topic/social-structure.

Bucero, A., & Müller, R. (2020). Sensemaking by project managers: Previous research, present findings, and future directions. In *Proceedings of the IPMA Research Conference, online, Sep 9–11, 2020,* Berlin, Germany. International Project Management Association.

Burchell, G. (1991). Peculiar interests: Civil society and governing "the system of natural liberty." In G. Burchell, C. Gordon, & P. Miller (Eds.), *The Foucault effect* (pp. 119–150). Chicago, IL: University of Chicago Press.

Burke, C. S., Fiore, S. M., & Salas, E. (2003). The role of shared cognition in enabling shared leadership and team adaptability. In C. L. Pearce & J. A. Conger (Eds.), *Shared leadership* (pp. 103–122). Thousand Oaks, CA: SAGE Publications.

Burke, C. S., Stagl, K. C., Klein, C., Goodwin, G. F., Salas. E., & Halpin, S. M. (2006). What type of leadership behaviors are functional in teams? A meta-analysis. *Leadership Quarterly, 17,* 288–307.

Burke, R. J., & Cooper, C. (2004). *Leading in turbulent times: Managing in the new world of work.* Oxford, UK: Blackwell.

Burns, T., & Stalker, G. M. (1994). *The management of innovation*. Oxford: Oxford University Press.

Buvik, M. P., & Rolfsen, M. (2015). Prior ties and trust development in project teams: A case study from the construction industry. *International Journal of Project Management, 33*, 1484–1494.

Cadbury, A. (1992). *The financial aspects of corporate governance*. London, UK: Gee (a division of Professional Publishing).

Cadbury, A. (2002). *Corporate governance and chairmanship: A personal view*. New York, NY: Oxford University Press.

Cain, S. (2013). *Quiet: The power of introverts in a world that can't stop talking*. London, UK: Penguin Books.

Cheong, M., Spain, S. M., Yammarino, F. J., & Yun, S. (2016). Two faces of empowering leadership: Enabling and burdening. *Leadership Quarterly, 27*(4), 602–616. https://doi.org/10.1016/j.leaqua.2016.01.006.

Chiocchio, F., Kelloway, E. K., & Hobbs, B. (2015). *The psychology and management of project teams*. Oxford: Oxford University Press.

Church, A. H., & Rotolo, C. T. (2013). How are top companies assessing their high-potentials and senior leaders? A talent management benchmark study. *Consulting Psychology Journal: Practice and Research, 65*, 199–223.

Clarke, N. (2010a). Projects are emotional. *International Journal of Managing Projects in Business, 3*(4), 604–624.

Clarke, N. (2010b). The impact of a training programme designed to target the emotional intelligence abilities of project managers. *International Journal of Project Management, 28*(5), 461–468. https://doi.org/10.1016/j.ijproman.2009.08.004.

Clases, C., Bachmann, R., & Wehner, T. (2003). Studying trust in virtual organizations. *International Studies of Management & Organization, 33*(3), 7–27.

Clegg, S. (2019). Governmentality. *Project Management Journal, 50*(3), 1–4. https://doi.org/10.1177/8756972819841260.

Clegg, S. R., Pitsis, T. S., Rura-Polley, T., & Marosszeky, M. (2002). Governmentality matters: Designing an alliance culture of inter-organizational collaboration for managing projects. *Organization Studies, 23*(3), 317=337.

Cohen, J. (1988). *Statistical power analysis for the behavioral sciences*. Hillsdale, NJ: Lawrence Erlbaum Associates.

Cook, S., & Brown, J. (1999). Bridging epistemologies: The generative knowledge between organizational knowledge and organizational knowing, *Organization Science, 10*(4), 381–400.

Cooper, R. G., & Kleinschmidt, E. J. (1994). Determinants of timeliness in product development. *Journal of Product Innovation Management, 11*(5), 381–396. https://doi.org/10.1111/1540-5885.1150381.

Cox, J. F., Pearce, C. L., & Perry, M. L. (2003). Toward a model of shared leadership and distributed influence in the innovation process: How shared leadership can enhance new product development team dynamics and effectiveness. In C. L. Pearce & J. A. Conger (Eds.), *Shared leadership* (pp. 48–76). Thousand Oaks, CA: SAGE Publications.

Crawford, L., & Da Ros, V. (2002). Politics and the project manager. *Australian Project Manager, 22*(4), 20–21.

Crevani, L., Lindgren, M., & Packendorff, J. (2007). Shared leadership: A post-heroic perspective on leadership as a collective construction. *International Journal of Leadership Studies, 3*(1), 40–67.

Cullen, C., & Leavy, B. (2017). The lived experience of project leadership in a loosely coupled transient context. *International Journal of Managing Projects in Business, 10*(3), 600–620. https://doi.org/10.1108/IJMPB-10-2016-0075.

Cunningham, J., Salomone, J., & Wielgus, N. (2015). Project management leadership styles: A team member perspective. *International Journal of Global Business, 8*(2), 27–54.

Das, T. K., & Teng, B. S. (1998). Between trust and control: Developing confidence in partner cooperation in alliances. *Academy of Management Review, 23*(3), 491–512.

Dean, M. (2010). *Governmentality: Power and rule in modern society* (2nd ed.). London, UK: SAGE Publications.

Denis, J. L., Langley, A., & Sergi, V. (2012). Leadership in the plural. *Academy of Management Annals, 6*(1), 211–283.

Dinsmore, P. C., & Rocha, L. (2012). *Enterprise project governance.* New York, NY: AMACOM.

Donaldson, L. (1985). Organizational design and life-cycle of products. *Journal of Management Studies, 22*(1), 25–37.

Donaldson, L. (2001). *The contingency theory of organizations.* Thousand Oaks, CA: SAGE Publications.

Drouin, N., Müller, R., Sankaran, S., & Vaagaasar, A. L. (2018). Balancing vertical and horizontal leadership in projects: Empirical studies from Australia, Canada, Norway and Sweden. *International Journal of Managing Projects in Business, 11*(4), 986–1006. https://doi.org/10.1108/IJMPB-01-2018-0002.

Drouin, N., Müller, R., Sankaran, S., Vaagaasar, A. L., Jain, K., & Nikolova, N. (2017). Balanced leadership in projects: Building a socio-cognitive-space as an organizational capability. The "project hat." In *Proceedings of the IRNOP 2017 Conference.* June 12–14, 2017, Boston, MA.

Duhig, C. (2016). What Google learned from its quest to build the perfect team. *New York Times Magazine,* February 25. Retrieved July, 7, 2021 from https://www.nytimes.com/2016/02/28/magazine/what-google-learned-from-its-quest-to-build-the-perfect-team.html.

Dunne, E. J., Stahl, M. J., & Melhart, L. J. (1978). Influence sources of project and functional managers in matrix organizations. *Academy of Management Journal, 21*(1), 135–140.

Easton, G. (2010). Critical realism in case study research. *Industrial Marketing Management, 39*(1), 118–128. https://doi.org/10.1016/j.indmarman.2008.06.004.

Edmondson, A. C. (2012). *Teaming: How organizations learn, innovate, and competes in the knowledge economy.* San Francisco, CA: John Wiley & Sons.

Einsiedel, A. A. (1987). Profile of effective project managers. *Project Management Journal, 18*(5), 51–56.

Endres, S., & Weibler, J. (2017). Towards a three-component model of relational social constructionist leadership: A systematic review and critical interpretive synthesis. *International Journal of Management Reviews, 19*(2), 214–236. https://doi.org/10.1111/ijmr.12095.

Englund, R., & Graham, R. (1997). *Creating an environment for successful projects: The quest to manage project management.* San Francisco, CA: Jossey-Bass.

Fauconnier, G. (1994). *Mental Spaces.* New York, NY: Cambridge University Press.

Fauconnier, G., & Turner, M. (1998). Conceptual integration networks. *Cognitive Science, 22*(2), 133–187.

Fellows, R., & Liu, A. (2016). Sensemaking in the cross-cultural contexts of projects. *International Journal of Project Management, 34*(2), 246–257. https://doi.org/10.1016/j.ijproman.2015.03.010.

Fernández-Aráoz, C. (2014). 21st-century talent spotting, *Harvard Business Review, 92*(6), 46–54.

Ferris, G. R., & Davidson, S. L. (2005). *Political skills at work: Impact on work effectiveness.* Boston, MA: Nicholas Brealey.

Fitsilis, P., Gerogiannis, V., & Anthopoulos, L. (2015). Software project team selection based on enterprise social networks. In M. Gen, K. Kim, X. Huang, & Y. Hiroshi (Eds.), *Industrial engineering, management science and applications* 2015. Lecture Notes in Electrical Engineering, vol. 349. Berlin; Heidelberg: Springer. https://doi.org/10.1007/978-3-662-47200-2_40.

Flyvbjerg, B. (2014). What should you know about megaprojects and why. *Project Management Journal*, *45*(2), 6–19.

Foucault, M. (1991). Governmentality. In G. Burchel, C. Gordon, & P. Miller (Eds.), *The Foucault effect* (pp. 87–104). Chicago, IL: University of Chicago Press.

Frame, J. D. (1987). *Managing projects in organizations*. San Francisco, CA: Jossey-Bass.

Franck, E., & Jungwirth, C. (2003). Reconciling rent-seekers and donators: The governance structure of open source. *Journal of Management & Governance*, *7*(4), 401–421.

French, J. R. P., & Raven, B. (1959). The bases of social power. In D. Cartwright (Ed.), *Studies in social power* (pp. 150–167). Ann Arbor, MI: Institute of Social Research.

Future Transport 2056. (2020). *Future transport strategy*. Available at https://future.transport.nsw.gov.au/plans/future-transport-strategy/future-transport-greater-sydney.

Gacasan, E. M. P., & Wiggins, M. W. (2017). Sensemaking through cue utilisation in disaster recovery project management. *International Journal of Project Management*, *35*(5), 818–826. https://doi.org/10.1016/j.ijproman.2016.09.009.

George, B., & Sims, P. (2007), *True north: Discover your authentic leadership*. San Francisco, CA: Jossey Bass.

Goldberg, L. R. (1993). The structure of phenotypic personality traits. *American Psychologist*, *48*(1), 26–34.

Goleman, D., & Boyatzis, R. (2008). Social intelligence and the biology of leadership. *Harvard Business Review*, *86*(9), 74–81, 136. Retrieved from http://www.ncbi.nlm.nih.gov/pubmed/18777666.

Goleman, D., Boyatzis, R., & McKee, A. (2002). *Primal leadership: Learning to lead with emotional intelligence*. Boston, MA: Harvard Business School Press.

Gorla, N., & Lam, Y. H. (2004). Who should work with whom: Building effective software project teams. *Communications of the ACM*, *47*(6), 79–82.

Graen, G. B., & Schiemann, W. A. (2013). Leadership-motivated excellence theory: An extension of LMX. *Journal of Managerial Psychology*, *28*(5), 452–469.

Graen, G., & Uhl-Bien, M. (1995). Relationship-based approach leadership: Development of leader-member exchange (LMX) theory of leadership over 25 years: Applying a multi-level multi-domain perspective. *Leadership Quarterly*, *6*(2), 219–247.

Grant, A. (2020). *Goodbye to MBTI, the fad that won't die*. Retrieved September 9, 2020, from https://www.psychologytoday.com/gb/blog/give-and-take/201309/goodbye-mbti-the-fad-won-t-die.

Groover, S., & Gotian, R. (2020). Five "power skills" for becoming a team leader. *Nature*, *577*(7792), 721–722.

Henry, J. (2020). Transport for NSW trial machine learning to detect crash blackspots. *itnews*, November 19, available at https://www.itnews.com.au/news/transport-for-nsw-trials-machine-learning-to-detect-crash-blackspots-557980.

Hersey, P., & Blanchard, K. H. (1988). *Management of organizational behaviour*. Englewood Cliffs, NJ: Prentice Hall.

Higgins, C. A., Judge, T. A., & Ferris, G. (2003). Influence tactics and meta-analysis. *Journal of Organizational Behaviour*, *24*, 89–106.

Hoegl, M., Weinkauf, K., & Gemuenden, H. G. (2004). Inter-team coordination, project commitment, and teamwork in multiteam R&D projects: A longitudinal study. *Organization Science*, *15*(1), 38–55.

Hooghe, L., & Marks, G. (2003). Unraveling the central state, but how? Types of multi-level governance. *The American Political Science Review*, *97*(2), 233–243. Retrieved from https://www.jstor.org/stable/3118206.

Horchwarter, W. A., Jordan, S. L., Ezaj, A., & Maher, L. P. (2020). Perceptions of organizational politics research: Past, present and future. *Journal of Management*, *46*(6), 879–907.

Hosseini, S. M., & Akhavan, P. (2017). A model for project team formation in complex engineering projects under uncertainty: A knowledge-sharing approach. *Kybernetes, 46*(7), 1131–1157.

Jensen, M. C., & Meckling, W. H. (1976). Theory of the firm: Managerial behavior, agency costs, and ownership structure. *Journal of Financial Economics, 3*(4), 305–360.

Jing, R., & Van De Ven, A. H. (2016). Being versus becoming ontology of paradox management. *Cross Cultural and Strategic Management, 23*(4), 558–562. https://doi.org/10.1108/CCSM-05-2016-0104.

Johnson, T. E., Lee, Y., Khalil, M. K., & Huang, X. (2007). Measuring sharedness of team-related knowledge: Design and Validation of a shared mental model instrument. *Human Resource Development International, 10*(4), 437–454. https://doi.org/10.1080/13678860701723802.

Jones, E. E, & Pitman, T. S. (1982). Toward a general theory of strategic self-presentation. In J. Suls (Ed.), *Psychological perspectives on the self* (pp. 231–262). Hillsdale, NJ: Lawrence Erlbaum Associates.

Judge, T. A., & Bono, J. E. (2000). Five-factor model of personality and transformational leadership. *Journal of Applied Psychology, 85*(5), 751–765. https://doi.org/10.1037/0021-9010.85.5.751.

Katzenbach, J. R., & Smith, S. K. (1993). The discipline of teams. *Harvard Business Review, 71*(2), 111–120.

Katzenbach, J. R., & Smith, S. K. (2003). *The wisdom of teams: Creating the high-performance organization*. Boston, MA: HBR Press.

Keegan, A., & Den Hartog, D. N. (2004). Transformational leadership in a project-based environment: a comparative study of the leadership styles of project managers and line managers. *International Journal of Project Management, 22*(8), 609–618.

Keys, B., & Case, T. (1990). How to become an influential manager. *Academy of Management Perspectives, 4*(4), 38–51.

Khan, J., Jaafar, M., Javed, B., Mubarak, N., & Saudagar, T. (2020). Does inclusive leadership affect project success? The mediating role of perceived psychological empowerment and psychological safety. *International Journal of Managing Projects in Business, 13*(5), 1077–1096. https://doi.org/10.1108/IJMPB-10-2019-0267.

Kipnis, D., Schmidt, S. M., Swaffin-Smith, C., & Wilkinson, I. (1984). Patterns of managerial influences: Shotgun managers, tacticians and bystanders. *Organisational Dynamics, 12*(3), 58–67.

Kipnis, D., Schmidt, S. M, & Wilkinson, I. (1980). Interorganizational influence tactics: Explorations in getting one's way. *Journal of Applied Psychology,* 65(4), 440–452.

Kirkman, B. L., & Rosen, B. (1999). Beyond self-management: Antecedents and consequences of team empowerment. *Academy of Management Journal, 42*(1), 58–74. https://doi.org/10.5465/256874.

Klein, K. J., Lim, B. C., Saltz, J. L., & Mayer, D. M. (2004). How do they get there? An examination of the antecedents of centrality in team networks. *Academy of Management Journal, 47*(6), 952–963.

Kocher, M. G., Pogrebna, G., & Sutter, M. (2013). Other-regarding preferences and management styles. *Journal of Economic Behavior and Organization, 88*, 109–132. https://doi.org/10.1016/j.jebo.2013.01.004.

Kogler Hill, S. E. (2016). Team leadership. In P. G. Northouse (Ed.), *Leadership: Theory and practice* (7th ed., pp. 363–396). Los Angeles, CA: SAGE Publications.

Kotter, J. P. (1985). *Power and influence*. New York, NY: Free Press.

Kruse, K. (2013). What is leadership? *Forbes*. Retrieved from https://www.forbes.com/sites/kevinkruse/2013/04/09/what-is-leadership/#5c7a1f9a5b90.

Kvalnes, Ø. (2020). *Digital dilemmas: Exploring social media ethics in organizations*. Cham, Switzerland: Palgrave MacMillan. https://doi.org/10.1007/978-3-030-45927-7.

Lane, K., Larmaraud, A., & Yueh, E. (2017). Finding hidden leaders. *McKinsey Quarterly*, January 4.

Larcker, D., & Tayan, D. (2011). *Corporate governance matters*. Upper Saddle River, NJ: Pearson Education.

Leach, D. J., Wall, T. D., & Jackson, P. R. (2003). The effect of empowerment on job knowledge: An empirical test involving operators of complex technology. *Journal of Occupational and Organizational Psychology, 76*(1), 27–52.

Lee, D. R., & Bohlen, G. A. (1997). Influence strategies of project managers in the information-technology industry. *Engineering Management Journal, 9*(2), 7–14.

Lee, D. R., & Sweeney, P. J. (2001). An assessment of influence tactics used by project managers. *Engineering Management Journal, 13*(2), 16–24.

Lee, H. W., Hays, N. A., & Johnson, R. E. (2020). To thine own (empowered) self be true: Aligning social hierarchy. *Journal of Applied Psychology*, online. https://doi.org/http://dx.doi.org/10.1037/apl0000813.

Leidecker, J. K., & Hall, J. L. (1974). A new justification for participative management. *Human Resource Management, 13*(1), 28–31.

Lemke, T. (2001). The birth of bio-politics: Michel Foucault's lecture at Collège de France on neo-liberal governmentality. *Economy and Society, 30*(2), 190–207.

Lewin, K. (1945). The Research Center for Group Dynamics at Massachusetts Institute of Technology. *Sociometry, 8*(2), 126–136.

Li, L., Müller, R., Liu, B., Wang, Q., Zhou, S., & Wu, G. (forthcoming). Horizontal-leader identification in construction project teams in China: How Guanxi impacts coworkers' perceived justice and turnover intentions. *Project Management Journal*.

Lindgren, M., & Packendorff, J. (2009). Project leadership revisited: towards distributed leadership perspectives in project research. *International Journal of Project Organization and Management, 1*(3), 285–308.

Lindgren, M., & Packendorff, J. (2011). Issues, responsibilities and identities: A distributed leadership perspective on biotechnology R&D management. *Creativity and Innovation Management, 20*(3), 157–170.

Loorbach, D. (2010). Transition management for sustainable development: A prescriptive, complexity-based governance framework. *Governance, 23*(1), 161–183. https://doi.org/10.1111/j.1468-0491.2009.01471.x.

Loorbach, D., Frantzeskaki, N., & Lijnis Huffenreuter, R. (2015). Transition management: Taking stock from governance experimentation. *Journal of Corporate Citizenship, 2015*(58), 48–66. https://doi.org/10.9774/gleaf.4700.2015.ju.00008.

Loree, D. (2015). The art of early talent spotting. *Ivey Business Journal*, November–December. Available at https://iveybusinessjournal.com/the-art-of-early-talent-spotting/.

Lovell, R. J. (1993). Power and the project manager. *International Journal of Project Management, 11*(2), 73–78.

Lunkka, N., Pietiläinen, V., & Suhonen, M. (2019). A discursive sensemaking perspective on project-based work in public healthcare. *Project Management Journal, 50*(6), 657–672. https://doi.org/10.1177/8756972819847062.

Malik, M., Sarwar, S., & Orr, S. (2021). Agile practices and performance: Examining the role of psychological empowerment. *International Journal of Project Management, 39*(1) 10–20. https://doi.org/10.1016/j.ijproman.2020.09.002.

Markaki, E. N., Salas, D. P., & Chadjipantelis, T. (2011). Selecting the project teams' members' members: A challenging human resources management process for laboratory research. *Key Engineering Materials, 495*, 159–162.

Martinelli, R. J., Waddell, J. M., & Rahschulte, T. J. (2017). *Projects without boundaries: Successfully leading teams and managing projects in a virtual world*. Hoboken, NJ: John Wiley & Sons.

Mathieu, J. E., Tannenbaum, S. I., Donsbach, J. S., & Alliger, J. M. (2013). Achieving optimal team composition for success. In E. Salas (Ed.), *Developing and enhancing high-performance teams and advice* (pp. 520–551). San Francisco, CA: Jossey Bass.

May, C. R., Mair, F., Finch, T., MacFarlane, A., Dowrick, C., Treweek, S., Rapley, T., Ballini, L, Ong, B. N., Rogers, A., Murra, E., Elwyn, G., Légaré, F., Gunn, J., & Montori, V. M. (2009). Development of a theory of implementation and integration: Normalization Process Theory. *Implementation Science, 4*(1), 1–9. https://doi.org/10.1186/1748-5908-4-29.

Mayer, R. C., Davis, J. H., & Schoorman, F. D. (1995). An integrative model of organizational trust. *Academy of Management Review, 20*(3), 709–734.

Maylor, H., Vidgen, R., & Carver, S. (2008), Managerial complexity in project-based operations: A grounded model and its implications for practice. *Project Management Journal,* 39(Supplement), S15–S26.

Maynard, M. T., Gilson, L. L., & Mathieu, J. E. (2012). Empowerment: Fad or fab? A Multilevel review of the past two decades of research. *Journal of Management, 38*(4), 1231–1281. https://doi.org/10.1177/0149206312438773.

McCall, G., & Simmons, J. (1978). *Identities and interaction.* New York, NY: Free Press.

McClough, A. C., & Rogelberg, S. G. (2003). Selection in teams: An exploration of the teamwork knowledge, skills and ability test. *International Journal of Selection and Assessment, 11*(1), 56–66.

McDonough, E. F., & Barczak, G. (1991). Speeding up new product development: The effects of leadership style and source of technology. *Journal of Product Innovation Management, 8*(3), 203–211.

McKevitt, D., Carbery, R., & Lyons, A. (2017). A profession but not a career? Work identity and career satisfaction in project management. *International Journal of Project Management, 35*(8), 1673–1682. https://doi.org/10.1016/j.ijproman.2017.07.010.

Merton, R. K., & Merton, R. C. (1968). On sociological theories of the middle range. In *Social Theory and Social Structure* (pp. 39–72). New York, NY: Free Press.

Miller, R., & Hobbs, B. (2005). Governance regimes for large projects. *Project Management Journal, 36*(3), 42–51.

Mintzberg, H. (1987). The strategy concept I: Five Ps for strategy. *California Management Review, 30*(1), 11–24.

Mintzberg, H., Raisinghani, D., & Theoret, A. (1976). The structure of "unstructured" decision processes. *Administrative Science Quarterly,* 246–275.

Monks, A. A. G., & Minow, N. (1995). *Corporate governance* (4th ed.). Chichester, UK: John Wiley & Sons.

Morgeson, F. P., Reider, M. H., & Campion, M. A. (2005). Selecting individuals in team settings: The importance of social skills, personality characteristics and teamwork knowledge. *Personnel Psychology, 58*, 583–611.

Morris, T., Greenwood, R., & Fairglough, S. (2010). Decision making in professional service firms. in P. C. Nutt & D. C. Wilson (Eds.), *Handbook of decision making* (Vol. 6, pp. 275–306). New York, NY: John Wiley & Sons.

Morrow, P. C., & Muchinsky, P. M. (1980). Middle range theory: An overview and assessment for organizational research. In C. Pinder & L. F. Moore (Eds.), *Middle range theory and the study of organizations* (pp. 33–44). Dordrecht: Springer. https://doi.org/10.1080/00128775.1989.11648423.

Müller, R. (2017). Governance mechanisms in projects. In R Müller (Ed.), *Governance and governmentality for projects: Enablers, practices and consequences* (pp. 173–180). New York, NY: Routledge.

Müller, R. (2019). Governance, governmentality and project performance: The role of sovereignty. *International Journal of Information Systems and Project Management, 7*(2), 5–17. https://doi.org/10.12821/ijispm070201.

Müller, R., Drouin, N., & Sankaran, S. (2019). *Organizational project management: Theory and implementation*. Cheltenham, UK: Edward Elgar.

Müller, R, & Kvalnes, Ø. (2017). Project governance and project ethics. In R Müller (Ed.), *Governance and governmentality for projects: Enablers, practices and consequences* (pp. 181–194). New York, NY: Routledge.

Müller, R, Martinsuo, M., & Blomquist, T. (2008). Project portfolio control and portfolio management in different contexts. *Project Management Journal, 39*(3), 28–42.

Müller, R, Packendorff, J., & Sankaran, S. (2017). Balanced leadership: A new perspective for leadership in organizational project management. In S. Sankaran, R. Müller, & N. Drouin (Eds.), *Cambridge handbook of organizational project management* (pp. 180–193). Cambridge, UK: Cambridge University Press.

Müller, R, Sankaran, S., & Drouin, N. (2018a). Horizontal leadership's influence on project success and the role of the cognitive space. In *Proceedings of the EURAM Conference,* June 20–22, Reykjavik, Iceland.

Müller, R., Sankaran, S., Drouin, N., Vaagaasar, A. L., Bekker, M. C., & Jain, K. (2018b). A theory framework for balancing vertical and horizontal leadership in projects. *International Journal of Project Management, 36*(1), 83–94.

Müller, R., & Turner, J. R. (2007). Matching the project manager's leadership style to project type. *International Journal of Project Management, 25*(1), 21–32. https://doi.org/10.1016/j.ijproman.2006.04.003.

Müller, R., & Turner, R. (2010). Leadership competency profiles of successful project managers. *International Journal of Project Management, 28*(5), 437–448. https://doi.org/10.1016/j.ijproman.2009.09.003.

Müller, R., & Turner, J. R. (2010a). *Project-oriented leadership*. Aldershot, UK: Gower.

Müller, R., & Turner, J. R. (2010b). Attitudes and leadership competences for project success. *Baltic Journal of Management, 5*(3), 307–329.

Müller, R., Vaagaasar, A. L., Nikolova, N., Sankaran, S., & Drouin, N. (2015). The socio-cognitive space for linking horizontal and vertical leadership. In *Proceedings of the APROS/EGOS Conference 2015,* December 9–11, 2015, Sydney, Australia.

Müller, R., Zhai, L., & Wang, A. (2017). Governance and governmentality in projects: Profiles and relationships with success. *International Journal of Project Management, 35*(3), 378–392.

Müller, R., Zhu, F., Sun, X., Wang, L., & Yu, M. (2018). The identification of temporary horizontal leaders in projects: The case of China. *International Journal of Project Management, 36,* 95–107.

Nanjundeswaraswamy, T. S., & Swamy, D. R. (2014). Leadership styles. *Advances in Management, 7*(2), 57.

Nauman, S., Mansur Khan, A., & Ehsan, N. (2010). Patterns of empowerment and leadership style in project environment. *International Journal of Project Management, 28*(7), 638–649. https://doi.org/10.1016/j.ijproman.2009.11.013.

Nooteboom, B. (1996). Trust, opportunism and governance: A process and control model. *Organization Studies, 17*(6), 985–1010.

Northouse, P. G. (2007). *Leadership: Theory and practice* (4th ed.). Thousand Oaks, CA: SAGE Publications.

Northouse, P. G. (2016). *Leadership: Theory and practice* (7th ed.). Los Angeles, CA: SAGE Publications.

Nutt, P. C., & Wilson, D. C. (Eds.). (2010). *Handbook of decision making* (Vol. 6). New York, NY: John Wiley & Sons.

OECD. (2001). *Governance in the 21st century*. Paris, France: OECD Publications.

OECD. (2004). *OECD principles of corporate governance*. Paris, France: OECD Publications.

Ojokuku, R. M., Odetayo, T. A., & Sajuyigbe, A. S. (2012). Impact of leadership style on organizational performance: A case study of Nigerian banks. *American Journal of Business and Management, 1*(4), 202–207.

Oke, A. E. (2013). Project management leadership styles of Nigerian construction professionals. *International Journal of Construction Project Management, 5*(2), 159–169.

Ölander, F., & Thøgersen, J. (1995). Understanding of consumer behavior as a prerequisite for environmental protection. *Journal of Consumer Policy, 18,* 345–385. https://doi.org/10.1007/BF01024160.

Ouchi, W. G. (1980). Markets, bureaucracies and clans. *Administrative Science Quarterly, 25,* 129–141.

Oxford English Dictionary. (2008). Retrieved February 10, 2020 from https://www.pdfdrive.com/oxford-english-dictionary-d195222413.htm.

Oxford English Dictionary. (2021). Retrieved July 7, 2021 from https://www.lexico.com/definition/transition.

Parolia, N., Goodman, S., Li, Y., & Jiang, J. J. (2007). Mediators between coordination and IS project performance. *Information and Management, 44*(7), 635–645. https://doi.org/10.1016/j.im.2007.06.003.

Pearce, C. L., & Conger, J. A. (2003). *Shared leadership.* Thousand Oaks, CA: SAGE Publications.

Pearce, J. L., & Sims, H. P. (2000). Shared leadership: Toward a multi-level theory of leadership. In M. M. Beyerlein (Ed.), *Team development* (7th ed., pp. 115–139). Amsterdam, NL: Elsevier Science.

Pearce, C. L., & Sims, H. P. (2002). Vertical versus shared leadership as predictors of the effectiveness of change management teams: An examination of aversive, directive, transactional, transformational, and empowering leader behaviors. *Group Dynamics: Theory, Research, and Practice, 6*(2), 172–197. https://doi.org/10.1037/1089-2699.6.2.172.

Pertz, M., Okoniewski, A., Schlegel, U., & Thoma, P. (2020). Impairment of sociocognitive functions in patients with brain tumours. *Neuroscience and Biobehavioral Reviews, 108*(April 2019), 370–392. https://doi.org/10.1016/j.neubiorev.2019.11.018.

Peters, T. (1988). *Thriving on chaos.* New York, NY: Harper Collins.

Peverelli, P. J. (2000). *Cognitive space: A social-cognitive approach to Sino-foreign co-operation.* Delft, NL: Eburan. https://doi.org/10.1016/s0364-0213(99)80038-x.

Pilkienė, M., Alonderienė, R., Chmieliauskas, A., Šimkonis, S., & Müller, R. (2018). The governance of horizontal leadership in projects. *International Journal of Project Management, 36*(7), 913–924.

Pinto, J. K. (2000). Understanding the role of politics in successful project management. *International Journal of Project Management, 18*(2), 85–91.

Pinto, J. K. (2016). *Project management: Achieving competitive advantage* (4th ed.). Boston, MA: Pearson.

Pinto, J. (2017). Viewing team selection through a temporal lens. *Organizational Psychology Review, 7*(2), 171–194.

Pinto, J. K., & Slevin, D. P. (1987). Critical success factors in successful project implementation. *IEEE Transactions on Engineering Management, 34,* 22–27.

Pinto, J., & Slevin, D. (1988). Project success: Definitions and measurement techniques. *Project Management Journal, 19*(1), 67–73.

Pinto, J. K., Slevin, D. P., & English, B. (2009). Trust in projects: An empirical assessment of owner/contractor relationships. *International Journal of Project Management, 27*(6), 638–648.

PMI. (2017). *A guide to the project management body of knowledge* (6th ed.) Newtown Square, PA: Project Management Institute.

PMI's talent triangle.™ (2015). Available at https://www.pmi.org/-/media/pmi/documents/public/pdf/certifications/talent-triangle-flyer.pdf.

Prince2.com. (2020). PRINCE2. Retrieved July 10, 2020, from https://www.prince2.com/eur/prince2-methodology.

Popper, K. (1959). *The logic of scientific discovery*. New York, NY: Basic Books.

Pretorius, S., Steyn, H., & Bond-Barnard, T. J. (2017). Exploring project-related factors that influence leadership styles and their effect on project performance: A conceptual framework. *South African Journal of Industrial Engineering, 28*(4), 95–108.

Raelin, J. (2003). *Creating leaderful organisations: How to bring out leadership in everyone*. San Francisco, CA: Berrett-Koehler.

Riley, A., & Burke, P. J. (1995). Identities and self-verification in the small group. *Social Psychology Quarterly, 58*(2), 61–73.

Roach, E. (1978). Principles of categorization. In E. Roach & B. B. Lloyd (Eds.), *Cognition and categorization* (pp. 27–48). Hillsdale, NJ: Lawrence Erlbaum Associates.

Roccas, S., Sagiv, L., Schwartz, S. H., & Knafo, A. (2002). The Big Five personality factors and personal values. *Personality and Social Psychology Bulletin, 28*(6), 789–801. https://doi.org/10.1177/0146167202289008.

Salovey, P., & Mayer, J. D. (1990). Emotional intelligence. *Imagination, Cognition and Personality, 9*(3), 185–211.

Sankaran, S., Vaagaasar, A. L., & Bekker, M. C. (2020). Assignment of team members to projects: Project managers' influence strategies. *International Journal of Managing Projects in Business, 13*(6), 1381–1402.

Sayles, L. R. (1976). Matrix management: The structure with a future. *Organizational Dynamics, 5*(2), 2–17.

Schneider, M. (2017). Google spent 2 years studying 180 teams: The most successful ones shared these 5 traits. *Inc*, July 19. https://www.inc.com/michael-schneider/google-thought-they-knew-how-to-create-the-perfect.html.

Schoorman, F. D., Mayer, R. C., & Davis, J. H. (2007). An integrative model of organizational trust: Past, present, and future. *Academy of Management Review, 32*(2), 344–354.

Schriesheim, C. A., Neider, L. L., & Scandura, T. A. (1998). Delegation and leader-member exchange: Main effects, moderators, and measurement issues. *Academy of Management Journal, 41*(3), 298–318.

Scott. J. C., Church, A. H., & Mclellan, J. (2017). *Selecting leadership talent for the 21st century workforce*. SHRM Foundations' Effective Practice Guideline Series. Alexandria, VA: SHRM.

Scrumguides.org. (2020). *The scrum guide*. Retrieved July 10, 2020, from https://www.scrumguides.org/scrum-guide.html.

Seibert, S. E., Silver, S. R., & Randolph, W. A. (2004). Taking empowerment to the next level: A multiple-level model of empowerment, performance, and satisfaction. *Academy of Management Journal, 47*(3), 332–349. https://doi.org/10.2307/20159585.

Seibert, S. E., Wang, G., & Coutyright, S. H. (2011). Antecedents and consequences of psychological and team empowerment in organizations: A meta-analytic review. *Journal of Applied Psychology, 96*(5), 981–1003.

Sergeeva, N. (2017). Labeling projects as innovative: A social identity theory. *Project Management Journal, 48*(1), 51–64. https://doi.org/10.1177/875697281704800104.

Serrador, P., & Pinto, J. K. (2015). Does agile work? A quantitative analysis of agile project success. *International Journal of Project Management, 33*(5), 1040–1051. https://doi.org/10.1016/j.ijproman.2015.01.006.

Sharma, P. N., & Kirkman, B. L. (2015). Leveraging leaders: A literature review and future lines of inquiry for empowering leadership research. *Group & Organization Management, 40*(2), 193–237. https://doi.org/10.1177/1059601115574906.

Singh, A. (2009). Organizational power in perspective. *Journal of Management in Engineering, 9*(4), 165–176.

Smith, C. M. (2011). Scripts: A tool for cognitive rehearsal. *The Journal of Continuing Education in Nursing, 42*(12), 535–536.

Sotiriou, D., & Wittmer, D. (2001). Influence methods of project managers: Perceptions of team members and project managers. *Project Management Journal, 32*(3), 12–20.

Spreitzer, G. M. (1995). Psychological empowerment in the workplace: Dimensions, measurement, and validation. *Academy of Management Journal, 38*(5), 1442–1465.

Spreitzer, G. M. (2007). Toward the integration of two perspectives: A review of social-structural and psychological empowerment at work. In C. Cooper & J. Barling (Eds.), *The handbook of organizational behavior* (1st ed.). Thousand Oaks, CA: SAGE Publications.

Srivastava, P., & Jain, S. (2017), A leadership framework for distributed self-organized scrum teams. *Team Performance Management, 23*(5–6), 293–314. https://doi-org.ezproxy.lib.uts.edu.au/10.1108/TPM-06-2016-0033.

Stein, R., & Swan, A. B. (2019). Evaluating the validity of Myers-Briggs Type Indicator theory: A teaching tool and window into intuitive psychology. *Social and Personality Psychology Compass, 13*(2), 1–11. https://doi.org/10.1111/spc3.12434.

Stephens, J. C., & Graham, A. C. (2010). Toward an empirical research agenda for sustainability in higher education: Exploring the transition management framework. *Journal of Cleaner Production, 18*(7), 611–618.

Stern, T. V. (2017). *Lean and agile project management: How to make any project better, faster and more cost-effective.* Boca Raton, FL: CRC Press.

Stets, J. E., & Burke, P. J. (2000). Identity theory and social identity theory. *Social Psychology, 63*(3), 224–237.

Tannenbaum, S. I., Mathieu, J. I., & Cohen, D. (2012). Teams are changing: Are research and practice evolving fast enough? *Industrial and Organizational Psychology, 5*(2012), 2–24.

Thamhain, H. J., & Gemmill, G. R. (1974). Influence styles of project managers: Some project performance correlates. *Academy of Management Journal, 17*(2), 216–224.

Thomas, K. W., & Velthouse, B. A. (1990). Cognitive elements of empowerment: An "interpretive" model of intrinsic task motivation. *Academy of Management Review, 15*(4), 666–681. https://doi.org/10.5465/amr.1990.4310926.

Thomson, L. L. (2011). *Making the team: A guide for managers* (4th ed.). New York, NY: Pearson.

Too, E. G., & Weaver, P. (2014). The management of project management: A conceptual framework for project governance. *International Journal of Project Management, 32*(8), 1382–1394. https://doi.org/10.1016/j.ijproman.2013.07.006.

Trost, J. K., Skerlavaj, M., & Anzengruber, J. (2016). The ability-motivation-opportunity framework for team innovation: Efficacy beliefs, proactive personalities, supportive supervision and team innovation. *Economic and Business Review, 18*(1), 77–102.

Tuckman, B. W. (1965). Developmental sequence in small groups 1. *Psychological Bulletin, 63*(6), 384–399.

Turner, J. R., & Müller, R. (2004). Communication and cooperation on projects between the project owner as principal and the project manager as agent. *European Management Journal, 21*(3), 327–336.

Turner, J. R., & Müller, R. (2006). *Choosing appropriate project managers: Matching their leadership style to the type of project.* Newtown Square, PA: Project Management Institute.

Turner, R., Ledwith, A., & Kelly, J. (2010). Project management in small to medium-sized enterprises: Matching processes to the nature of the firm. *International Journal of Project Management, 28*(8), 744–755. https://doi.org/10.1016/j.ijproman.2010.06.005.

Turner, R., & Lloyd-Walker, B. (2008). Emotional intelligence (EI) capabilities training: Can it develop EI in project teams? *International Journal of Managing Projects in Business, 1*(4), 512–534. https://doi.org/10.1108/17538370810906237.

Tuuli, M. M. (2018). What has project characteristics got to do with the empowerment of individuals, teams and organisations? *International Journal of Managing Projects in Business, 11*(3), 708–733. https://doi.org/10.1108/IJMPB-08-2017-0097.

Useem, M. (2010). Spotlight on leadership lessons from the military: Four lessons in adaptive leadership. *Harvard Business Review*, (November), 86–90.

van Assen, M. F. (2020). Empowering leadership and contextual ambidexterity: The mediating role of committed leadership for continuous improvement. *European Management Journal*, *38*(3), 435–449. https://doi.org/10.1016/j.emj.2019.12.002.

van de Ven, A. H. (1989). Nothing is quite so practical as a good theory. *Academy of Management Review*, *14*(4), 486–489. https://doi.org/10.5465/amr.1989.4308370.

Van Oorschot, K. E. Van, Sengupta, K., & Wassenhove, L. N. Van. (2018). Under pressure: The effects of iteration lengths on agile software development performance. *Project Management Journal*, *49*(6), 78–102. https://doi.org/10.1177/8756972818802714.

Vincent, S., & Wapshott, R. (2014). Critical realism and the organizational case study. In P. K. Edwards, J. O'Mahoney, & S. Vincent (Eds.), *Studying organizations using critical realism* (pp. 148–167). Oxford, UK: Oxford University Press.

Voß, J. P., Smith, A., & Grin, J. (2009). Designing long-term policy: Rethinking transition management. *Policy Sciences*, *42*(4), 275–302.

Wegner, L. L. (2004). *Organizational leaders and empowered employees: The relationship between leadership styles, perception of styles, and the impact on organizational outcomes*. Minneapolis, MN: Capella University.

Weick, K. (1993). The collapse of sensemaking in organizations: The Mann Gulch disaster. *Administrative Science Quarterly*, *38*, 628–652.

Weick, K. E., Sutcliffe, K. M., & Obstfeld, D. (2005). Organizing and the process of sensemaking. *Organization Science*, *16*(4), 409–421. https://doi.org/10.1287/orsc.1050.0133.

Whetten, D. A. (2002). Modelling-as-theorizing: A Systematic methodology for theory development. In D. Partington (Ed.), *Essential skills for management research* (pp. 45–71). Thousand Oaks, CA: SAGE Publications.

Williamson, O. E. (1985). *The economic institutions of capitalism*. New York, NY: Free Press.

Williamson, O. E. (1991). Comparative economic organization: The analysis of discrete structural alternatives. *Administrative Science Quarterly*, *36*, 269–296.

Yu, M., Vaagaasar, A. L., Müller, R., Wang, L., & Zhu, F. (2018). Empowerment: The key to horizontal leadership in projects. *International Journal of Project Management*, *36*(7), 992–1006. https://doi.org/https://doi.org/10.1016/j. ijproman.2018.04.003.

Yukl, G. (2002). *Leadership in organizations*. Upper Saddle River, NJ: Prentice Hall.

Yukl, G., & Falbe, C. M. (1990). Influence tactics and objectives in upward, downward and lateral influence attempts. *Journal of Applied Psychology*, *75*(2), 132–140.

Yukl, G., & Mahsud, R. (2010). Why flexible and adaptive leadership is essential. *Consulting Psychology Journal: Practice and Research*, *62*(2), 81–93.

Yukl, G., & Tracey, R. (1992). Consequences of influence tactics used with subordinates, peers and the boss. *Journal of Applied Psychology*, *77*(4), 525–535.

Zabojnik, J. (2002). Centralized and decentralized decision making in organizations. *Journal of Labor Economics*, *20*(1), 1–22.

Zhang, L., Cao, T., & Wang, Y. (2018). The mediation role of leadership styles in integrated project collaboration: An emotional intelligence perspective. *International Journal of Project Management*, *36*(2), 317–330. https://doi.org/10.1016/j.ijproman.2017.08.014.

Zhu, F., Wang, L., Sun, M., Sun, X., & Müller, R. (2019). Influencing factors of horizontal leaders' role identity in projects: A sequential mixed method approach. *International Journal of Project Management*, *37*(4), 582–598. https://doi.org/10.1016/j.ijproman.2019.02.006.

Zimmermann, M. A. (2000). Empowerment theory. In J. Rappaport & E. Seidman (Eds.), *Handbook of community psychology* (pp. 43–63). Boston, MA: Springer Link.

Zurcher, A. (2014). *Debunking the Myers-Briggs personality test*. Retrieved October 21, 2020, from https://www.bbc.com/news/blogs-echochambers-28315137.

Index